TOURISTS, TRAVELLERS AND PILGRIMS

TOURISTS, TRAVELLERS AND PILGRIMS

GEOFFREY HINDLEY

Hutchinson

London Melbourne Sydney Auckland Johannesburg

For Diana

Hutchinson & Co. (Publishers) Ltd
An imprint of the Hutchinson Publishing Group
17–21 Conway Street, London W1P 6JD

Hutchinson Group (Australia) Pty Ltd
30–32 Cremorne Street, Richmond South, Victoria 3121
PO Box 151, Broadway, New South Wales 2007

Hutchinson Group (NZ) Ltd
32–34 View Road, PO Box 40–086, Glenfield, Auckland 10

Hutchinson Group (SA) Pty Ltd
PO Box 337, Bergvlei 2012, South Africa

First published in 1983

Designed and produced for Hutchinson & Co. by
Bellew & Higton Publishers Ltd
17–21 Conway Street, London W1P 6JD

Copyright © Geoffrey Hindley 1983

British Library Cataloguing in Publication Data
Hindley, Geoffrey, 1935 –
  Tourists, Travellers and Pilgrims
  1. Europe – Description and travel
  I. Title
  914′.042′0922   D907
ISBN 0–09–149460–5

Typeset by V & M Graphics Ltd, Aylesbury, Bucks
Printed in Great Britain by The Anchor Press
and bound by Wm Brendon & Son Ltd,
both of Tiptree, Essex

CONTENTS

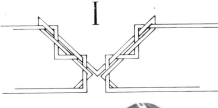

I

DELIGHTS AND
HAZARDS
OF THE ROAD

'The Postilion has been struck by lightning ...'

S ince he is the subject of the most famous quote in the history of travellers' phrase books, and since he was for two and a half centuries the principal hazard of the road, it seems only fair to start with the postilion.

The young John Ruskin, on tour in the 1840s observed that the French horses were well up to their work though 'good-humouredly licentious' and were driven by one postilion riding the shaft horse. Like many another before him, Ruskin was astonished by the footwear of his young postilion, 'half his weight being in his boots which were brought out slung from the saddle like two buckets, the youth, after the horses were harnessed, walking along the pole and getting into them'. In France even the light

Details from TRAVELLERS ARRIVING AT THE INN John Boyne

postchaise was accompanied by a postilion, 'clad in a dirty sheepskin coat, greasy night cap and vast jack boots', like oyster barrels rimmed with iron, to protect the legs in case of accident.

Continental postilions were not well loved by English travellers. Smollett, the novelist, found the French variety 'lazy, lounging, greedy and impertinent. If you chide them for lingering, they will continue to delay you longer; if you chastise them with sword, cane, cudgel or horsewhip they will either disappear entirely, or they will find means of vengeance by overturning your carriage.'

UNSPRUNG HEROES

By the eighteenth century, the traveller had a variety of vehicles to choose from. The *carosse*, similar to the English stage coach, carried six passengers in reasonable comfort. The *coche* (English 'coach', derived from the Hungarian *kutche*), carrying sixteen passengers, had two vast wicker-work baskets slung fore and aft piled high with luggage and even, on occasion, passengers. In Italy the run from Turin to Venice was generally by *calesce*, a very select mode of transport carrying only two passengers and two trunks behind.

The usual mode of transport for the modestly well-to-do traveller was the diligence. This was a large public coach, picking up and depositing passengers en route; with a change of horses every twelve miles, it was capable of covering eighty miles in a long day's journey in ideal conditions, though most travellers were content with as much as fifty. The body of the carriage rested upon large thongs of leather, fastened to heavy blocks of wood. The classic French diligence, 'a huge, lofty, lumbering machine, something between an English stage and a broadwheeled wagon', consisted of three parts or bodies joined together. The front division was called the *coupé*; 'it was shaped like a chariot or postchaise, holding three persons quite distinct from the rest of the passengers, so that ladies may resort to it without inconvenience, and, by securing all three places to themselves, may travel nearly as comfortably as in a private carriage.' Behind this came the *interieur* which seated six. At the back of the strange conveyance was attached the *rotonde*, 'the receptacle of dust, dirt and bad company, the least desirable part of the diligence and the cheapest except the *banquette*, or imperial, an outside seat on the roof of the *coupé* tolerably well protected from rain and cold by a hood and leather apron, but somewhat difficult of access until you are accustomed to climb up into it'.

The *banquette* had the advantage of fresh air, a splendid view and, because it was so high up, comparative freedom from dust. One might, however, 'sometimes meet rough and low-bred companions, for the

French do not like to travel outside, and few persons of the better class resort to it'. The English, renowned for their love of fresh air, were the exception, preferring 'the *banquette* to all other parts of the diligence'.

When John Ruskin took his bride on their honeymoon in the 1840s, he followed the advice of the travel writers on the pleasures of the *coupé* in the diligence and found it 'just like one's own chariot and six – and no trouble with postilions'. Effie was equally delighted: 'John took the *coupé* for himself, and me, we were very comfortable and saw the six grey horses prancing in front of us in very fine style.' She noted that the *coupé* was expensive; 'they would not give it except for all the way to Caen so there is 16 half francs – multiplied by 3, plus 3 francs extra for luggage'. There was an additional disadvantage. To maintain its speed, a heavily laden diligence needed seven horses, but the operators did not always provide a full team. Effie noted ruefully on the run from Caen to Falaise: 'the diligence goes very slow when there are only two horses.'

Ruskin looked back with nostalgia to the family journeys of his youth, when weeks of planning and improvements were needed before the travelling coach was reckoned ready to start. They began 'with the choice of a suitable carriage from Mr Hopkinson's of Long Acre'. Even this master of his craft could not produce the carriage that would satisfy Mr Ruskin senior. Once the vehicle had been selected it had to be arranged. There was 'the cunning design and distribution of store-cellars under the seats, secret drawers under front windows, invisible pockets under padded lining safe from dust, and accessible only by insidious slits, the fitting of cushions where they would not slip, the rounding of corners for more delicate repose, the prudent attachment of springs to blinds'. The man remembers the delights of these youthful family excursions with cosy pleasure. 'The little apartment was to be virtually one's home for six months and the very arranging of it was an imaginary journey itself. With every pleasure, and none of the discomfort of practical travelling.'

DESTINATION CULTURE

Even on his honeymoon, Ruskin did not neglect his true passion, Europe's medieval architecture. His father once remarked: 'John occupies himself with the architecture of the Cathedral – a lovely edifice, but I find it very slow.' John was not deterred and in due course became England's most revered authority on architecture in an age when nostalgia for the Middle Ages was flooding Europe in the wake of the Romantic movement.

Both in the places he visited and in the devout spirit in which he approached the great churches, Ruskin's architectural journeys seem almost to have been pilgrimages. And yet the people of the Middle Ages would hardly have been at ease in his company. No doubt they marvelled at the great cathedrals, but it was the relics of the saints within them that they had come to see. Often enough the travellers had a long and perilous journey, but wherever they went they brought trade and profit. Many a small European town drew its chief revenue from the pilgrims; special hostels were built to accommodate them and guided tours organized for their benefit.

The Protestant Reformation of the early sixteenth century discredited the cult of saints and divided Europe along religious battle lines which travellers crossed at their peril. Yet the lure of Rome still attracted the adventurous from Protestant countries. If they were prudent, they travelled incognito and slept at a different inn each night. Only the foolhardy lodged in the city of the Popes over the Easter festival when the Inquisition was especially vigilant, checking inns for any guests who had failed to take the sacrament.

The English traveller Fynes Moryson, going from Rome to Naples in the year 1591, joined a party travelling under guard of sixty musketeers as protection against bandits. His journey through the Low Countries had been yet more hazardous. The coastal roads of Holland were crawling with freebooters from the Spanish army of the Netherlands who preyed on foreigners and particularly relished plundering Protestant Englishmen. Moryson adopted the disguise of a poor Bohemian wearing 'an old Brunswick thrummed hat, a poor Dutch suit which I rubbed with dust to make it seem old, so as my tailor said he took more pains to spoil it as to make it'. He stained his face and hands and so, 'without cloak or sword' (that necessary passport of a gentleman on the Continent) he took his place in a poor wagon. Most nights, taken for a pauper, 'with servile countenance and eyes cast on the ground', he was told to bed down on a bench in the taproom.

During the seventeenth century young Englishmen fanned out across Europe, through Flanders and Holland, France and Germany to Italy. Their destinations were not the shrines of the Christian faith, but the monuments of the pagan past and the centres of the new learning of Renaissance Europe. The 'grand tour', as it soon became known, was the prelude to a training in the diplomatic corps or other public service, or merely an opportunity to study Continental fashions and architecture with a view to later improvements for the ancestral home.

In 1725 Lord Annendale advised his nephew to take 'particular note of the French way of furnishing rooms, especially with double doors and windows ... and finishing them with looking glasses, marble, painting and gilded stucco'. The model tourist asked questions about everything – the

10

history, trade, climate, politics, law, art and customs of the country – and noted down his observations. Arriving at a new town, his first visit was to a high steeple or other vantage point for a birds-eye view of the place and its most notable buildings, all of which had to be studied and sketched in due course.

Some critics reckoned that even the conscientious derived little benefit from the exercise. Dr Samuel Johnson defined the grand tourist as one 'who enters a town at night and surveys it in the morning and then hastens away to another place', acquiring in the process, 'a confused remembrance of palaces and churches'. And, of course, many of the young blades travelling at their fathers' expense did not pay even that much attention to the serious aspects of the tour. In Paris the young Lord Chesterfield 'rose very late and breakfasted with other milords to the loss of two good morning hours – by coach to the Palais, then on to the English coffee-house where a party was made for dinner. From dinner they adjourned in clusters to the play, where they crowd up the stage drest in very fine clothes. From the play to the tavern again, where they get very drunk, and where they either quarrel among themselves or sally forth, commit some riot in the streets and are taken up by the watch.'

When the young Earl of Carlisle arrived at Spa in the Netherlands in 1768 after three years on the grand tour, he found it full of English friends. He rose at six, was out riding until breakfast, played cricket till dinner, and then danced in the evening until he could 'scarcely crawl'; this, he observed, was the life. He had travelled in luxury, and the revels at Spa were a fitting end to an aristocrat's progress. Less prosperous gentlemen, too, could be handsomely entertained by the European nobility.

During his stay at the German court of Anhalt-Dessau, James Boswell was invited to join the hunt.

At last the stag was slain, a cold collation of meat, bread and butter and wine was served round. Prince Diederic then presented me with the stag's foot, saying, 'My dear sir, this is a mark of distinction.' This pleased me. It shall be laid up in the museum at Auchinleck, with an inscription on a plate of gold or silver, telling that Laird James the Fourth had it in a present from a German prince with whom he had the honour of hunting, when upon his travels.

We know that Boswell did take it home, from an elegant Latin inscription composed for the display case by Sir David Dalrymple.

Pilgrims had brought back innumerable relics, many of them fakes; the grand tourists were souvenir hunters in the modern manner. Thomas Coryat(e), famous and far-travelled eccentric, even brought back the worn-out shoes in which he claimed to have walked all the way to Venice.

OVERSET Thomas Rowlandson

They hung in the parish church of his native Odcome in Somerset for more than a hundred years. A rather more useful memento of his 1610 Italian tour was an eating fork. A decade after this the fifteen-year-old Lord Montagu was delighted by the tourist souvenirs on sale in Dieppe – knick-knacks in tortoiseshell and whalebone, and carved ornaments in ivory.

About this time the more serious art lovers among Britain's aristocracy were beginning their two-century buying spree in the European art market. The great collections they brought back to England's country houses still constitute a major element in Europe's heritage of Classical and Renaissance art. They also imported foreign, and above all Italian, styles of architecture. Holkham Hall in Norfolk was built for Thomas Coke in the Palladian style by William Kent, whom he met while on the grand tour in 1715.

The young Coke was accompanied by his tutor Dr Howard. The tutor, more commonly called the 'bear leader', was an essential companion for any young gentleman. The wise father chose him with care. Unscrupulous 'needy bold men' had been known to sub-contract a boy's tuition to second-rate academies and pocket the difference in fees, or even take bribes from scheming foreigners to entrap the youngster into an unsuitable marriage. But there were times when any tutor allowed his young bear a certain amount of rope, if only for a quiet life. Few had pupils so keen on culture as Thomas Coke, and even he escaped in Vienna. Bored at last with his civilizing education, he decided to join the Austrian army in the Balkans, purchased equipment and horses and would indisputably have gone off to war against the Turks had not Dr Howard persuaded the Austrian authorities to put him under polite house arrest.

As the tour might last for as long as three years, it is not surprising that the young bloods looked for diversion from the ruins and languages they had been sent to study. Robert Walpole, son of the famous prime minister, admitted: 'I have left off screaming Lord, this! and Lord, that! The farther I travel, the less I wonder at anything: a few days reconcile me to a new spot, or an unseen custom.' Nevertheless, the flood of young travellers grew ever greater towards the end of the eighteenth century. A contemporary observed: 'To such a pitch is the spirit of travelling come in the kingdom that there is scarce a citizen of large fortune but takes a flying view of France, Italy and Germany.' To the countries through which they passed, they presented a spectacle that was to make the term 'milord' part of the vocabulary of Europe. The entourage of William Beckford, son of a former Lord Mayor of London, was mistaken in the 1780s for a progress of the Tsar of Russia. One guidebook of the time actually told its readers that to spend lavishly was the way to be respected. In an age when extravagance was a way of life, few needed further prompting. The *Gentleman's Guide* for 1770 noted apprehensively that 'our young nobility and gentry collect mobs in the street by throwing money from the windows. People in trade find the English custom so vastly beneficial that they have their lookers-out on purpose to bring them to their shops and taverns.'

TRAVEL DOCUMENTS

It is sometimes supposed that the visa, the passport and the health certificate are inventions of the twentieth century's bureaucrats and that in the past the traveller wandered at will across frontiers, unhampered by customs officials or border guards. This was very rarely the case. More typical is the unhappy ordeal of Lord and Lady Cashell on reaching Calais after a deperately rough passage of five hours. The party of the great British milord was subject to the full rigours of the frontier post. There was a 'cruel' delay before they were permitted to land, 'our names being written down and reported to the municipality on shore, reeling after our sufferings, we were taken to the Custom House, and thence to examination of the commissaires'. Even after 'trunks, pocket books, green baize bags, etc., had been meekly handed over for inspection, the customs men put their hands into our pockets and then felt down our sides, even to our ankles, for contraband'. In fairness to the French customs service, it should be said that a few years earlier Boswell had found their advice on the quality of the Paris brothels entirely reliable.

With the little formalities of the customs house completed, Lord Cashell and his fellow passengers had to get new passports, the ones issued in England not being valid for the outward journey through France. This complication may have been the fault of whoever booked the passage, because by the 1830s it was certainly possible to get a passport valid for France at the French passport office in London. Anyone travelling on a British Foreign Office passport was liable to find it taken away at the French frontiers, as at any other. In its place, the traveller received a *passe provisoire* while the passport itself was sent on to Paris, there to be countersigned by the minister of the interior. It was necessary to have this done, as the *gendarmes* could 'stop you on the highway, or waylay you as you descend from the diligence – force themselves into the *salle à manger* or enter your bedroom to demand a sight of it. It is needless to expatiate, it is the custom of the country.'

Strangely enough, a traveller finding himself in a country at war with his own might find no more obstruction to the obtaining of his passport than

LOADING THE FERRY George Morland

the normal bureaucratic delays. Laurence Sterne tells us in the *Sentimental Journey* that he got all the way to Paris without a passport, even though he 'had left London with so much precipitation, that it never entered my mind that we were at war with France'. He had passed through Calais in the company of a French count, which may have helped matters but, inevitably, the *lieutenant de police* arrived, in due course, at his hostel. On learning that he had no passport 'the master of the hotel retired three steps from me, as from an infected person', and when he heard that Sterne had no friends in Paris who could procure him one, the landlord assured his guest that he would certainly be sent off to the Bastille the following morning. But the resourceful author equipped himself with the vital document merely by making application to a member of the court at Versailles.

Elsewhere, things could be much more complicated than that. The visitor to Lucca needed a local permit at the city gates before being accepted at an inn and the wise traveller in Italy provided himself with two health certificates: one stating that he was in good health, so that he could travel at all; the other stating that he had a mild indisposition, so that he could eat meat during Lent. In addition, most people carried letters of credit; the *port fueille*, or document case, was one of the tourist's principal pieces of baggage.

Letters of introduction were as necessary as letters of credit for the gentleman traveller. 'I have no letters for Nice,' wrote Arthur Young, a gentleman from Suffolk, in September 1789, 'therefore, knowing nothing of the inside of the houses, I must be content with what meets the eye.' When the young John Milton left England in May 1638, his portfolio contained both a passport signed by the Warden of the Cinq Ports and a letter of introduction to Lord Thomas Scudamore, the British ambassador in Paris. A century later the irrepressible James Boswell proudly presented the privy councillor of the Duke of Brunswick with a letter from Count Bentinck of the Hague. Four hours later he had been presented to 'all the Grand etcs, and to the Dames d'honneur' and was sitting down to dinner with the Duke and Duchess. 'Here now do I find myself in the very sphere of magnificence', runs his exultant journal. 'I live with princes and a court is my home ... I went home in vast spirits. I could scarcely sleep.'

17

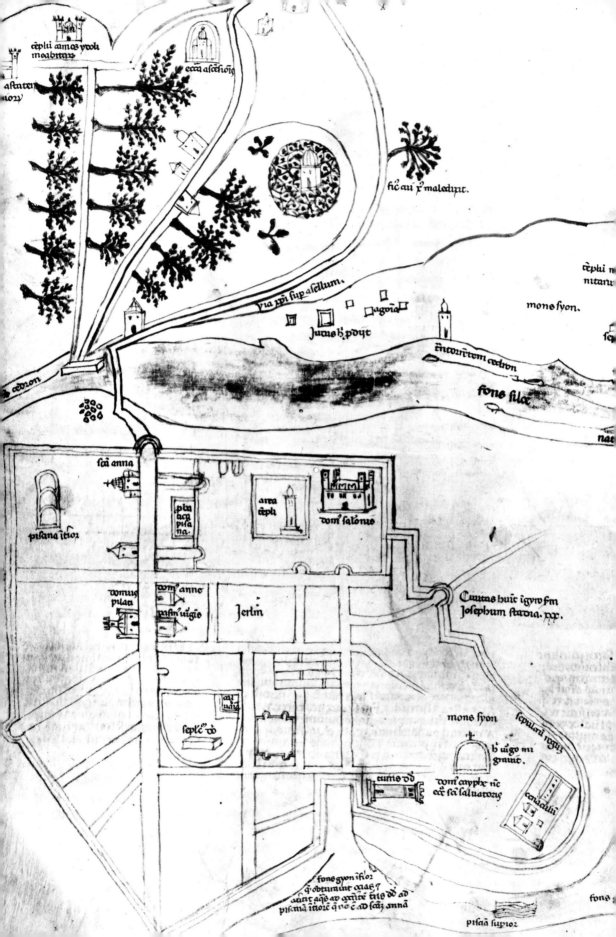

cepli camoz yroli
moabitaz

astaten
nioz

ecca ascecionis

hic aui xp maledipit.

cepli m
nitani

mons syon.

via xpi sup asellum.

Jutas h pdyt

agoia

encountem cedron

fons silce

de cedron

scā anna

piscina itioz

area
ceph

dom salonis

pha
aca
pisa
na

domus
pilati

dom anne

pastm uigis

Jerlm

cum od

sepulcri regis

ault
nona

mons syon

sepl̄c od

h uigo mi
gratie

cumis od

dom cayphe nc
ecc scī salnatoris

cenaculū

Cinitas huic igitis sm
Josephum stadia. xx.

fons gyon istoz
qz obtunaint ociaez
auin aqe ao occlrte tyle od ao
piscina itioe q uo c ao scā anna

piscina supioz

fons

II

DESTINATION
JERUSALEM

One warm Mediterranean evening in the spring of 1458, John Tiptoft, Earl of Worcester, sat over his wine with the English Castellan of the international crusading order of the Knights of St John of Jerusalem, putting the world to rights and ruminating on the sad state of Christendom. Five years earlier the great city of Constantinople, for a thousand years Christianity's eastern bastion, had fallen to the infidel armies of the Turk. The Castellan and his knights, drawn from all the countries of Europe, manned the island stronghold of Cyprus and their galleys kept the sea-lanes open for Christian ships. The Earl was on a pilgrimage to Jerusalem.

The battle lines of Islam and Christendom were criss-crossed by trade

Opposite   Town plan of Jerusalem from SECRETA FIDELIUM CRUCIS,
a handbook for crusaders written in 1321
Above   'First Day', an illustration from A CANTERBURY PILGRIMAGE
by J. E. Pennell, 1885

and travel. Even the dyers who manufactured the richly coloured robes of the papal court imported the alum to fix their colours from mines in Turkey. Today, the western tourist marvels at the glories of the Kremlin in Communist Russia; in the fifteenth century, pilgrims also journeyed through territory governed by the ideological enemy.

When Earl John embarked on his voyage, the history of western European pilgrimage was already a thousand years old. As early as the fourth century, Pope Damasus had instituted a system of signposting in the catacombs; by the early seventh century, pilgrims could buy a guide to a route round the principal churches of Rome. From the ninth century, when the supposed body of St James the Apostle was discovered there, Compostela in the western Spanish province of Galicia, made up the trinity of medieval Europe's great shrines. Travellers to Jerusalem were often distinguished from visitors to the other two sanctuaries as 'palmers' because they brought back palm leaves as a token of their journey. Visitors to the holy city of Rome were sometimes colloquially known as 'Romers', while some purists, the poet Dante among them, reserved the term 'pilgrim' for those who made the lengthy trek to Compostela.

The word 'pilgrim' derives from the Latin *peregrinus* meaning 'foreigner' or 'stranger' and so, by natural transference of ideas, became a synonym for 'traveller'. No doubt, to an Italian and a Florentine at that, a visit to Rome hardly counted as a journey compared to the long haul to Spanish Galicia. The word is found in English at least as early as 1200, with the neutral sense of 'traveller' or 'stranger', and continued to be used in this general sense, as well as the specific one of a traveller to holy places, into the sixteenth century. In John Wycliffe's translation of the Bible, which he completed in the 1380s, he even used the verb 'to pilgrimage' meaning to travel or live abroad. Thus, in its very history, the word 'pilgrim' betrays that, whatever reason they gave for their wanderings, medieval people who set out for the holy places often did so for much the same reasons that motivate the modern tourist. The English translation of a pilgrim journal ends with the words 'the further ye go, the more ye shall see and know'. The fascination of travel, it would seem, is no modern discovery.

In our own day people will travel thousands of miles to see the house of Elvis Presley and compete at auction for a pair of his jeans. Medieval pilgrims flocked with almost equal devotion to the Church of the Holy Sepulchre, built over the supposed tomb of Jesus Christ, to gaze in wonder at the various pieces of the True Cross scattered in churches across half Europe, and willingly suspend their disbelief to purchase from some itinerant pedling palmer putative relics of every kind. It was understandable. To the medieval mind, relics were not merely immediate mementos of the saint but radiant sources of a mystic power which sanctified the building in which they were housed, and charged people and even objects that came into contact with them. It was believed that this power could be tapped and preserved so that when a pilgrim left his or her home town neighbours begged them to carry a piece of jewellery to the shrine, that it might be imbued with the heavenly mana.

In an age when the 1980 Formula One motor racing champion confesses to patching his underpants with fragments of the red pants he wore at the beginning of his career, and humbler motorists charm their car keys with a St Christopher token, we should, perhaps, not sneer too easily at other people's superstitions. However, even in the thirteenth century there were cynics ready to calculate that the portions of the True Cross surviving into their day would provide sufficient timber to rebuild the Ark of Noah. It would have been interesting to have their comments on the reliquary at St Thomas's shrine at Canterbury, which was said to contain a piece of the clay from which Adam had been created.

The quest for relics was by no means the only reason for undertaking a pilgrimage. The Church offered indulgence of sins to those who made their devotions at the great shrines; notable sinners were often ordered to undertake the journey as a penance. Wisely perhaps, they were sometimes instructed to return with letters proving they had actually been to the designated sanctuary. Others made a voluntary penance. The brilliant and rakish scholar Aeneas Silvius Piccolomini, who began his career as a rising man in the anti-papal Conciliar movement, underwent a conversion in 1445, submitted to the Pope, and a decade later became Pope himself as Pius II. He suffered from gout. No doubt he felt it a just penance since he had contracted it on pilgrimage to Our Lady of Whitekirk in East Lothian, Scotland, when, in an access of devotion he had walked the last stage of the journey barefoot in the snow.

Kings and noblemen went on pilgrimage. Duke William V of Aquitaine visited either Rome or Compostela once a year and was renowned for his piety. One of his contemporaries, Fulk the Black of Anjou, reputedly descended from the Devil, suffered no such misappraisal from his peers. Yet he punctuated his career of rapine and conquest with 'several visits to the Holy Land'. After his time the clergy at the Church of the Holy Sepulchre offered a special service for their truly noble clients – membership of the Order of Knights of the Sepulchre. The ceremony was the more coveted because the tomb of Christ was believed to be at the centre of the world. It was certainly impressive as witnessed by one pilgrim in the 1480s. The accolyte was solemnly summoned 'into the inner cave of the Lord's monument' and invested with the sword and spurs of knighthood. He was then instructed to kneel before the Lord's tomb 'so that his knees rested upon the pavement, and his breast and arms lay upon the lid of the tomb'.

In this position the young gentleman was duly dubbed and, no doubt, swelled at the thought of the dashing role he might one day play if the potentates of Europe should combine to drive the Infidel Turks from the Holy Land. For by this time Jerusalem had been in Moslem hands for just three centuries. The triumph of the First Crusade, which had won the city for Christendom in 1099, was reversed by the genius of Saladin the Kurd in 1187. For eighty years, then, it had been a province of Latin Christendom, and the pilgrims who visited in those years came back with travellers' tales of the strange Franco-Syrian society of the conquerors' descendants, already 'gone native'.

The first crusaders presented themselves as champions of the Cross, but in truth many of the leaders were landgrabbers and others were profiteers. There were, of course, some honourable men, and among the common soldiers many more. But even at the height of the crusading movement there were western Christians cynical about the motives of their heroes. 'Some were weighed down by debt; others were known criminals flying from the deserved penalties of their crimes; others were ready to fight not only the enemies of Christ but even their fellow Christians, if there seemed any chance of plunder; and others, eager for novelty, went for the sake merely of learning about strange lands.'

Some of the pilgrims to Palestine during the Christian period served for a few months in the defence forces. Others were too shocked by the oriental life style of their co-religionists, and their readiness to compromise in the politics of the region, to stay longer than was absolutely necessary. One pilgrim was outraged to discover that although the al Aqsa mosque had been duly consecrated as a Christian temple, one of the porches was still reserved for the Arab population of the city. Seeing a Moslem infidel practising his abominable creed, the Christian rushed up to him and swung him roughly round to face the East, crying out: 'This is the way thou shouldst pray.' He was summarily thrown out of the building by the Templar knights who acted as custodians. They were on the best of terms with the locals during times of peace and, having ejected the fanatic, hastened to mollify the Arab gentleman, explaining that the offender had but recently come from Europe, and could not be expected to know better.

It was indeed a strange world for the European visitor. At Damascus there was a holy image that healed Jews, Christians and Moslems without distinction of creed. Near to Nazareth bubbled a spring of holy water where the Virgin Mary had washed the clothes of the infant Christ, which was venerated equally by Moslems and Christians. Syrian Christian gentlemen of middling rank and *nouveaux riches* Italian merchants covered their houses in mosaic and marble; carpets lay on the floors and the beds were spread with regularly laundered linen. At meal times, their tables were laid with gold and silver cutlery and, instead of using their fingers like men, they followed the effeminate Byzantine custom and picked at their meat with a fork-shaped eating prong. The chaplain of King Baldwin I, a first-generation settler, had boasted: 'We have become true Easterners. The Roman and the Frank are transformed into the Galilean or Palestinian.' Staying too briefly in the new country to accept its ways, the average western tourist-pilgrim could only give his shocked assent.

The local Arabs watched these uncouth visitors with wondering eyes. 'The Franks (May Allah Render them Helpless!) possess none of the virtues of men except courage', was the general opinion. Nothing revealed them for the barbarians they were more clearly than their conduct in the public baths. Virtually unknown in twelfth-century Europe, the steam bath had been a standard luxury of Eastern life since the days of the Roman empire. Newcomers and tourists from Europe eagerly explored the experience. But they scorned to wear towels round their waists as Arab conventions of modesty demanded. A boisterous European, visiting the baths at Damascus for the first time, whipped off the towel of one of the attendants. He stared in amazement, for the man's pubic hair had been shaved. Calling the fellow over he 'stretched out his hand over the place and said, "An excellent idea. By the truth of my religion, do the same for me."' When the shave was completed to his satisfaction he ordered his servant to bring his wife into the steam room. What followed might cause a few raised eyebrows even in a modern unisex sauna. Ordering his wife to lie on the marble slab, the knight pulled up her skirts with his own hands and supervised the appalled Arab attendant as he shaved off the lady's pubic hair.

Preparations for Adventure

The fall of Jerusalem to the Moslem armies of Saladin spurred Europe to a new crusade. The Kings of France and England and the Emperor of Germany pledged themselves to the campaign, but the Emperor died on the march and his huge army dispersed, while Philip of France returned home even before the march on Jerusalem had begun. Under the inspiring generalship of Richard the Lionheart of England the cosmopolitan army very nearly achieved its aim. But realizing that, even if the city were won, it could not be held, the King came to terms with Saladin. Their agreement meant that thousands of soldiers, who had joined the colours as much for the pilgrimage as for the war, were permitted to visit the holy places. King Richard refused to go with them, for shame that he had failed in his oath to recapture the city for Christ.

The Third Crusade did not win back Jerusalem, but King Richard's emissary, Hubert Walter, Bishop of Salisbury, did win Saladin's agreement that Latin priests should be allowed to celebrate Catholic rites at the Church of the Holy Sepulchre, Bethlehem and Nazareth. In the centuries that followed, pilgrims from Europe sometimes found routes to the Holy City closed by war or politics, but access was possible more often than not and, thanks to the negotiating skill of Bishop Walter, when they arrived they were able to share in the familiar rites of the western liturgy.

Most pilgrims set out with lofty ideals and many remained true to them. Yet months away from the settled community of their home towns or villages, the dangers of the road and the delights of new experience that travel in foreign parts had to offer, not only broadened the mind but encouraged a free style of life which, in the context of the age, was rich in temptation. Many churchmen lamented the irony that journeys undertaken as a penance for sin could lead the pilgrims to the peril of their souls. In the eighth century St Boniface warned women pilgrims that many before them had made the holy journey to Rome only to lose their virtue in some casual encounter on the road.

At this period the Irish were renowned as pilgrims. A contemporary observed that there were so many on the roads 'that it would appear that the habit of travelling is part of their nature', but the Irish themselves realized that there was more to the spiritual life than the pursuit of relics. In the words of an eighth-century Irish poem: 'To go to Rome means great labour and little profit; the king you seek can only be found there if you bring him within yourself.' In the twelfth century St Bernard, who preached the Second Crusade, nevertheless deplored the superstitious pride that some monks took in the relics at their monasteries, 'Your cell', he told them, 'is Jerusalem.'

Serious churchmen have always taught that true religion is to be found in the inner life of the devout spirit. In 1370 Canterbury celebrated the jubilee of St Thomas à Becket. Distribution points were set up along the road from London to Canterbury, where pilgrims could get free food and drink. To Simon Sudbury, Bishop of London, it seemed that the holy day of the Church had turned into a carnival. On his way to pay his devotions to the saint's shrine, he overtook a party of cheerful pilgrims looking forward to the plenary indulgence of their sins that the pilgrimage would earn. 'Better hope ye might have of Salvation', he admonished them, 'had ye stayed at home and brought forth fruits meet for repentance.' An English moralist of the next century denounced the idea of pilgrimage even more harshly. 'There are many who keep their pilgrimages not for God but for the devil ... who sin more freely when away from home or go on pilgrimage to succeed in foolish love.' The words echo the warning of St Boniface and remind us that for a thousand years people saw the pilgrimage as an opportunity for adventure as well as for spiritual reward.

The Zurich-born friar Felix Fabri, who made the journey twice in the late fifteenth century, entitled the account of his travels not *The Pilgrimage* but *The Wanderings of Brother Felix*. He received ecclesiastical permission for the second trip on the grounds that the first one had allowed too little time to see the Holy Places properly. The title of his book and the fact that on the second journey he travelled as chaplain to a group of young German noblemen suggest that at heart Brother Felix was bitten by the travel bug.

The lengthy preparations needed for a pilgrimage ranged from the practical to the ceremonial. One packed as if for a camping holiday. William Wey, a Devon man who travelled with the Earl of Worcester's party in 1458 recommended a long list of necessaries, including 'a little cauldron and frying pan, dishes, bowls and glasses'. Travel documents were necessary. Laymen were required to get a licence for the journey from their bishop; monks needed permission from their abbot. These *testimoniales*, an early variant of the passport, were no mere formality; failure to produce them on demand could result in summary arrest as a vagrant. The conscientious pilgrims adopted the 'outward signs' of his vocation. His beard was left to grow; he donned a long grey gown with a large red cross sewn on to it, and a black or grey hat also marked with a red cross; and finally shouldered a scrip, or small pouch, containing basic provisions.

The pilgrim was finally required to put his affairs in order. He had to make a will and warn creditors of his impending departure by announcements read in the church. As departure day approached there was the ritual blessing of his accoutrements. The scrip was sprinkled with holy water and placed round his neck by the priest; the staff was next placed in his hands; and finally the cross was blessed and the gown, sprinkled with holy water, was handed over.

On the day of departure the whole town turned out. Friends and neighbours thronged the traveller asking to be remembered in his prayers at the holy places and perhaps pressing into his hand some ring or jewel to be sanctified at the shrine. Friar Fabri proclaimed his departure with a valedictory sermon. At the end he begged for the prayers of his congregation and invited them to join in a hymn. Many broke down in tears, anxious and alarmed, 'fearing, even as I myself feared, that I should perish in the terrible dangers of the journey'.

FIRST STOP VENICE

Setting out from the southern German city of Ulm, Fabri naturally headed for Venice, where one could either charter a ship or take passage on one of the galleys organized by the city government. This was the most popular route for all pilgrims from northern Europe. Then as now, the English set out from their island either by a North Sea crossing – usually Yarmouth to Zeeland and thence down the Rhine valley and the Inn valley for the Alps – or Dover-Calais, crossing the Alps by the Great Saint Bernard or the Saint Gotthard pass, to approach Venice along the River Po.

On the Great Saint Bernard the famous hospice of Mont-Joux offered quite decent accommodation for the traveller, with stabling and laundry facilities, but the journey over the mountains was dangerous and frightening. Bandits lurked to cut off stragglers and, for some, the plunging gorges and jagged heights were frightening in themselves. The Welshman Adam of Usk, who made the trip early in the fifteenth century, had himself blindfolded and carried in a litter rather than face the horrors of the Saint Gotthard.

In view of the dangers that lay ahead, it was only common sense to travel with a party. Brother Fabri was safe enough with his band of sword-bearing young gentlemen, others attached themselves to a group as soon as possible. English guide books of the period, such as John Poloner's *Description of the Holy Land* or the anonymous *Information for Pilgrims*, stressed the importance of keeping on good terms with one's travelling companions. Parties generally formed themselves on the channel crossing. Sometimes one member was appointed treasurer and, since well-to-do pilgrims might be carrying twenty pounds or more, it could be a responsible job. Even the poorer members of the party might have jewellery and precious stones belonging to friends who had helped finance their trip. On the pilgrim's return the stone was incorporated into a rosary or some other object of devotion, en route it needed protection.

Margery Kempe, who made her pilgrimage in the 1420s, was the wife of a well-to-do merchant of Lynne in Norfolk. The author of the first autobiography in English, notorious in her home town for her fits of religious possession, and considered by some to be a mystic, she was headstrong and flamboyantly independent. She was a woman of powerful sexuality and still more powerful will who, despite the protests of her hapless husband and the objections of the local bishop, had persuaded a

Top   DOME OF THE ROCK, JERUSALEM David Roberts
Above   THE CRYPT OF THE HOLY SEPULCHRE, JERUSALEM David Roberts

cleric to absolve her from the duties of the marriage bed. It was a wrench for her, too, since she writes in her book that they had 'great delectation either of them in using of other', but Margery was persuaded that the pleasures of the bed were a betrayal of her vocation. Such a woman was not easily to be withstood.

Margery set off on her pilgrimage in triumph. The Bishop of Lincoln attended her farewell and was among those who asked her to pray for them when she reached the Holy City. It is not surprising that such a woman found it difficult to follow the guide books' advice and 'keep on good terms with her travelling companions'. By the time her party reached Constance they were frankly fed up with their imperious and self-opinionated would-be leader. They refused to let her stay for the rest of the journey. Margery, of course, thought them a bunch of misguided fools. But she was not dismayed. She had money, and set about finding a companion and guide among the pilgrim riff-raff in the city who had run out of funds.

Margery Kempe was a loner; Brother Fabri, very much the reverse. He and his young patrons made cheeful progress on to Innsbruck, through the village of Tramin, famous for its traminer grapes and wine, and over the Brenner Pass to Trent. Further into Italy they came to Feltre and here some of them rode to the top of a hill from which they had been promised by the guide a first glimpse of the Mediterranean, 'the sea which perchance would be our tomb'. In the middle distance the setting sun glowed on the waves, but 'the rest of the ocean, the end of which none of us could see, seemed to be a lofty, thick black cloud; it had a terrible appearance.' A few days later they reached the shores of the Lagoon and took passage for the city. At length they saw before their eyes 'the famous, wealthy and noble city of Venice, mistress of the Mediterranean, standing in wondrous fashion in the midst of the waters, with lofty towers, great churches, splendid houses and palaces'. It seemed almost beyond belief that 'such weighty and tall structures' should have their foundations in the water.

The glorious city was one of Europe's most powerful trading states and also one of the wonders of Christendom. Her multitudinous churches were themselves almost worthy of a pilgrimage, and few travellers embarked for the next great stage of their journey without a visit to some of them, above all the church of St Christopher. Sound businessmen, the city fathers recognized the considerable revenue they derived from the pilgrim traffic and set up a special department of state for the welfare of the travellers. This employed twelve full-time guides, who were decently paid and forbidden to accept tips, either from the pilgrims or from the Venetian shopkeepers. They conducted sightseeing tours and could be consulted on problems of accommodation and currency.

The party from Ulm needed no such advice. Their rooms were already reserved at the St George Inn, owned by a rich Frankfurt merchant and run by a German manager and his wife. Fabri and his companions heaved a sigh of relief as their canal barge was moored at the hostelry. The landlady and her husband gave him a special welcome, as he had lodged with them on his first pilgrimage, and the rest of the party were delighted to find themselves among compatriots. 'The entire staff was German and there was not a word of Italian to be heard in the house, which was a great comfort.' The very dog was a good German. He leapt up to greet the travellers, licking them on the face 'as dogs do upon those they know', and any German could be assured of such a welcome. Even other German dogs and German beggars were treated as friends by this excellent dog, but foreigners, Italian beggars, and the local curs, were warned off with angry barks.

The well-organized traveller aimed to reach Venice shortly before one of the quarterly galley sailings. Bad timing could mean having to charter a private ship, rarely so reliable as the closely supervised galleys authorized by the Venetian city government, and involved bargaining in a foreign language with a tough, professional and rarely scrupulous sea captain.

It was considered wiser to take passage on one of the republic's galleys. Each year two were deputed for the pilgrim traffic. The ship owners were among the leading families of the Venetian state, but they were obliged to follow stringent government regulations in the fitting out of their boats, at least in the parts of the vessel reserved for the better class of traveller. When it came to booking a passage, probably the largest single item of expenditure, the pilgrim who turned to the city guides who had proved so helpful on his tours of the churches, found himself disappointed. The merchant princes who ran the galley service reserved to themselves the right of settling the fares.

Reservations were made at booths set up at the great door of St Mark's. Two 'costly' white banners, blazoned with the pilgrim emblem of the red cross, floated from a couple of lofty spears. 'By these banners we understood that two galleys had been appointed for the transport of the pilgrims.' In 1483 the two owners were Messer Pietro de Lando and Messer Augustino Contarini. 'The servants of these two noblemen stood beside the banners, and each invited the pilgrims to sail with their master; the one party praised Augustino and abused Pietro, the other did the reverse.' Both captains promised to sail at once, which Fabri, who had travelled with Contarini three years earlier, 'knew to be a lie'. Eventually the leader of his party came to terms with de Lando's captain.

As Fabri had warned, the sailing was delayed. The galley was to sail by the first fair wind after twenty-six days had elapsed. However, there would have been much the same delay if they had sailed with Contarini. Both captains had shown them over the accommodation and both had provided generous hospitality before the deal was agreed. They chose de Lando's because it was the larger and the newer. Contracts were signed and sealed at the notary's office in the Doge's palace; these specified the standard of accommodation and meals to be served, and the fare – forty ducats, one way. Twenty ducats were to be paid in Venice, the balance on arrival at Jaffa.

The Germans now had about a month's delay. Most pilgrims used the waiting period visiting the shrines and making preparations for the voyage and the journey to Jerusalem. Currency was the first problem. For travellers from the remoter parts of Europe, especially England, it had been a problem all the way. Used to a single coin of the realm accepted as legal tender from Cornwall to Northumberland, the inexperienced English were startled by the multiplicity of currencies in the numerous principalities of Germany. William Wey urged the reader of his *Itineraries* to change all his money each time he crossed a frontier, 'for the coins of the one lordship will not go in the next lordship'. In Venice one had to buy gold and silver money freshly minted in the republic herself, 'otherwise', according to the Milanese Santo Brasca, 'the Moors will not accept the coins, even if they be ten grains overweight'.

Brasca had much practical advice for 'the man who loves his life and is accustomed to live delicately at home'. His *Advice to Pilgrims* of 1480 was clearly aimed at an 'A – B' readership. The traveller should have two bags in his luggage, 'one right full of patience', the other containing at least one hundred and fifty Venetian ducats: one hundred for the voyage and fifty for medical fees and other emergencies. Syrup of ginger was a good remedy against travel sickness; a warm cloak was necessary for the cold nights at sea; fruit syrup was essential to keep a man alive in the great heat of Palestine; and a supply of clean shirts would at least lessen the annoyance from 'lice and other unclean things'. It was possible, as William Wey found, to hire bedding in Venice. A pillow, two pairs of sheets and a quilt could be had for the all-in price of three ducats – half of this was described as a deposit, returnable if the goods were brought back in decent condition. It is unlikely that many deposits were successfully claimed.

JOURNEY TO THE CENTRE OF THE WORLD

Even during the darkest centuries the idea of Palestine kept a window in the European mind open to the world beyond. The fifteenth century, the age of the first great explorers, witnessed an upsurge of interest in things foreign. One of the most popular books, *The Travels of Sir John Mandeville*, purported to be a description of the world and was particularly aimed at the pilgrim-tourist market. Written in French, probably at Liège, about the year 1375, it was supposedly the travel journal of an English knight. Why the anonymous Flemish author settled on an Englishman for his hero is not clear; perhaps the English were thought to be especially venturesome – or credulous. The book was soon translated into all the major European languages and for thousands of readers the stories of the fictional Mandeville represented the sober truth about the strange world of the East and the awe-inspiring sites of the Holy Land.

Familiar from Bible stories and sermons, the Holy Land was probably the only foreign place, apart from Rome, that the average person could conceive. Mount Olivet, Calvary, Bethlehem and the Holy Sepulchre, all evoked quite precise responses while places such as Rouen or Paris had only the most misty associations. The better informed were aware that the Church of the Holy Sepulchre was, in addition to its religious importance, the very centre of the world. The knowledge gave extra excitement to the anticipation of the journey ahead. Before it was over, the pilgrim would need all his imagination to keep his enthusiasm alive.

The forty-ducat single fare charged to Fabri and his friends should have ensured first-class conditions. Poor travellers had to be content with what they could get. The cheapest rate was fifty or sixty ducats for the round trip. Beside transport to and from Jaffa, this included subsistence rations on shipboard and the admission charges to the principal sites in Jerusalem, Bethlehem and Nazareth. It was a common saying with stay-at-homes that the voyage from Venice to the Holy Land was 'a mere pleasant excursion'. But this forerunner of the modern package tour had pretty severe drawbacks.

Even the privileged traveller found conditions rather squalid. 'The chief occupation among seafarers, which, though loathsome, is yet very common, daily and necessary, is the hunting of lice and vermin. Unless a man spends several hours in this work when he is on pilgrimage, he will have unquiet slumbers.' As to conditions on the galley deck, they were 'right evil, smouldering hot and stinking'. Bedding, laid out according to rectangles chalked out by the ship's crew, covered the whole deck, travellers sleeping head to toe, like Negroes transported in an eighteenth-century slaver. Congestion was compounded by the bedlam of cackling from the hen coops belonging to passengers with the funds to supplement the meagre ship diet. In the stampede at meal times the clumsy, weak, or merely drunk, were not infrequently bowled overboard. And when a strange sail was sighted, panic reigned for fear it should be a Barbary corsair.

Money, enough of it, could buy something approaching comfort. John Tiptoft, Earl of Worcester, ate at the captain's table; he had his quarters on the poop deck, up wind of the stench below; there was even an awning over his bed; but then he had hired the captain as his personal guide and courier. It was a wise precaution. A group of German gentlemen had to argue long and hard with their captain to get a stack of planking removed from their quarters. 'Some of it jutted into the space where we wished to put our shoes and chamber pots.'

The galley put in at various ports along the route and the pilgrim who could afford it took every opportunity to 'furnish himself with eggs, fowls, bread, sweetmeats and fruits'. The poorer passengers stretched their legs with relief and treated themselves to a drink in the taverns by the quayside or explored the local sights. As we have seen, when his ship put in at Cyprus, the Earl of Worcester and his party made their way to the comforts of the Castellan's house. They were entertained in princely style. A Milanese gentleman, Robert Sanseverino, had been invited to join the party, and has left a description of the evening.

The guests rode through olive groves, where sweet herbs, crushed by their horses' hooves, scented the air. At length they came to a spreading garden, 'planted with beautiful trees, especially cedars and chestnuts; there were orange groves, thickets of bay and the whole garden was graced with ornamental fountains.' Low tables were set in the dappled shade, finely woven tapestries and carpets hung over the bushes, and garlands of fragrant flowers were everywhere. As the shadows lengthened, the two Englishmen, Earl and Castellan, talked, as travellers always do, of things back home and the journey ahead.

Meanwhile, more devout pilgrims paid a visit to the Abbey on the Hill of the Holy Cross. Unfortunately, they were swindled: at least, those who had not read their *Mandeville*. There, they could have discovered that the Abbey's relic was not, in fact, the True Cross, but the cross on which Dismas the Good Thief, crucified with Christ, was hanged. 'But, for the profit of the offerings', the Abbey authorities claimed that it was 'the cross of Our Lord Jesus Christ'. It was the first of many frauds awaiting the gullible.

At Jaffa their troubles began in earnest. Local Christian barrow-boys peddled phoney relics; Moslem traders employed street urchins to start street brawls so that they could demand 'compensation' for damaged goods. The Franciscan community of Mount Syon made some attempt to introduce the newcomers to the customs and hazards of the land in a sermon preached by one of their number at Ramlah, the last stage on the road to Jerusalem. At the end of his harangue the friar pleaded with his hearers not to carve their names or coats of arms on shrines and buildings and, above all, not to help themselves to souvenirs.

But despite the pleas people did carve their names and coats of arms on buildings and altars and holy statues; some even knocked bits off them as trophies. The redoubtable William Wey got back to England with stones from Calvary, the Holy Sepulchre, the place where the True Cross had been discovered, and the cave of the nativity at Bethlehem. The writer of one of Europe's earliest guide books, he is also, it must be admitted, one of the earliest examples for the critics of the tourist menace, whose ineffectual voices rose in vain protest from the secluded beauty spots and sacred places of the old continent. However, since our concern in the chapters which follow is the travellers rather than the stay-at-homes, we will merely give a censorious nod in the direction of Mr Wey and press cheerfully on with the travellers who succeeded him.

THE MOUNT OF OLIVES, an illustration from SYRIA, THE HOLY LAND AND ASIA MINOR ILLUSTRATED IN 120 VIEWS drawn by W. H. Bartlett, W. Purser, 1836–38

EDINBURGH

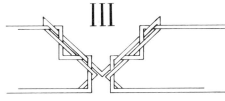

III ISLAND KINGDOM

The England from which Margery Kempe, William Wey and the Earl of Worcester embarked for their pilgrimages to the Holy Land had a mixed reputation in Europe. It was admired for its music – the composers Lionel Power and John Dunstable were considered by their fifteenth-century contemporaries to have transformed the art, and their trombone players were reckoned to have achieved unequalled mastery of the new instrument. It was a time when, because of their long wars with France, the English were well known, and not universally liked, on the Continent. A thoughtful Spaniard observed: 'They have no wish to live in peace, for peace does not suit them, seeing that they are so numerous that they cannot keep within their country and in time of peace many cannot

Opposite LADY GLENORCHY'S CHAPEL, EDINBURGH John Ruskin
Above STAGE COACH PASSENGERS AT BREAKFAST James Pollard

find subsistence there. They have no liking for any other nation.' Generally, they were considered the odd men out of Europe. The legend that the English had tails was centuries old. When, in the spring of 1436, they were finally expelled from Paris, the French collaborators who had supported the régime were driven from the city to cries of, 'After the foxes! Have their tails!'

The English soldier's favourite oath of 'Goddam' earned him in France the nickname of *godon* and his superstition had become a proverb. The Flemish chronicler Commines spoke of the English love of prophecies, 'of which they are never short'. But pilgrim-tourists throughout Europe knew England as the home of one of the greatest shrines of Christendom. Within months of his murder on 29 December, the tomb of Thomas à Becket was the scene of miracles and his canonization followed three years later. In July 1174 King Henry II, generally considered responsible for the outrage, made the pilgrimage and a public penance. Three miles away from Canterbury he dismounted from his horse and, taking off his shoes, walked barefoot to the shrine, dressed in a rough woollen gown. In an age when kings were venerated almost as gods by the simple minded, it was an awesome sight. A foreign visitor recorded that his footsteps 'seemed to be covered in blood, and so it really was; for his tender feet were cut by the hard stones, and much blood flowed from them to the ground.'

Five years later King Louis VII of France made the pilgrimage to pray for the health of his son; shortly after, the towns-people of Canterbury were dazzled by the exotic splendour of the procession of Heraclius, Patriarch of Jerusalem. For the next three and a half centuries, thousands of common people flocked to the shrine from all over Europe. Its halidom of relics was impressive. In addition to the body of the patron himself, the devout could pay their devotions at the reliquaries containing the heads of three saints, the bed of the Blessed Virgin, the stone on which Christ stood before His Ascension and many other sacred objects.

Chaucer's immortal picture of the pilgrimage depicts the pilgrims themselves as a cheerful company, travel hungry rather than excessively religious, fired with enthusiasm for pilgrimages by the invigorating air of springtime rather than deep devotion. Many, perhaps most, took the road to Canterbury because it was one of the great sights of England. They were not disappointed.

The tomb of St Thomas the Martyr [wrote an anonymous Venetian about the year 1500] excels all belief. It is of great size, yet it is entirely covered with plates of pure gold and even this is hardly visible because it, in turn, is encrusted with precious stones, such as sapphires, diamonds, rubies and emeralds ... In addition there are the most beautiful sculptured gems as well as agates, onyxes, cornelians and cameos carved in relief.

But all these wonders were surpassed, in the opinion of the Italian visitor, by a great ruby, as large as a man's thumb-nail. He arrived in the cathedral just before sunset and the interior was somewhat dark and yet, he wrote, 'I saw that ruby as if I had it in my hand.' When the shrine was stripped of its treasures on the orders of King Henry VIII during the Reformation, the glorious ruby of the martyr became an ornament for the royal person.

The England of the early sixteenth century was a landscape of small market towns and cities of modest size, densely wooded by our standards and aglow with the shining new stone of churches and bridges put up in the burst of building of the previous century. The countryside was rich in legends and wreathed in mysteries. The homely River Wye, the traveller was told, ran through a valley 'where spirits suffer torments, and there is the marvellous entrance into the earth of the Peak where souls are tortured'. William Worcester, who wrote the first topographical survey of the country in the 1460s, learnt about the harbours of the Isle of Man from a Dublin merchant he met on the road. Another traveller told him of the fabulous Aran Isles off the coast of Ireland itself, 'where men cannot die; but when they decide, in extreme old age, that the time has come to depart this world, they have themselves carried out of the island'.

Travellers' tales like these are scarcely more fabulous, for us, than the stories that Europeans took home from England. If they are to be believed, and if we accept the views of the English nurtured by modern Europeans, the country must have been populated by an entirely different race of people. Erasmus of Rotterdam, the renowned Dutch Renaissance scholar, was astonished by a country which seemed populated by 'goddess girls, divinely fair ... They come to see you and drink your health in kisses, wherever you go the world is full of kisses waiting.' In the mid-sixteenth century a Greek traveller observed: 'The English display great absence of jealousy in their usage towards females; even those who have never seen them kiss them on the mouth with salutations and embraces and to themselves this appears by no means indecent.' A Venetian was equally startled at the easy way 'most beautiful ladies, and most pleasant' kissed all and sundry; while a German was shocked to find the custom as freely practised in the street, even the church, as in the home.

At this time, Calais 'a fortified town in Picardy', was still a possession of the English King. Ever since the mid-fourteenth century the walls of Calais represented for many European travellers the English frontier. In the many periods of war between England and France the approach could be hazardous. Andrea Badoer, a Venetian ambassador, 'experienced greater difficulty in getting into the town than had befallen me during the rest of my journey, there being numerous fortified towns belonging to the French on the borders which are strictly guarded'.

For centuries the usual port of entry was Dover, 'a small town, full of inns'. To Nicander, a Greek who travelled to England on business in the mid-sixteenth century, the first impression of strangeness was made by the language. 'It is curious,' he wrote, 'having contributions from almost all the rest, as I conjecture. They speak somewhat barbarously, yet their language has a certain charm and allurement, being sweeter than that of the Germans and the Flemings.' A member of a diplomatic mission, he found the nobility 'replete with benevolence and ... courteous to strangers'. Unfortunately, 'the rabble and the mob' were 'turbulent and barbarous in their manner' and not particularly well affected towards foreigners. The courteous gentry were less xenophobic but he never once encountered 'a kindly sentiment of goodwill' towards the French.

Elizabethan England struck many foreigners as a swaggering, extrovert country. The German travel writer Hentzner summed up the wealthy classes as 'lovers of show, liking to be followed wherever they go by whole troops of servants, who wear their masters' arms in silver, fastened to their left sleeves'. The population in general 'excelled in dancing and music, for they are active and lively. They are good sailors, and better pirates, cunning, treacherous, and thievish; above three hundred are said to be hanged annually at London.' The figure may not be exact, but few contemporaries would have questioned the analysis. Perversely enough, the English were proud even of this. A century before, Sir John Fortescue, an exile in France during the Wars of the Roses, chafed at the company he was obliged to keep and fumed at the pusilanimity of the French compared with his brave and warlike compatriots. He rested his proof on the criminal statistics for the two countries. More were hung for robbery and man-slaughter in a single year in England than were hung in France in seven years and the reason was 'that they have no heart to do so terrible an act'.

No doubt Fortescue would have been disgusted by the comment of his contemporary the Flemish chronicler Philippe de Commines to the effect that the English were 'polite'. Yet in the next century Hentzner made the same observation. He found the English 'more polite in eating than the French, devouring also less bread but more meat, which they roast to perfection'. He also noted the English penchant for sugar, a great deal of which they put in their drink. The general level of prosperity seemed to be high. Even humble farmers could afford to cover their beds with tapestry. The Venetian Daniele Barbaro was struck by the wealth of the country too. He noted the rich reserves of tin and lead, the famous prosperity of the wool trade, and the country's magnificent pasturage. Indeed, it seemed to him that the corn yield would be still higher 'if the people did not shirk toil. But they have what they need and do not seek more.'

The same point struck Hentzner. 'The soil is fruitful, and abounds with cattle, which inclines the inhabitants rather to feeding than ploughing, so that near a third part of the land is left uncultivated for grazing.' Perhaps he did not understand the part which the enclosure of grazing lands was playing in the increasingly money based economy of sixteenth-century English agriculture. But the prosperity of the country was unmistakable. 'Lodgings are excellent and commodious here,' wrote an Italian 'a sure sign of a country's wealth.' At the end of the century another German, Thomas Platter, found a 'splendid profusion' of crops – cereals, garden produce, apples, pears, purple plums, cherries and hops. The country could afford to import the finest wines from Gascony, Spain and the Rhineland while the local ale, 'which is prepared from barley, is excellent well tasted, but strong, and soon fuddles'. It was not in short supply.

London had a great many inns, taverns and beer-gardens 'where much amusement may be had with eating, drinking, playing the fiddle and other entertainments. What is particularly curious ... women ... frequent the taverns more often than the men.' If one woman was invited she would bring three or four others and they would 'gaily toast each other' late into the evening. It was in London that Platter first saw tobacco smoked, in the year 1599.

The powder is lit in a small pipe, the smoke sucked into the mouth, after which a good draught of Spanish wine follows. They always carry the instrument upon them, and light up on all occasions, at the play, in the taverns and elsewhere. The herb, imported from Indies, makes them riotous and merry, and rather drowsy, just as if they were drunk, though the effect soon passes. Their preachers cry out on them for their self destruction.

The strange freedom allowed to English women, who could even be seen in the markets 'employed undisguisedly in affairs of trade', and the men's passion for smoking, merely confirmed for visitors what Europeans already knew – the English were strange people. 'The English', thought a German, 'are impatient of anything like slavery. If they see a foreigner very well made, or particularly handsome, they will say: "It is a pity he is not an Englishman."' In the 1720s the French political theorist Montesquieu found the same atmosphere. 'This nation is passionately fond of liberty ... each considers himself a monarch.' Fifty years later Karl Philip Moritz was

Top A PEEP BEHIND THE SCENES, COVENT GARDEN THEATRE
John Nixon, 1802
Above Thomas Rowlandson's engraving of a pub in Wapping, 1807

as impressed by the popular interest in politics as he was shocked by the open abuse which members of parliament flung at each other. 'When one sees how the lowliest carter here shows an interest in public affairs; how everyone feels himself to be a man and an Englishman – as good as the King and his King's ministers – it brings to mind thoughts very different from those we know when we watch the soldiers drilling in Berlin.'

LONDON

'This city', wrote an Italian in the early sixteenth century, 'abounds with every article of luxury. In a street named the Strand there are fifty-two goldsmiths' shops, full of silver vessels such as salt-cellars, drinking cups and basins.' Over the next two centuries London rose to become the preeminent city of northern European trade and visitors stared astonished at the 'prodigious heaps of gold and silver in the windows'. A Prussian gentleman, Herr Archeholtz, waxed eloquent at the magnificence of the shops 'which sometimes extend without interruption for an English mile. Each shop front has large glass windows and a glass door; the variety and symmetrical arrangement of all that is finest and most modern provide the most brilliant spectacle for the passers-by.'

Samuel Johnson considered that the walk from Charing Cross to Whitechapel took one through the 'greatest series of shops in the world' and Karl Philip Moritz was also impressed by the Strand. 'One shop jostles another, people of very different trades often live in the same house which from top to bottom displays large signboards.' It is not perhaps surprising that in the London of Hogarth's *Gin Lane* the most frequent signboard he observed was 'Dealer in Spirituous Liquors'. According to Moritz, an entire street could 'resemble a well-arranged show cabinet, with onlookers standing stock still in the middle of the street to admire paintings, machines, precious objects – all advantageously displayed behind great clear glass windows'.

The streets of the capital were a ceaseless bustle of noise and traffic. 'Carts and coaches make such a thundering as if the world ran upon wheels; hammers are beating in one place, tubs hooping in another, pots clinking in a third. Here are porters sweating under burdens, there, merchants' men bearing bags of money.' Coaches had been part of the scene since the 1560s when Guylliam Boonen, a Dutchman and Queen Elizabeth's coachman, is believed to have 'brought the use of coaches into England. By little and little they grew usual among the nobility and others of sort'. In 1634 a carriage rank was licensed in the Strand and carriages permitted to ply for public hire.

The development was not welcomed by Thames watermen. In Thomas

Platter's day it had been customary to travel up and down the town by attractive pleasure craft. Crowds of boatmen, their wherries moored at the end of tiny streets that led to the Thames, jostled for clients who were free to choose the boat they found most attractive and pleasing. The wherries, generally carrying no more than two people, were charmingly upholstered with embroidered cushions laid across the seat, often protected by an awning. But seventy years after Platter depicted this colourful scene the hackney carriages had taken much of the river traffic. A pamphlet of 1679 presented the complaint of the watermen. 'Coaches and sedans deserve both to be thrown into the Thames, and but for stopping the channel I would they were, for I am sure where I was wont to have eight or ten fares in a morning I now scarce get two in a whole day.' Nevertheless, water traffic continued into the eighteenth century, and on 1 August 1716 Thomas Doggett, the actor, inaugurated his race for Thames watermen from London Bridge to Chelsea. It quickly became a tourist attraction and Boswell, for one, had great sport watching the 1763 race. Even today Doggett's Badge is still competed for.

The multiplication of public vehicles congested the already crowded and filthy streets. Moritz was disgusted by the 'detestable butchers stalls, especially in the neighbourhood of the Tower. The guts and refuse being thrown all on the street and setting up an unbearable stink.' Eventually this nuisance was stopped so that, when she visited France in the 1840s, Effie Ruskin was able to record as an unpleasant surprise the stench from the offal in the streets.

In eighteenth-century London everyone took care to walk down the side of the street, keeping to the paved sidewalks introduced in the 1760s and avoiding the filth flung from the windows. Dr Johnson recalled that when his mother lived in the capital there were two sorts of people 'those who gave the wall, and those who took it. Now it is fixed that every man keeps to the right: or, if one is taking the wall, another yields it.' Not that hygiene was the chief concern of London pedestrians in those days. Footpads were a scourge. A German visitor, Wenderborn, thought that there were more people to be seen in London at midnight 'than in many considerable towns of Europe at noonday'. It is to be hoped that they looked to their purses. In the 1750s King George II had been relieved of his watch, while taking a stroll in the gardens of Kensington Palace. Early in the next century, we find the management of Sadlers Wells Theatre advising ladies that their return home to the elegant safety of Grosvenor Square would be protected by an armed horse patrol.

London's international reputation as a theatre centre, so important a draw to modern tourists, was firmly established during the lifetime of

Shakespeare. Touring companies took his plays, and many others, to audiences in Denmark and Germany; at home, travelling players were already part of tavern entertainment. In the 1590s, a German tourist was delighted to find that his hostlery was 'visited by players almost daily'. Unfortunately he does not tell us what plays they performed, but we can be sure that the charge was a good deal less than the prices in the theatres.

Moritz, who attended a performance at the Haymarket in the 1780s, jotted in his notebook that a seat in a box cost five shillings and the cheapest seats in the house, the gallery, were a shilling. The gallery customers got their money's worth. Moritz, who had paid three shillings for his seat in the pit, found that the gallery made a great noise. 'Every moment a rotten orange came hurtling past me, one hit my hat, but I dared not turn round for fear one hit me in the face.' Behind him sat a young fop 'who continually put his foot on my bench in order to show off the buckles on his shoes; if I didn't make way for his precious shoes, he put his foot on my coat tails'.

After the show he soothed his spirits at a coffee shop. It was an institution that fascinated foreigners. As a Frenchman observed, 'you have all manner of news; you have a good fire which you may sit by as long as you please; you have a dish of coffee; you meet your friends for the transaction of business – and all for a penny, if you don't care to spend more.' Other visitors were astonished by the freedom of political discussion and at the way gentlemen mixed freely with tradespeople and even servants. Between the opening of the first coffee room under the Commonwealth, to the decline of the institution in the early nineteenth century, more than two thousand coffee shops opened their doors for business. Some had long and even distinguished careers, others failed after a few years. Few visitors to the city missed taking a cup of coffee, or a glass of something stronger, at one of these intriguing and novel establishments.

By the mid-nineteenth century, the ale-house and the private club had largely displaced the coffee shop. The American Bayard Taylor, who saw most of what there was to see in the capital, makes no mention of the once famous institution. He was impressed by the bustle of the great metropolis and puzzled by the 'antique appearance' of some districts. In Fleet Street the shops seemed distinctly old-fashioned and the medieval aspect was heightened by the old gate of Temple Bar, the western boundary of medieval London. But all hints of medievalism disappeared as one approached the Strand and Trafalgar Square. 'Fancy every house in Broadway a store all built of light granite, a lofty column in the centre, double the crowd and the tumult of business and you will have some idea of the view.' He visited the National Gallery, opened just six years before, and was not greatly impressed by the prize exhibit of the growing collection, Sebastian Piombo's *The Raising of Lazarus*. But he was not disappointed by London's other tourist attractions.

He marvelled at St Paul's, trembled within the lowering walls of the Tower, and mused rhapsodically in Poet's Corner in Westminster Abbey. He duly inspected the coronation chair, noting that on the bottom, someone had carved his name with the fact that he once slept in it. This establishes that at least two people, other than bored churchgoers, have slept in the Abbey.

Fifty years before Taylor's visit, François de Chateaubriand, then a nonentity unflatteringly described on his passport as 'a French officer in the emigrant army, five feet four inches, thin shape, brown hair, and pitted with the small Pox', had passed the night there. 'Wishing to contemplate the interior of the basilica by twilight and lost in admiration of its bold and capricious architecture,' he found the doors locked on him. His shouts and hammering on the doors spread out in the silence and were lost; he had to resign himself to sleeping among the dead.

A poor but proud emigrant, who refused the daily shilling doled out to royalist exiles by the British government, Chateaubriand was in lodgings at six shillings a month, 'under the lathes of a garret at the end of a little street off the Tottenham Court Road'. When there was a court reception he could only watch the ladies go by, sitting sideways in their sedan-chairs – 'their great hoop-petticoats protruding through the door of the chair like altar hangings'. Thirty years later, the daughters and grand-daughters of those same young ladies were dancing at his home in Portland Place. For, in 1822, 'His Lordship the Vicomte de Chateaubriand' came once again to London, but this time as ambassador of the restored Bourbon monarchy. By then his passport carried no description. 'My greatness was such as to make my face known wherever I went.'

In all his glory he sometimes yearned for the cameraderie of the exiles in the bad times – to go into the country, into the little garden of some unfrequented tavern, and drink a cup of bad tea on a wooden bench and talk of insane hopes'. Once the hopes had been realized, he found the only relief for his nostalgic melancholy was the less oppressive melancholy of Kensington Gardens. But the gardens were now no longer fashionable. In years gone by the 'loveliest of Frenchwomen, Mme Recamier, used to walk there followed by the crowd'; now the fashionable set drove in Hyde Park. Playing truant from the embassy and acting the role of 'poor little emigrant noble' he would watch them from the deserted lawns of Kensington Gardens.

ON THE ROAD

As the industrialization of England gathered momentum in the second half of the eighteenth century, the population of London grew at an accelerating rate. But the eighteenth century also saw a marked improvement in the roads of England, caused by the turnpike companies which sprang up all over the country. The first turnpike trust was set up in the 1660s and from then on the movement gathered speed.

The trusts were empowered by parliament to collect tolls over defined stretches of road and, in return, undertook the upkeep and maintenance. The concessions were granted in the first instance for a period of twenty-one years, on the theory that after that time the road could be maintained by the traditional system of parish and forced labour. By the end of the eighteenth century more than 20,000 miles of British roads were under the supervision of turnpike trusts.

They derived their name from the form of barrier at the toll points. This was originally a pivoted bar, looking like a spear or pike, similar in fact to the barriers at modern unmanned railway crossings. Inefficiency and corruption were to give the turnpikes a bad reputation, but they did effect real improvements in numerous sections of the road network. By and large, travellers welcomed the toll-gate as an earnest of at least a few miles of tolerable road, just as the modern driver appreciates even a brief stretch of dual carriageway.

The essential weakness of the system lay at the collection point. Without machinery at the gate to register the number of vehicles passing through, the trusts had virtually no means of checking what their revenues should be. The 'pike keepers' made the most of the situation and trusts came to farm out the concessions. Inevitably they received less than the real value of the tolls, while travellers were left to combat the extortions of unscrupulous concessionaires. For all its drawbacks, the system did make for better roads and Arthur Young, writing in 1771, reckoned that the improvement of the roads had reached a point where it was having social consequences. 'Now a country fellow, one hundred miles from London, jumps on a coach box in the morning and for eight or ten shillings gets to Town by night.'

Actually, as the wide-eyed rustic discovered, travelling to London was not always a smooth ride. The odds on reaching the capital without being delayed by some 'gentleman of the road' were hardly even. The danger increased as one approached the city for within a twenty-mile radius of the centre, highwaymen and robbers of all kinds were especially active.

This was hardly a novel situation. In the late thirteenth century, King Edward I had ordered the clearing of 200-foot swathes along the roads to remove the cover for lurking criminals; his grandson Edward III repeated the injunction with particular reference to the approaches to the capital. In the seventeenth century the profession of common robber was dignified by the addition to its ranks of a number of gentlemen impoverished by the Civil War. Taking a lead from their plight, ordinary ruffians would assert that they had only been forced into their nefarious way of life by the confiscations of the Parliamentarians and protest that they robbed only men of known Republican sympathies.

This convenient fiction was not available to one of the most notorious of England's road robbers. When she died, aged about seventy-five in 1659, Mary Frith, known as Moll Cutpurse, had amassed a considerable fortune and was something of a public figure. A play based on her life, called *The Roaring Girle*, had delighted Jacobean theatre audiences and antedated the Newgate pastoral *The Beggars' Opera* by nearly a century. Both these immensely successful works exploited the air of romantic fascination with which the English continued to regard their criminal classes, well into the nineteenth century.

The highwaymen, for the most part a ruffianly bunch, played up to the part expected of them. Their public executions were set pieces of sham heroics in which the thief played the part of the dashing adventurer, joking with the hangman and ignoring the priest. The crowds loved it: ladies swooned away and men fought for possession of the corpses, believed to have magical powers. The idea of capital punishment as a deterrent was never more in vogue than in the eighteenth century, and will never be more thoroughly discredited. If the traveller's brains were not spilled by a bullet from Dick Turpin's pistol, his stomach was liable to be turned at every crossroads and vantage point along the road by the sight of decaying corpses, in 'ingeniously made' iron cages, hanging from the public gibbets. Yet ineffective as these were in their deterrent role, they did have their uses. Particularly valuable was the help they afforded writers of guide books in giving directions such as 'first left past the second gibbet'. Highwaymen, too, seem to have appreciated the merits of these unmistakable landmarks; for many a robbery took place in the shadow of the gibbet.

The profession had its occupational hazards. It also required a degree of social grace from its more serious devotees. Some were, as they claimed, petty noblemen fallen on bad times – often as a result of the gaming table; others were sons of clergymen and, as befitted such gentlefolk, demanded money with great civility – until they were crossed. The wise traveller carried a second purse for the 'collectors', as they were euphemistically known. Foreign visitors to England were astonished by the numbers of robbers on the roads, but equally astonished at their often charming and courtly ways. Foreigners were accustomed to bloodthirstier things. In September 1723, three English gentlemen and their servants, were waylaid on their journey from the Silver Lion Inn at Calais to Boulogne. Unarmed, they were forced to give up their possessions and then, as their French coachman looked on, were made to lie face down in the road; they were then shot to death and their bodies mutilated.

It was a far cry from the best standards of English robbery. Gentleman Harry, with his headquarters at the White Swan in Whitechapel, boasted that he was an old Etonian; Dandy Jack Rann wore sixteen tassels at his knee, one for each of his prison terms. Karl Moritz placed the highwayman second in the hierarchy of the English criminal fraternity to the pickpocket 'to be found in the best company'. These, he was told, were often men of rank 'reduced to this way of living by reason of their past extravagance'.

The roads were dangerous, but Britain's hostelries enjoyed a generally good reputation. The best were furnished in mahogany and graced with needlework bell-pulls; even modest establishments offered reasonable accommodation and, if one was a devotee of ham and eggs, decent enough food. An Irish gentleman found the Lion at Liverpool, one of the city's better inns, served an excellent sixpenny supper of 'veal cutlets, pigeons, asparagus, lamb and salad, apple pie and tarts'. The Blue Boar in London's Holborn, with its forty bedrooms, select private apartments and seven coach houses, was a premier establishment but even here the food was not always to the Continental taste. A German tourist, who admired the English tea, 'with its slices of bread and butter as thin as poppy leaves', found English roast beef too rare for his taste and complained bitterly of cabbage leaves boiled in plain water. He also found that the service was, on occasion, 'impudent'. This complaint was sometimes echoed by Englishmen.

In 1825 William Cobbett, author of the famous *Rural Rides* and scathing critic of government agricultural policies, stayed one October evening at the George Inn, Andover. Sutton, the landlord, was 'a rich old fellow, who wore a dirty white apron with an air of mastership quite incompatible with the meanness of his dress and the vulgarity of his manners'. After dinner, Cobbett was called on for a speech. His tirade against the government's ill treatment of farmers was going well, when Sutton 'finding that my speech-making had suspended all intercourse between the dining room and the bar and supposing that, if my tongue were not stopped from running, his taps would be had, though an old man, forced his way up the thronged stairs and was beginning to bawl out at me, in so many words, that my speech injured his sale of liquor'.

The landlord having been unceremoniously ejected from his own dining room, the speech reached its conclusion to great acclaim. The company, now ready for drinking, found an embargo had been enforced until Cobbett should leave the premises. At length, however, the 'old fustian-jacketted fellow,' abandoned the 'insolence of wealth for the servility of avarice' and came up 'bringing pipes, tobacco, wine, grog, sling and seeming to be as pleased as if he had just sprung a mile of gold'. Songs, toasts and speeches filled up the time until half past two on the following Sunday morning.

Outside London, Oxford was one of the great sights. 'Environed round with hills adorned with woods and enclosures', it stood 'pleasant and compact'. Sir Christopher Wren's Sheldonian Theatre was a prominent landmark 'encompassed with the several colleges and churches and other buildings whose towers and spires appear very well at a distance'. The High Street was considered very noble and its famous Mitre Inn was a favourite haunt of dons and undergraduates. A German hotel guest observed that the latter were always dropping in for 'a chat, a pot of ale and a short parley with the landlord's daughter', who, he had discovered for himself, was a well-behaved wench.

The baths and spas of England were much frequented. Karl Philip Moritz was drawn by the fame of Matlock Baths in Derbyshire and found that the town surpassed all he had expected. 'On the right were several elegant houses for those taking the treatment; on the left ran the river in a deep ravine.' The place was thronged with horses and carriages, but as a fashionable resort it could not match Bath.

Supervised during the season by a master of ceremonies, Bath was second only to London in fashionable England during the eighteenth century. Europeans were impressed by the care with which its elegance was policed. 'There is a serjeant, that all the bathing time walks in the galleries and takes notice that order is observed. Most people of fashion send to him when they begin to bathe, then he takes particular care of them – which deserves its reward at the end of the season.' At the side of the bath there were rings 'that you may hold by and so walk a little way, but the springs bubble up fast and strong and are hot against the bottom of one's feet, especially in what they call the Kitching in the King's Bath, which is a great cross with seats in the middle and many hot springs rise there'. The famous pump room was opened in 1704 and the first Assembly Rooms four years later. In the middle of the century the fashionable season presided over by the renowned Beau Nash made the London-Bath coach service the most frequented in the country. Many a tourist found that the season at Bath was an extension of the high life of the capital.

THE AMERICAN EXPERIENCE OF BRITAIN

Nathaniel Hawthorne, novelist and New Englander, had always looked upon England as 'the old home'. When he actually arrived in the country in the summer of 1853, he was impressed with uncanny force by the idea that he had been there before. The illusion was so powerful that he 'almost doubted whether such airy remembrances might not be a sort of innate idea, the print of a recollection in some ancestral mind, transmitted with fainter and fainter impress through several descents, to my own'. He had come to the country in the hope that the post of American consul in Liverpool, to which he had been appointed, would ease his financial troubles. Unfortunately his hopes were mistaken. The family remained short of funds and the hospitality they enjoyed in the luxurious homes of Liverpool's chief citizens provoked his wife Sarah to frank, rather vulgar and almost envious admiration. She was even more impressed by the splendour of the English women's dresses; her husband merely found English women 'massive, not seemingly pure fat, but with solid beef, making an awful ponderosity of frame'.

After two years, when it was becoming apparent that his career was not progressing as well as he had hoped, Hawthorne was deeply disillusioned. The family had begun its stay by renting a smart, furnished house at an annual rent of a hundred and sixty pounds. This was below the going rate but it was still too much for Hawthorne and he moved into a lodging house. The guests had to provide their own food and necessaries, 'even to the candles you burn and the soap on your wash stands', and the writer came to the conclusion that an English lodging house was 'a contrivance for carrying the domestic cares of home about with you'. His initial reaction to the country had been reversed. 'I HATE England;' he wrote, 'though I love some Englishmen.' It was very much a love-hate relationship, one feels, for later he wrote: 'An American is not very apt to love the English people.' But there was one institution that Americans could not resist. 'There is something in royalty', he mused, 'that turns the republican brain.'

A VISIT TO SCOTLAND

The idea of visiting the wild landscape of Scotland for pleasure did not become popular until the nineteenth century. Dr Johnson had allowed Boswell to persuade him on a journey to the Hebrides back in the 1770s and the famous journal of their excursion is an entertaining comment on the views of one British citizen on the rugged world of the northern kingdom. Johnson did not consider the novelty of the trip a match for the familiar streets and coffee houses of his beloved London. But the rise of

London decorated for Queen Victoria's Diamond Jubilee in 1897

Romanticism put a premium on landscape for its own sake and Scotland came into her own. Cook's first tours outside England were to Scotland and in the 1840s an American visitor had already discovered the romance and beauty of the country.

On 1 July 1844 Bayard Taylor climbed the gang plank to the deck of the sailing ship *Oxford* as she lay in New York harbour. He had not 'accumulated so large a sum as tourists usually spend on their travels' but he was determined to see Europe, 'what has hitherto been deemed the privilege of the wealthy few'. Over the ensuing months he completed a heroic itinerary, travelling mostly on foot, and published an account of his adventures to which we shall return in later chapters of this book.

The *Oxford*'s destination was Liverpool. Taylor took a berth in the second cabin communicating with the deck by a hatch, having bought his provisions on shore to be prepared by the ship's cook. On-board entertainment was provided by a group of ebullient Iowa Indians, headed by their chief White Cloud, who were on a visit to England for an exhibition of their dancing. Taylor later looked in on the display in London's Piccadilly but he, and the rest of the passengers of the *Oxford*, were treated to a preview of one of the war dances of the tribe. What for a modern audience would be a fascinating spectacle, struck Taylor as 'a most ludicrous scene'.

Apart from this diversion, life on board the little ship had not much to offer and, because they were becalmed for three days, it was a slow crossing. But then, on the morning of the twenty-fifth, coming up from his cramped quarters below deck Taylor experienced one of those magical moments which compensated for all the hardships of the days of sail. They were still out of sight of land when suddenly they caught the 'meadow freshness of the Irish bogs on the morning wind'. The next day, this harbinger of landfall was confirmed by a glimpse of the lighthouse on Tory Island. Then, 'just under the golden flood of light that streamed through the morning clouds, southwards, blended in with the hue of the veiling cloud, loomed a lofty mountain'. As the sun set, Taylor had his first sight of Scottish soil, the islands of Islay and Jura, then 'the wind being ahead, we tacked from shore to shore, running so near the Irish coast, that we could see the little thatched huts, stacks of peat, and even rows of potatoes'.

Late in the afternoon of the twenty-eighth, the passengers at the ship's rail watched the sun setting behind the mountains of North Wales, beyond coastal headlands studded with windmills. Soon after that, the distant spires of Liverpool one by one slowly pricked upwards from the horizon. They docked the next day, and Taylor took the ferry to northern Ireland for a day trip to the Giants' Causeway. Formations among the huge granite blocks seemed like the pipes of a great church organ and it was only with reluctance that the American left the enchanted coasts of Ireland the next morning.

He embarked at Port Rush on the steamboat *Londonderry*, economizing as always by taking a deck passage, rather than paying six times as much for a place in the cabin. The boat put in at Greenock and then steamed on to Dumbarton. At the castle, Bayard Taylor, who felt that his Scottish trip had now truly begun, tested the weight of the great sword of William Wallace, the ancient Scottish hero. After this, a walk to Loch Lomond and the little steamer *Water Witch* for a cruise on the crystal waters of the Loch. 'Under a clear sky and the golden light of the declining sun, we entered the Highlands, hearing on every side names we had learned long ago in the lays of Sir Walter Scott.'

After exploring Rob Roy's Cave, the travellers took another steamer through the thickets that lined the bank of a channel 'hardly wider than the boat'. Taylor revelled in some of the finest scenery of the Highlands; he breakfasted on Loch Lomond trout; he climbed Ben Lomond; he passed a glorious summer morning on the banks of Loch Katrine; and, at last, he took an English coach to Falkirk and thence, by railway, on to Glasgow.

The climax of this Scottish tour came at the Burns Festival being held at Ayr that August. The ships in the little harbour hung out all their flags; the streets of the town were crowded with people carrying banners and wreaths. But the American was displeased by the beggars 'seated at regular distances along the road' and outraged to find the sign 'Licensed to retail spirits to be drunk on the premises', hanging over the door of Burns's birthplace, 'a neat little thatched cot'.

At the very goal of their pilgrimage, their minds suitably prepared to pay their devotions at the shrine, Taylor and his friends shuddered at the unseemly crowd of happy drinkers in the very birthplace of Robert Burns. They shouldered a determined way through the throng to inspect 'a fine original portrait' of the poet on the far wall and then to muse before the wall recess in which wayward genius had been born. But they lingered too long and the landlady looked towards them, as if to enquire what they would take to drink. Too shocked for words, 'there was profanity even in the thought', the three Americans hastened from the scene, as bitterly disillusioned, one feels, as any medieval pilgrim by the huckstering in the Church of the Holy Sepulchre.

The town procession in honour of the poet somewhat raised the tone of the celebrations. The parade was led by the local freemasons and they were followed by a group of shepherds, some archers in Lincoln green and finally a party of highlanders 'in their most picturesque costume'. On the saluting platform the 'quality', represented by Lord Elgintoun and Professor Wilson, stood with all the amiability they could muster, shoulder to shoulder with the sons of the poet, his sister and her children.

The occasion had turned out happily after all and the American party returned to Glasgow in high spirits. There they entrained for Edinburgh, buying six shilling tickets in the open cars. 'On leaving the depot we were plunged into the heart of the hill on which Glasgow cathedral stands and were whisked through the darkness and sulphury smoke to the daylight again.' After the stirring events of the Burns Festival 'Edinburgh's palace-like edifices', Cannongate and the Castle, merit merely a paragraph in Bayard Taylor's journal and after a stay of just thirty-six hours, he and his companions 'buckled on their knapsacks and marched out of the northern Athens'.

QUEEN VICTORIA'S JUBILEE PROCESSION OF 1897

'So far as I can see', wrote Mark Twain, introducing his account of the great celebration, 'a procession has value in but two ways – as a show and as a symbol; its minor function being to delight the eye, its major one to compel thought, exalt the spirit, stir the heart, and inflame the imagination. As a mere show, and meaningless – like a Mardi-Gras march – a magnificent procession is a sight worth a long journey to see.'

As one of the thousands of foreign tourists in London for the solemnities of that year, he contributed to Britain's invisible export earnings. But neither he, nor any other spectator of the stunning show, considered the economic aspect of the affair. It 'set one reflecting upon what a large feature of this world England is today'. The time had not yet come when the cynical could regard a British royal pageant as a calculated tourist attraction. The Britain of Victoria appeared too solidly established as the world's great power for cash calculations to play any part in the homage to the Queen's glorious sixty years. The very scaffolding built to accommodate the spectators seemed designed to endure until Doomsday. 'The Englishman', Twain reflected, 'requires that everything about him shall be stable, strong, and permanent, except the house which he builds to rent. His own private house is as strong as a fort. The rod which holds up the lace curtains could hold up an hippopotamus ... Everything he constructs is a deal heavier and stronger than it needs to be.' Those 'ten miles of terraced benches' for the spectators, intended for only two days' service had enough timber to make them 'a permanent contribution to the solidities of the world'. An American, watching them being dismantled, said: 'Don't do it – save them for the Resurrection.'

Mark Twain got to the seat reserved for him in the Strand at five past ten. As far as the eye could see, in both directions, the windows of the buildings 'suggested boxes in a theatre snugly packed'; there had never been 'such a massed and multitudinous array of bright colours and fine clothes'. The display mounted storey by storey, 'all the balconies and windows being packed, and also the battlements stretching along the roofs. The sidewalks were filled with standing people ... fenced from the roadway by red-coated soldiers, a double stripe of vivid color which extended throughout the six miles which the procession would traverse.'

The American had reached his place just in time for this quick survey of the spectators and by a quarter past ten the head of the procession came in sight, led by Captain Ames, the tallest man in the British Army. 'And then the cheering began.' Twain quickly decided that it was going to be impossible to do full justice to the spectacle. 'There was going to be too much of it, and too much variety in it, ... it was to be a spectacle for the kodak, not the pen.' He 'was not dreaming of so stunning a show'. Nevertheless, fortunately for us, he attempted a description.

Presently the procession was without visible beginning or end, but stretched to the limit of sight in both directions – bodies of soldiery in blue, followed by a block of soldiers in buff, then a block of red, a block of buff, a block of yellow, and so on, an interminable drift of swaying and swinging splotches of strong colour sparkling and flashing with shifty light reflected from bayonets, lance heads, brazen helmets and burnished breastplates.

All the nations of the world seemed to be there: '... the procession was the human race on exhibition ... a sort of allegorical suggestion of the Last Day.' Chinese, Japanese, Koreans, Africans, Indians and Pacific Islanders were all represented 'and with them samples of all the whites that inhabit the wide reach of the Queen's dominions'. The Indian princes, 'men of stately build and princely carriage', in the most splendid, beautiful and costly ceremonial dress clothes of the whole procession, made the greatest impact on the crowd and 'wherever they passed the applause burst forth'. Prince Rupert of Bavaria provided, for the knowledgeable, a still more intriguing sight. He was representing his mother, Princess Ludwig, who was the direct descendant of the House of Stuart and was recognized by a tiny band of eccentric enthusiasts as the rightful Queen of England. 'The microbe of Jacobite loyalty,' Mark Twain wrote in a somewhat lordly aside, 'is a thing which is not exterminable by time, force, or argument.'

Rupert was among thirty-one foreign princes who paid their homage; they had been preceded by the prime ministers of the colonies and dominions and each group of dignitaries was escorted before and behind, by troops of soldiers. The parade was so immense that the first carriages did not come into view for an hour and a half.

The excitement was growing now; interest was rising to the boiling point. Finally a landau driven by eight cream-colored horses, most lavishly upholstered in gold stuffs, with postilions and no drivers ... came bowling along, followed by the Prince of Wales, and all the world rose to its feet and uncovered. The Queen Empress was come.

Thus America's staunchest and most irreverent patriot draws to the end of his account. He had first visited Britain in 1872 intending to collect material for a lightly satirical book on English manners and customs. Once in the country he found that he liked it and its people too much to go ahead with the project. Besides, in the words of one of his editors, 'he was so busy entertaining, and being entertained, that he had little time for critical observation'.

The famous humorist himself wrote to a friend: 'I do hate to go away from these English folks; they make a stranger feel entirely at home, and they laugh so easily that it is a comfort to make after-dinner speeches here.'

'THE SCEPTERED ISLE' – ENGLAND AS SHE WAS

On that first trip, Mark Twain had interspersed his lionizing at the great houses of England with journalism for the New York press. One of his commissions was to cover the state reception given for the Shah of Persia in the summer of 1873. The splendours of that event make a story in themselves; yet one senses that the American correspondent was still more impressed by the beauties of the host country than the oriental magnificence of the visitor. The press corps was sent over to Ostend to accompany the Shah on the last stage of his journey and the trip from London to Dover seems to have delighted Twain. He gives a picture of England in the high summer of her greatness which provides a natural conclusion to this survey of the foreign experience of Britain.

The first surprise was the smoothness and speed of English railways. Once out of Victoria, Mark Twain found himself 'whistling over the housetops as if in a sleigh'. He added: 'One can never have anything but a very vague idea of what speed is until he travels over an English railway. Our "lightning" expresses are sleepy and indolent by comparison.' Through the back windows of the rows of houses lining the railway embankment the passengers saw 'many a homelike family of early birds sitting at their breakfasts'.

The sheer extent of the great city took the American visitor's breath away. Once out of the city he shook off the drowsiness of his early morning start to revel in 'the brilliant sunshine pouring down, the balmy wind blowing through the open windows, and the Garden of Eden spread all abroad'. They swept along through fields of golden grain with 'not an unsightly fence or an ill-kept hedge, through broad meadows covered with fresh green grass as clean swept as if a broom had been at work, the little brooks wandering up and down them, noble trees here and there, cows in the shade, groves in the distance and church spire projection out of them.' Like many an American after him, Mark Twain was delighted by the 'quaint old-fashioned houses set in the midst of smooth lawns or partly hiding themselves among the fine old forest trees'. These 'quaint' homes were clearly prosperous residences, but equally enchanting were the humble cottages, one 'clothed in a shining mail of ivy leaves!' It was a fairytale landscape, fragmented now and ravaged by a century of ruthless progress. Like the nineteenth-century Americans for whom Mark Twain wrote, the English of today can only 'imagine those dainty little homes surrounded by flowering shrubs and bright green grass and all sorts of trees – and then go on and try to imagine something more bewitching'.

A scene from THE FOREIGN TOUR OF MESSRS. BROWN, JONES AND ROBINSON by Richard Dolye, 1855

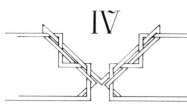

IV

THE FRENCH EXPERIENCE

'Calais the busy – the bustling – the – I had almost said the beautiful . . . It is a little France. Every traveller must love Calais, a place where he first found himself in a strange world.' These rhapsodic words of John Ruskin would not strike sympathetic chords in the hearts of travellers today. The only 'bustling' is the bustle to clear the car ferry approach roads and beat the traffic out of the town. But most modern tourists from Britain share at least this with their predecessors: the ports of northern France are still for many their first sight of things foreign. And there is another experience which some queasy voyagers may find familiar from the past. At five o'clock in the afternoon of 14 May 1608 the undoubtedly bustling Tom Coryat arrived in Calais after he had 'varnished the exterior parts of

Opposite CONVERSATION UNDER THE STATUE, LUXEMBOURG
GARDENS lithograph by J. M. Whistler, 1893
Above Detail from an early twentieth-century photograph of a
railway scene

the ship with the excremental ebullitions of my tumultuous stomach'.

Coryat made a seven-hour crossing and that was slow, even for the days of sail. Two hundred years later, there was a regular peace-time service from Dover which rarely took longer than six hours in the crossing. From a little book on Dover, published in 1799, we learn that, before the war against France, five packets were established there under the direction of the general Post Office, one sailing on Wednesday the other on Saturday with the mails to Calais and Ostende. 'In addition, thirty of the handsomest sloops in the kingdom sailed the straits.' With a good wind they were able to reach Calais in three hours and go into the harbour with the same tide.

If the packet missed the tide and arrived after the water had ebbed back out of the harbour, 'the passengers had to go ashore in boats, which is usually affected without inconvenience as the boatmen are extremely expert and careful', which was just as well, since the last stage of the trip to the beach was – at least for the better class of passengers – on piggy-back by those same boatmen. The fare for this service was one guinea for gentlemen and five shillings for their servants. Once the harbour was reached and the custom house cleared, most grand tourists – that 'army of peregrine martyrs; young gentlemen transported by the cruelty of parents and guardians, and travelling under the direction of governors recommended by Oxford, Aberdeen and Glasgow' – were looking for a good meal and a comfortable bed. Everybody who was anybody headed for the Hotel d'Angleterre, whose proprietor was Monsieur Dessein.

When Laurence Sterne stayed there in the 1760s, Dessein's excellent and expensive table was already renowned. Twenty years later it was still the resort of the 'peregrine martyrs'. The Russian historian Karamzin was sorely troubled by seven or eight young Englismen who had just crossed the Channel with the intention of travelling through Europe. They had a noisy supper, calling for 'Wine! Wine! The very best!' and kept it up into the small hours, banging their fists on the table and stamping their feet. Eventually, 'after several God damns', they consented to desist.

The traveller left Calais, as like as not, in a chaise or carriage supplied by M. Dessein whose coach hire business brought him a sizable fortune. Sterne was offered the choice of 'a couple of chaises which had been purchased by my Lord A. and B. to go the Grand Tour, but had gone no further than Paris; so were as good as new. They were too good, so I passed on to a third, which stood behind and forthwith began to chaffer for the price.'

The Hotel d'Angleterre remained the most fashionable place to stay well into the 1840s. By that time, not only Laurence Sterne but also Sir Walter

Scott had slept there and, as John Murray recorded in his handbook to France, the rooms where they had stayed were named after them. By then a new type of tourist was on the roads: no eighteenth-century gentleman would have cared that he had the choice of rooms once used by mere writers. Even in Murray's day, the links between northern France and Britain went much deeper than a couple of visiting celebrities. He noted, with smug satisfaction, that Boulogne, 'the very spot where Napoleon had proposed the invasion of our shores', had become one of the chief British colonies abroad. 'The town,' he went on, 'is enriched by English money; warmed, lighted and smoked by English coal; English signs and advertisements decorate every other shop door, in tavern and lodging-house; and every third person you meet is either a countryman or speaking our language.'

Caen, Rouen and Avranches also had sizable English populations – 'people with a moderate income which in England would be looked on as barely enough to keep a family at all respectable, are looked upon by the peasantry as milords'. Their touring compatriots were amused to find these precursors of the modern tax exile 'endeavouring to be taken for French; and when they are found out they talk of their châteaux and forests here, as big and majestic as they possibly can, but in general they have a broken-down, shabby-genteel appearance about them – not at all the thing.' Half a century earlier, at the French royal leather factory at Pont au de Mer, Honfleur, Arthur Young had found a group of Englishmen with a different tale to tell. Lured by the promise of good living, they were workers who had come over the Channel to seek employment. A Yorkshire labourer had told Young that though they were well paid, they found things 'very dear, instead of very cheap as they had been given to understand'.

LODGINGS, HOSTELRIES AND THE TABLE D'HÔTE

'Is there anything worth seeing in Corsica? Is there any sublimity or beauty in the scenery? Have I taken too much baggage? Am I not an idiot for coming at all? Are there not banditti? Should I not carry clothes for all sorts of weathers, boxes of quinine pills, flea powders?' For Edward Lear, landscape painter by trade, nonsense poet by renown, his 1868 trip to Corsica was a working journey. Nevertheless, his second thoughts on what John Ruskin called the 'discomforts of practical travelling', have been echoed by many a holiday tourist.

Like earlier travellers in France, Lear bemoaned the prevailing conditions of filth in the hotels. Outside the precincts of Dessein's famous establishment, French accommodation was chancy. The Croix Blanche Inn at St Girons, in the remote region of the Basses Pyrennées seems to have established the bench mark for absolute ghastliness. It was 'the most execrable receptacle of filth, vermin, impudence and imposition that ever wounded the feeling of a traveller'. Presided over by 'a withered hag, the demon of beastliness', this remarkable hostelry offered as its best room 'a chamber over a stable, whose effluvia through the broken floor were the least offensive of the perfumes afforded by this hideous place'.

French landlords of all but the very finest hotels despised the idea of clean floors and yet 'even the filthy cabaret, whose kitchen and salon are scarcely endurable to look at, commonly affords napkins and table-cloths, clean though coarse and rough, and beds of unsullied sheets and white draperies with well-stuffed pillows and mattresses'.

Almost any French landlord would offer a well-dressed dinner of eight or ten dishes at almost any hour of the day. Outside Paris the price was reasonable and at the host's table one could eat very cheaply. To eat at the *table d'hôte* meant to share a common meal with other guests at a long table generally presided over by the innkeeper himself. When the other diners were locals, one had a chance to observe something of the manners of the people, though there were occasions when the French, surrounded by foreign tourists, curbed their volubility. 'We sat down thirty or forty at every meal,' recorded one visitor to the country, 'a most motley collection of French, Italians, Spaniards and Germans, and one Armenian.' But although he had come to France expecting to have his ears constantly fatigued, he was surprised on this occasion by 'the taciturnity of the French'.

The experience of William Hazlitt, critic and essayist, was rather different. While carving the meat, his host flourished the knife about 'in such a manner as to endanger those near him'. From time to time he stopped, 'with the wing of a duck suspended on the point of his fork, to spout a speech out of some play'. With dinner barely over, he collected 'all the bottles and glasses on the table, beer, wine, porter, emptied them into his own, heaped his plate with the remnants of fricassees, gravy, vegetables, mustard, melted butter and sopped them all up with a large piece of bread'. He finished the performance by picking his teeth with a sharp-pointed knife.

It was John Murray's view that respectable people should not consider sitting at the *table d'hôte*, which he considered to be the preserve of commercial travellers 'of a stamp very inferior to those of the same class in England. In France they commonly sit down to table with their hats on, and scramble for the dishes, so that the stranger who is not alert is likely to fare very ill.'

By the mid-nineteenth century, in fact, well-to-do travellers could fare pretty well in France. At the Hotel d'Albion in Rouen, Effie and John Ruskin paid twelve francs a day for a large sitting room with a 'nice' piano, and a bedroom and a dressing room. Stopping on the road at a Norman farm house, they were served excellent coffee in bowls, roast chicken, boiled greens, cider and, for dessert, strawberries and pears. Another traveller found the chief inn at Rheims large and well served, providing an excellent bottle of wine with a first-class dinner.

For Arthur Young, some years before, Rheims had proved a memorable stop on his French tour. 'The first view of the city from the hills at the distance of about four miles, is magnificent. The cathedral makes a great figure, and the church of St Rémy terminates the town proudly.' In Young's experience the beautiful prospect of a French town from the distance all too often proved a delusion. When you entered them they proved to be 'a clutter of narrow, crooked, dark and dirty lanes'. At Rheims it was very different. The streets were almost all broad, straight and well built. More important, they led to that excellent inn, with its fine wines and good food.

Rheims, the cathedral city of the Champagne region, seems to have been a hospitable place. Horace Walpole, prime minister's son, and Thomas Gray, poet, certainly found it so. They fell in with a party of men and women 'of the best fashion' and one evening, walking in the public gardens, one of the ladies suggested an *al fresco* supper. 'Immediately the cloth was laid by the side of a fountain under the trees, and a very elegant supper was shortly served up.' When servants and waiters had cleared the remains of the meal, the company set to singing and dancing. It was a warm, velvet night and, with everyone in the mood, a 'company of violins' was immediately ordered. The minuets and country dances followed one another until four in the morning, 'at which time such as were weary got into their coaches'. The cavalcade made its cheerful way homewards, the more lively revellers 'dancing before the coaches with the music in the van, and in this way we paraded through the principal streets of the city, and waked everybody in it'. The story seems a world away from the contrived *fêtes galantes* of Louis XV's Versailles.

PALACE LIFE

Young, who in Rheims had discovered that 'the *vin mousseux* of Champagne absolutely banished the writhes of rheumatism', visited Versailles in 1788, the year before the French Revolution. The palace had been conceived by the ambition of King Louis XIV as a monumental stage set for the drama of royal pomp in every particular. He had lived an unbelievably public life. His morning levée, his meals and his retiring to rest were all public functions watched by scores of people with tourists among the courtiers. In fact, admission was granted to anyone from virtually any walk of life, so long as he wore a sword, the badge of gentlemanly rank. Swords could conveniently be hired for a modest charge at the gate.

Even in the days of the Sun King Louis not everyone was impressed with the amenities of the palace. One courtier called Versailles a 'sad place', another described it as a 'favourite without merit'. In a hard winter the wine was liable to freeze in the carafes on the royal table. Louis XIV's mistress Madame de Maintenon caustically observed that the bedrooms were swept with draughts 'like American hurricanes'; she had built a special inner room, big enough to hold an armchair and a bed. The King's doctor, determined to preserve at least his own health, was to be seen complacently sitting in a sedan chair before the fires of its marbled halls. The terrain was a mixture of unstable sandy soil and marshlands and the air was notoriously unhealthy. The palace fell from court favour for a time after Louis's death. When his successor Louis XV returned there in the 1740s, he preferred the mansion of the Petit Trianon in the grounds.

But when Horace Walpole visited Versailles in the mid-eighteenth century, the aura of Bourbon monarchy had been a little tarnished. 'Stand by, clear the way, make room for the pompous appearance of Versailles le Grand! But no: it fell short of my idea of it. They say I am to like it better next Sunday; when the sun is to shine; the King is to be fine; the waterworks are to play.' Yet, despite the carping criticisms of envious gentry and even the informed criticism of long suffering courtiers, by the middle of the eighteenth century Versailles was an obsession of autocrats everywhere, so that imitations, from the grandiose to the modest, sprang up all over Europe.

Arthur Young, a Suffolk country gentleman who had embarked for France to research a book on French methods of agriculture, found the town of Versailles a sizable place with a population of sixty thousand. In the time-honoured manner of tourists to France, he relaxed over a drink in one of the coffee houses on the boulevards, watching the street girls, deafened by the music and noise, and depressed by the absence of street cleaners and street lighting. The palace itself interested him hardly at all. It was not in the least 'striking'; it lacked unity; it was 'an assemblage of buildings, but not an edifice'. However, he was impressed by the 'careless indifference and freedom from suspicion' which allowed even the poorest citizens to walk uncontrolled about the palace, 'even in the royal bed chamber'. And, however little he admired the palace, even the practically minded Young could not suppress the frison afforded by the nearness of monarchy. When he viewed the King's apartment, 'which he had not left a quarter of an hour', he enjoyed 'those slight traits of disorder that showed he *lived* in it'.

Nothing in Young's account of the great palace suggests that the cataclysm of revolution was little more than a year away. The pomp of court pageantry progressed along its immemorial way with the careless indifference of a secure institution. The gentleman from Suffolk joined the throng watching the King invest the Duke of Berri with the cordon bleu. 'During the service, the King seemed by his inattentiveness to wish himself hunting. He would certainly have been as well employed, as hearing from his throne a feudal oath of chivalry administered to a boy ten years old.' Innocently, the Englishman asked a court lady whether it was the Dauphin who was being honoured. She laughed in his face 'because, as all the world knows, the Dauphin has the cordon bleu as soon as he is born. So unpardonable was it for a foreigner to be ignorant of such an important part of French history.' According to other travellers the whole French people were fascinated with royal protocol, 'showing by the eagerness of their attention not curiosity only, but love. Where, how, and in whom these gentlemen discovered this I know not.' Young, who was by no means deceived by the insouciance of the court, was already developing a sceptical attitude to the state of France.

He continued his tour, aiming to combine sightseeing with his researches into agricultural affairs. He much preferred the château of Chambord on the Loire to Versailles, particularly admiring the stone staircase in the centre of the house. With its 'interwoven ascents and descents whereby persons can go up and down without meeting', it is still one of the chief tourist attractions of the Loire Valley. But though he admired the architecture of the place, as he stood surveying the great park from the battlements, Young pondered on utility and splendour.

I could not help thinking [he wrote] that if the King of France ever formed the idea of establishing one complete and perfect farm under the turnip culture of England, here is the place for it. The château for the residence of the director and all his attendants; the barracks for stalls of cattle. The profits of the wood would be sufficient to stock and support the whole undertaking.

TOURING THE REVOLUTION

Two years later, Young found his researches into the agronomy of France hampered by the turmoil of the coming Revolution. On 9 June 1789, he wrote:

The business going forward at present in the pamphlet shops in Paris is incredible, such that one can scarcely squeeze from the door to the counter. Nineteen twentieths of these productions are in favour of liberty. The coffee houses in the Palais Royal are crowded within and expectant crowds are at the doors and windows, listening, mouth agape, to certain orators, each haranguing his little audience from chair or table in terms of more than common violence against the present government. The thunders of applause cannot be easily imagined.

Later the same month he commented: 'It is impossible to have any other employment at so critical a moment, than going from house to house demanding news. The doctrine of the times runs every day more and more to *a republic*. In the streets one is stunned by the number of hawkers of seditious pamphlets.'

A few days after this, Young encountered a French officer who had served with the American Revolutionary armies. The man accosted him in English as he was having a drink at an inn; the conversation went as follows.

French officer: 'In Paris the *tiers état* are running mad and need wholesome correction. They want to establish a republic – Absurd!'

Young: 'Pray sir, what did you fight for in America?'

Officer: 'But, of course, to establish a republic.'

Young: 'What was so good for the Americans, is it so bad for the French?'

Officer: 'Aye, damme! That is the way the English want to be revenged.'

In fact, everyone Young met supposed that the English were delighted at the confusion reigning in France. Some were openly suspicious of this wandering foreigner.

In some districts he met with suspicion verging on hostility. Near L'Isle sur le Doubs he was questioned for not having a cockade of the *tiers état* in his hat.

It was clear that this was no moment for joking. I immediately purchased a cockade, but the hussey pinned it into my hat so loosely that it blew into the river and I was soon again in the same danger when I reached Lisle. A crowd gathered and I did not like my situation at all. I assured them that I was English and cried 'Vive le tiers', whereupon they gave me a bit of a huzza. I got, however, another cockade which I took care to have so fastened not to lose it no more.

His stay in Paris should have forewarned him. There he had seen the King walking in the Tuileries gardens guarded by six militia men and had been shocked by the casual disrespect shown him by the commoners strolling in the park. The Queen, on her morning walks, barely received the acknowledgement due to any lady. At Versailles he had found things

A Visit to Château Lafite, Medoc, France *c.* 1890

very different from the situation on his previous visit. The ceremonial of the court was in abeyance while the population of the town was, 'to the last person, in the interest of the commons'. Young commented with characteristic shrewdness: 'This town is absolutely fed by the palace, and if the cause of the court is not popular here, it is easy to suppose what it must be in all the rest of the kingdom.' Nevertheless, these sage observations in his journal did not prepare him for the incident at L'Isle sur le Doubs.

It was a bad time for travellers altogether. The social and political unrest made for danger on the roads and yet, with the country on the verge of cataclysm, the French hotelier held to his traditional ways. At Guignes, Young relieved his 'sadness' by watching an itinerant dancing master fiddling a tune for some children by the roadside. 'With great magnificence' he gave twelve sous pieces to buy cake for the children, 'which made them dance with fresh animation'. It was a mistake. His landlord, seeing the Englishman 'so rich', made him pay nine livres and ten sous 'for a miserable tough chicken, a salad and a bottle of very sorry wine'.

The Revolution left its scars. The Rogets, a family of Swiss descent travelling in the early 1800s, found the château of Fontainebleau converted into a school. It was in a dilapidated condition 'from the fury of the mob and stood as a monument to the devastation produced by the revolutionary storms'. At Lyons, too, the 'direful effects of the Revolution were everywhere visible'. In 1793 the city had been sacked by the army of the National Convention and hundreds of its defenders shot. When the Rogets visited the place many of the finest parts were still in ruins and they could only surmise that it must once have been very fine.

PARIS

We are fortunate that observers of the quality of Young and Roget have left us their records of the French provinces. The majority of tourists of their generation merely followed the roads that led southwards to Italy. In France the capital and the royal town of Versailles were the prime destinations, but there were mixed feelings about the one as about the other. 'Paris', wrote William Hazlitt, 'is the beast of a city.' Rousseau revealed that all the time he was in it, he was only trying to leave it. For Hazlitt the Englishman and for Rousseau the Swiss, as for many travellers before and since, half the trouble with Paris was the Parisians. Lord Chesterfield wrote:

I shall not give my opinion of the French because many a Frenchman has paid me the highest compliment they think that they can pay to anyone, which is 'Sir, you are just like one of us.' I shall only tell you that I am insolent; I talk a great deal; I am very loud and peremptory; I sing and dance as I go along and lastly I spend a monstrous deal of money in powder.

The powder was, of course, for that essential ornament of a gentleman, his wig. The Parisian concern for personal elegance infected even Dr Johnson, that pontifical sage whose dictionary Chesterfield, so unwisely for his future reputation, failed to sponsor. Visiting Paris for the first time at the age of sixty-six, Johnson, we are told, 'abandoned the black stockings, brown coat and plain shirt he customarily wore in London, and appeared in white stockings, a new hat and a French-made wig of handsome construction'. A Scottish architect and designer also willingly succumbed and adopted 'a most Frenchified head of hair, a complete suit of cut velvet of two colours set off with a satin linings; white stockings; pumps with red heels; stone buckles like diamonds on knees and shoes; and Brussels lace at breast and hands.'

In those days it was generally agreed that when an Englishman came to Paris, he could not appear until he had undergone 'a total metamorphosis. At his first arrival it is necessary to send for the taylor, perruquier, hatter and shoemaker. It is also necessary to watch the bills for, as the *Gentleman's Guide* of 1770 observed, you will meet nowhere greater cheats than the French taylors'.

Few modern tourists need concern themselves with the rates charged by Parisian tailors, but the city herself has the knack of unsettling foreigners. 'The returned New Yorker cannot fail to be deeply impressed with the finish, the organic perfection, the elegance and reserve of the Paris scene mirrored in his memory.' Thus wrote William C. Brownell in the 1890s. For him 'the shop windows' show' was one of the great spectacles of the French capital.

However, in the immediate aftermath of the Napoleonic wars the shops were not the aspect of Paris that most impressed. On the contrary, they were very poor: 'all they have is displayed in the window; they have no magazine of goods, being deficient in capital and the walls are covered with inscriptions which dazzle the eye.' On the walls were frequently painted the objects sold in the shops, such as bread or vegetables. A garland was the sign that wine was sold within. Yet these food shops had an iron grating over their windows 'to defend them from the mob, in case of any tumult'.

But even in the years of defeat Paris struck the visitor with its bustle. 'Before you have finished your question, the Parisian has answered you, bowed and taken his leave. Everywhere there are crowds of people, everywhere noise and hubbub. Even at one and two o'clock people are still about. At five in the morning artisans begin to appear in the streets and little by little the whole city comes alive again.'

Worst of all was the traffic. 'Coaches, chaises and cabriolets drive with amazing rapidity over an irregular pavement with a deafening noise, splashing through the gutters which run in the middle of the streets.' Unlike London, there was

a total want of foot pavements and the poor foot passengers are driven like frightened sheep. There are an infinity of one-horse cabriolets, driven by young men of fashion. I saw a young poor child run over and probably killed. If young noblemen in London were to drive their chaises in streets without footways as their brethren do in Paris, they would speedily and justly get very well threshed and rolled in the kennel.

For a few hours, on the great feast days of the church year, even the traffic nuisance in the city itself abated. On Corpus Christi the whole town swarmed with processions, and coaches were not allowed to stir till these were over. The streets were lined with tapestry or, failing that, with bed curtains and old petticoats. Dr Burney found that

the better sort of people all go out of town on these days, to avoid the *embarras* of going to mass, or the ennuis of staying at home. Whenever the host stops, which frequently happens, all the people fall on their knees in the middle of the street, whether dirty or clean. I readily complied with this ceremony rather than become remarkable, so that I found it incumbent on me to kneel down twenty times ere I reached Notre Dame.

Burney was careful to touch the filthy ground with only one knee, but many elegant Frenchmen virtually prostrated themselves.

In more relaxed mood, one could stroll along the boulevard outside the gates of the city. It was laid out in walks, with a wide carriageway running down the middle. Coffee houses, conjurors and shows of all kinds lined the walks and every summer evening the place thronged with well-dressed people and clattered with splendid equipages. In warm weather there was dancing in an illuminated courtyard, from which an elegant colonnade gave onto a ballroom where the minuets, allemands, cotillons and contre danses continued when the weather was cold. The busy coffee houses along the boulevard had 'bands of music and singing, the Sadler's Wells way, but worse'.

In the late nineteenth century, when the boulevard park outside the city was hardly a memory, Parisian entertainments were more like the night spots of the modern city. Ladies anxious for their reputations had to take care. They might, 'without impropriety', visit the best cafés or sit at the tables outside, but should on no account enter the cafés on the north side of the boulevards between the Opera and the rue St Denis. For the more daring revellers there were the can-can establishments which, even in the 1880s according to one purse-lipped guide book, still retained 'some attraction to the visitor on account of the fast reputation which they formerly had'. However, using the wet-blanket treatment favoured by the more sophisticated puritans of all periods, the writer advised against them, not on the grounds of their sinful delights, but rather because they 'are now of the most dreary description', offering an 'altogether unnatural and forced abandon'. One was invited to suppose that the censorious writer rather favoured natural and unforced abandon and turned away from these establishments, 'where the can-can is danced by paid performers', with the world-weariness of the mature roué.

Whatever he thought of his guide book, the tourist in late nineteenth-century Paris would certainly know all about the night life. From the mid-1860s the city had burst out in coloured wall posters which introduced art into the business of advertising for the first time in its history. The medium was the recently perfected technique of colour lithography; the pioneer was Jules Cheret. He became famous overnight and was later awarded the Legion of Honour for 'applying art to commercial printing'. By then, his vigorous and brilliant innovation had become part of the Paris scene. A visitor said: 'Paris without its Cherets, would be a Paris without one of its most prominent characteristics; a Paris, moreover, with its gaiety of aspect materially diminished.' Cheret's commissions came from cosmetic firms, department stores and night club owners. Many a tourist must first have seen the magic words 'Folies Bergère' on a Cheret poster, and the night club advertisements by his still more famous successor Toulouse-Lautrec now occupy a venerated place in the history of art.

To some the gaiety of la vie Parisienne was a regrettable distraction from the serious business of picture galleries and culture. But this view was a minority one. Even Joseph Addison, journalist, classical playwright and censor of London's morals in the early 1700s, seems to have surrendered to the mood of cynical flippancy that pervaded the French capital. He had once planned a guide book of Italy based on the classical antiquities there, but did not seem able to take the art treasures of Paris so seriously. 'What particularly recommends 'em to me,' he wrote, 'is that they don't speak French and have a very good quality, rarely to be met with in this country, of not being too talkative.'

Today it is impossible to visualize Paris at night without its restaurants. However, up to the mid-eighteenth century, haute cuisine was confined largely to the houses of the rich and the dining rooms of a few select hotels. With the opening of the first public restaurant during the reign of Louis XVI, a splendid new institution joined the repertoire of Parisian entertainment. Twenty years later there were more than one hundred restaurants in the capital and in the years following the defeat of Napoleon one in particular became the favourite haunt of visiting Englishmen. This was the establishment known as the Café de Mille Collone, at the Palais Royale, where the Junoesque charms of the proprietress were as much admired as the specialities of her chef and the mysteries of her cellar.

The early restaurants must have been welcomed by tourists. Lodgings in Paris were not generally so available as in London and tended to be dearer. If one 'searched with trouble' it was possible to find a room in a family house, for a moderate sum which might include two meals a day with a pint of wine at each. But more usually one had to negotiate separately for meals and might have to be satisfied with the *table d'hôte* at some second-rate inn. The average charge for accommodation without board ran at about £2.00 a month, and if one could not afford a suite of rooms at a hotel 'you must probably mount three, four or five pairs of stairs and in general have nothing but a bed chamber'. In the 1790s Tom Paine, author of *The Rights of Man*, lived in Paris in 'a mean set of rooms up half a dozen flights of stairs in a remote part of town'. He shared with a friend, whose two sons, aged four and five, put everybody out of patience except the author. In fact Paine was very much at home. So long as celebrity hunters remembered that 'vanity is his ruling passion' and could stomach his 'surprising ugliness' and his 'abominably dirty' state, they found him 'easy and benevolent and his conversation remarkably entertaining'.

ON TOUR IN FRANCE

The bustle of life in Paris stopped abruptly at the city gates. Approaching the city for the first time, down the Calais road, Arthur Young was bewildered by the deserted highway and the almost lifeless landscape through which he travelled. His astonishment deepened a few days later as he headed south for Orleans. 'In ten miles we met not a tenth of what would have been met had we been leaving London at the same hour.'

Early in the next century, Dr Roget recorded the almost physical impact made by the contrast between town and country as his coach rolled through one of the toll-gates guarding the main entrances to the city.

Of a sudden we emerged from the busy scenes of a large and gay metropolis, upon extensive plains, deserted and forlorn. There you glide along lengthened avenues of trees, perfectly straight and uniform, where the sight of an inhabitant, or even traces of a human's footsteps are rarely met with. Whilst the din of carriages is yet vibrating in the ear, one is astonished at the silence that prevails in these unfrequented roads.

The scenery was beautiful enough, but travelling could be arduous. Roget and his party found the attentions of the village smiths a particular trial. 'At every village the vulcans of the place are very officious, expecting the carriage may have broken a spring or something of the sort.' The

Rogets were also disappointed, as others before them, by the conditions at the country inns. They had hoped to break their journey to Lyons with a siesta each afternoon, but 'never found comfortable inns at the time we wanted them, and generally found our chaise more cool and pleasant than the close rooms we were shown into'. So they rattled on uncomfortably through the heat of the day.

By the mid-nineteenth century the fashion for rambling through rural retreats was growing apace, yet some of today's most famous tourist sights were hardly visited. When the Ruskins reached Mont St Michel they found, not a tourist resort, but a castle occupied by five hundred convicts, beyond which stretched 'a grey dune sand of soft, clay granite dust mixed with mud, covered by the tide only once every six days, trusted to by the inhabitants for ablution of all foulness but remaining for the rest of the week with a pool or two of thick salt water. It is surrounded by a flat and filthy sand, channelled by brown and stinking rivulets of slow discharge – and spotted by fragments and remnants of fish and offal and street cleansings.' Even John Ruskin, 'prepared to bear this kind of thing in pursuit of the picturesque', was almost defeated by the stench.

For all but the most adventurous, places like the Mount were too far off the beaten track to consider. The southern French ports, on the other hand, which served as embarkation points for the Italian riviera, were frequently visited. During his travels in the south, the redoubtable Arthur Young found the Maison Carré at Nîmes, 'beyond all comparison the most light, elegant and pleasing building I ever beheld'. At Marseilles there was the exotic spectacle of the galley slaves, 'miserable caitiffs, all commanded by an imperious and cruel seaman'. One visitor found them 'cheerful and full of knavery' while the ineffable James Boswell, passing through on his way to Corsica, offered them the comforts of philosophy. As he pointed out, 'custom makes all things easy' and this being the case, the fact that some of them had been chained to their oars for thirty years would help them to bear even that hardship philosophically.

CORSICA

The island of Napoleon's birth was a remote and uncultured outpost of Europe. Boswell the lionizer was one of its few early visitors. His safaris in pursuit of the famous generally took him to the salons of the fashionable world, but in October 1765 he landed upon the wild Corsican shore bearing introductions from Jean-Jacques Rousseau to General Pasquale Paoli, leader of the island's independence struggle against its then colonial master, Genoa. Boswell's plan was to make himself spokesman of the patriots and so amplify his reputation in a new dimension.

He applied for his passport at Corte, the island's capital. 'When the passport was finished and ready to have the seal put to it, the chancellor desired a little boy who was playing in the room by us to run with his mother and bring the great seal of the kingdom. I was much pleased with this simple incident.' His *Journal to Corsica* duly extended the author's fame, but his advocacy did nothing for the patriot cause. In 1768 Genoa abandoned the attempt to control the island and handed it over, not to independence but, for a consideration, to the French. The Bourbon soon routed Paoli's forces. The following year, the general fled to London and to a certain drawing room fame as Boswell's protégé.

In the August of that year the wife of Carlo Buonoparte, a petty nobleman and lawyer in Ajaccio, gave birth to a son. Formerly a staunch patriot, Buonaparte senior quickly became a zealous supporter of the French régime, while his old leader, Paoli, was later governor of the island for Revolutionary France. Yet, without Paoli's freedom fight, Napoleon Bonaparte would not have been born of French nationality.

A century after this momentous event Edward Lear found himself staying at the major's house in Ajaccio. A tired and lonely fifty-five-year-old, he relaxed gratefully in the hospitality of Monsieur and Madame Quenza. After dinner he was shown 'a large collection of letters, written by the first emperor Napoleon and by General Paoli, to the great-grandfather of M. Quenza. Those of the former are on coarse paper and coarsely written. There was an orderly book, too, with enough signatures of Buonaparte to make the fortune of an autograph seller.'

Lear's first few days on the island had passed in drizzling rain and low spirits. Spring was the 'right and perhaps the only time for a sketching tour of Corsica, earlier, the snow would have made the higher districts unavailable to the landscape painter; later, the heat would prevent work.' So, regretfully, Lear had taken ship at Cannes just as the most pleasant and beautiful season was beginning. He set out in great excitement at the prospect of seeing 'that grand chain of Corsican Alps' but was doomed to disappointment as nothing was visible 'beyond the leaden, unlovely waves, except a low line of dark grey-green coast and glimpses between thick folds of cloud, of mysterious heights of far snow and rock.'

He found the customs officials civil and obliging but his hotel room was 'far too near the kitchen to be agreeable, and where abundant noises, odours and flies may be expected'. The hotel entrance and staircase were 'extremely dirty, and encumbered by small children who clung parasitically to the steps and balustrades'. But he ate well. His first meal was a late breakfast of fresh whiting, omelette and the famous *broccio* or cream cheese of the region. Everywhere he went he was to be delighted by the careful and obliging manners of Corsican innkeepers and at Mme Paolini's establishment, deep in the heart of the island, he was served a veritable banquet of a breakfast – trout and beef-steak, brains and caper sauce, Irish stew, *broccio*, and even an etcetera, 'all good in quality and profuse in quantity'. One suspects, it must be said, that this remarkable landlady had a soft spot for her winsome and good natured guest. When Lear came to leave, she urged him not to settle the bill but to stay at her hotel on his return and pay her then. When he pointed out that he might die and she would lose her money, she replied: 'In that case, although we are poor and should miss your money, we should not feel the loss so much, because our sorrow for your death would be greater.'

Château Azay-de-Rideau, Lorraine

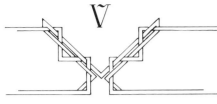

V
THE NETHERLANDS: AUSTRIAN, SPANISH AND DUTCH

D uring the two hundred years of the era of tourism known as the age of the grand tour – that is roughly from 1630 to 1830 – the countries we now call the Netherlands, Belgium and Luxembourg provided the chief cockpit for the wars of Continental Europe and had their political geography rearranged several times. At the beginning of the sixteenth century the duchies, counties and prosperous trading cities of the region were provinces of an empire ruled by Spain. The United Provinces of the North (now called the Netherlands) won their independence from Spain, and were formally recognized in 1648. However, Spain kept her hold on the southern provinces, the Spanish Netherlands, until 1714 when they passed to Austria. Eighty years later

Opposite   A FAIR IN AMSTERDAM J. H. Prins
Above   An artist at work in Bruges

these Austrian Netherlands were absorbed into Napoleonic France. The Congress of Vienna (1814–15) redrew the boundaries once again by incorporating the whole region into the new Protestant Kingdom of the Netherlands. Catholic Belgium rebelled in 1830 and the Kingdom of the Belgians was founded; at the end of the nineteenth century Luxembourg also won her independence.

ON THE ROAD

Compared with most countries in Europe, the Low Countries had superb roads. From Antwerp to Brussels one rattled along a paved surface constructed 'as well as the best streets in London', and kept in better repair. The thirty miles from Brussels to Ghent was along a well-engineered causeway. These roads were exceptional; moreover they were served by some of the best inns in Europe. As in many Continental wayside inns the guests slept in a common bedroom, but at least the Dutch landlord provided individual bunks let into the walls, with comfortable mattresses and clean linen. The Dutch habit of placing spitoons on the tables did not suit every tourist's notion of decorum, but in other respects the well-scoured and clean-sanded dining room was a pleasure to share with other guests at the *table d'hôte*.

The English sometimes preferred to stay at English establishments, of which there were many – The Queen of Hungary, at The Hague, for instance. This was not only because they were cheap – about one-third of the price of comparable establishments in London – but also because the landlords did present a bill in the English fashion. For there was one drawback about the Dutch hostelry. The landlord did not itemize the charges, merely demanded the total by word of mouth, offering neither bill nor receipt. Anyone foolhardy enough to query the sum was liable to be hauled before the magistrates.

Not only were the roads better and the inns more hospitable, but the Dutch and Flemish vehicles tended to be more comfortable than the diligences elsewhere. The most luxurious mode of travel in the Low Countries, or indeed all Europe, was the hotel barge plying between Ghent and Bruges. Two dozen passengers were transported in comfort for the moderate charge of a penny a mile. In summer they could laze on the deck; in winter, recline in the airy saloon, spotlessly clean and heated with its own coal fire. There were also private compartments to be hired. One could take a snack and a drink during the half-hour stops at bank-side taverns, but the seven course dinner in the saloon was as moderately priced as at any inn. A typical menu offered soup, pickled herrings, duck, salmon, veal, mutton, beef and vegetables, followed by desserts. Bread and beer were free, and a variety of good wines could be had cheaply.

These comforts were matched by the delights of the journey. 'The whole country appears a large garden; the roads are shaded on each side with rows of trees and bordered with large canals, full of boats.' Approaching the towns one heard the distant sound of carillon music ringing across the fields. These innocent sounding tunes could be used as coded signals against an invader; for the average tourist they were the most characteristic memory of his visit. At Ghent there was a half-hour performance just before noon on Sundays, Mondays, Wednesdays and Fridays. Dr Burney, the historian of music, went up into the belfry to see the carilloneur on the keyboard which sounded the bells, 'in his shirt with the collar unbuttoned and in a violent sweat'. The mechanism was operated by hand levers struck by the fist, which were linked to the bell clappers by long wires and other levers called trackers.

The countryside was dotted with neat villages, their red roofs shining among the 'level scenery of enamelled meadows, with stripes of clear water across them, and barges gliding busily along', and 'large herds of beautifully spotted cattle were enjoying the plenty of their pastures'. The cities themselves did not disgrace this model landscape. The streets were paved with broad stones; each housewife saw to it that her maid scrubbed down the pavement before her door every morning; the streets were regularly swept; and the floors and benches of the ale-houses cleaned. The Dutch obsession with cleanliness may have been something of a joke, but it is clear that foreigners relished the unique experience of hygiene and comfort, so unlike any other European country.

THE TOWNS

The long drawn out history of political unrest in the south was reflected in the homely concerns of daily life. Travelling in Luxembourg in 1828 one tourist found the landlord of his inn at the little town of Chiny bitterly incensed with Dutch King William over the price of wine. By royal decree French wine could only be imported by sea. '"Now really," growled the inn-keeper, "after the wine has been sent from Champagne to Paris, and from Paris to Havre, and from Havre to Antwerp, and from Antwerp to Chiny, one would have to be as rich as the King himself to drink it."' And the 'Champagne' under discussion was not the famous *vin mousseux* of that region but its humble *vin ordinaire*.

Approached from the sea, Antwerp did not fire the imagination. As his ship edged its way through the numerous sandbanks of the dreary Scheldt, the tourist saw little of interest. A traveller in the 1840s noticed 'a few Flemish fishing boats with painted hulls, sandbanks without end, roofs of villages, many of them lower than the river, and a few church towers until the tall steeple of Antwerp cathedral appeared on the horizon'.

Antwerp's golden age was already three centuries in the past. Early in the sixteenth century the Antwerp Exchange was the money capital of Europe. But the religious wars, during which she endured a fourteen-month seige, began the strangulation of the city. The dead hand of Spanish rule, and the subsequent closing of the River Scheldt by Spain's agreement with the Netherlands, put the Dutch port of Amsterdam in the ascendant. John Evelyn, who visited the 'magnificent and famous city' of Antwerp in the 1640s, admired its majestic buildings and the lovely walk on the outskirts, but found the place gloomy, lifeless and thinly populated.

In the mid-eighteenth century tourists found Antwerp a city 'to fill the mind with melancholy reflection concerning the transient state of worldly glory'. The Exchange building still rose imperiously over the centre but was 'as useless to the inhabitants as the Coloseo at Rome'. The churches, the palaces, the squares and even whole streets were almost abandoned. 'Scarce a fishing boat can now be discovered in the numerous canals, cut with such labour and expense, or on the noble River Scheldt.' To the millionaire William Beckford, Antwerp seemed an ideal place for retirement. 'No village among the Alps is less disturbed. In its two hundred and twelve streets and twenty-two squares the grass grows in deep silence.'

Only on the high days of the Church festivals did this somnolent city come to life. Then 'a prodigious number of priests, singing psalms all the way processed to the church with wax tapers in their hands, accompanied by French horns and serpents. Behind them comes a large silver crucifix and a Madonna and Child as big as the life, of the same metal'. All night long, the usually deserted streets were alight with the glow of bonfires and reverberated to the huzzas of the crowds and the reports of rockets, squibs and crackers.

By contrast, Amsterdam continued in an upward curve of prosperity. This had taken off in the 1590s after the fall of Antwerp to the Spaniards. In that decade foreigners found new houses going up all over the town and the harbour bustling with the loading and unloading of ships from all over Europe. The building of Amsterdam was a major engineering enterprise. The main buildings, such as the fourteenth-century Old Church, the fifteenth-century New Church, the synagogues and the Guildhall and the fabled Bank, had to have their foundations shored up on hundreds of wooden piles driven into the marshy earth.

The streets of Amsterdam throbbed with life from dawn to dusk. Rope dancers, musicians and buskers of all kinds entertained the passer-by;

hundreds of street traders set their stalls round the bridges that criss-crossed the canals. Money-changers clinking their black coin bags jostled with bakers turning out pies and pancakes from portable ovens. Booksellers' premises and bars were open to the street, and, as the nights drew in, brilliantly lighted shop windows flooded the pavements with warm squares of light.

The well-stocked shelves supplied the people of Amsterdam with the produce of the world and its tourists with the specialities of the city. The skill of her optical instrument makers and gem-cutters had long been famous, but Amsterdam was also one of Europe's chief centres of printing, renowned for maps and finely printed English books.

Then, as now, one of the chief glories of the Netherlands was the tulip harvest. In the 1710s, Joseph Addison was enraptured by 'the glorious show of these gay vegetables'; another Englishman spent his last guilder in Amsterdam on tulip bulbs for a generous uncle. Everywhere in the Netherlands, foreigners were impressed by the signs of wealth and a kind of public domesticity. William Beckford carpingly described the well-ordered gardens of Amsterdam's bourgeoisie as 'endless avenues of stiff parterres, formal gardens scrawled and flourished in patterns like the embroidery of an old maid's work bag'. But he admired the regularity of the houses and gardens of the more opulent citizens, whose carefully designed flower-beds and trim hedges stretched out of the city for miles along the road to Utrecht.

Considered the 'handsomest, the most fashionable and the most modern looking town in the Netherlands' by nineteenth-century visitors, The Hague had long been popular with European gentlemen on the grand tour. On his eighteen-month tour of England, France and Italy in the 1690s, Duke Frederick III of Gotha passed through the Netherlands with an impressive entourage. Accompanying the Duke were his major-domo, two gentlemen-in-waiting, a secretary, the ducal chaplain, a physician, the treasurer of the court, two pages, a valet, a lackey and the cook and two servants. The Hague had been an important seat of government for close on a century. Its palaces included the Prins Maurits Huis with its superb collection of pictures, but for many tourists a more interesting attraction of the stylish town were the gambling rooms. Nearby, Scheveningen grew in popularity as the craze for sea-bathing spread, and coastal watering places all over Europe attracted a more and more fashionable clientele.

During the seventeenth and eighteenth centuries sledging was a favourite winter diversion with the Dutch aristocracy and winter sports were popular with all classes of society. At Leyden, the birthplace of Rembrandt and famous for its university, one winter visitor found 'every

Dice throwers in an ancient inn at Volendam, Holland,
photographed by Donald McLeish

house forsaken and all the people of the ice'. There he saw 'sleds drawn by horses and skating' and ice yachts which, if his report is to be believed, with all sails spread would go more than a mile and a half a minute.

To the south of Leyden, the thriving town of Rotterdam presented a very different aspect from its modern appearance. The old town, largely destroyed by German bombing in 1941, was 'a beautiful confusion of chimneys, intermixed with the tops of trees with which the canals are planted and the masts of vessels', so that the visitor had difficulty in determining whether he was approaching a fleet, a city or a forest. The streets were a model of Dutch urban house-keeping. Well-paved, they were kept so clean that a lady wrote home that she had walked all over town in her house shoes without picking up a spot of dirt. 'The common servants and the little shop women here are more cleanly nice than most of our ladies', she observed. The crippled beggars, so common in the other great cities of Europe, were virtually unknown.

BRUSSELS

One of the great cities of the fifteenth-century Dukes of Burgundy, who then ruled most of the Netherlands, Brussels was also a favourite resort of their sixteenth-century descendant, the Emperor Charles V. Although it was an important centre in the revolutionary struggles against Spain, it remained in Spanish hands and was the principal city of the Spanish and Austrian Netherlands.

From the mid-eighteenth century there was a fine view of the city to be had from the nearby Château Charles, built by the Archduke Charles of Lorraine. This stood on a hill at the edge of the forest of Soignes and commanded a sweeping panoramic view. Far to the north could be seen the spires of Antwerp, nearer stood Mechlin and to the north-east lay the university city of Louvain with its superb medieval town hall. Even more interesting than the view was the château itself. Its luxuriously appointed rooms included one panelled and furnished in the, then, fashionable style of japanning; but the most remarkable thing in the house, indeed one of the rarest sights in all Europe, was 'a chair which goes up to the top of the house by machinery'.

Arriving in Brussels, few tourists failed to be impressed by the Grande Place of the Hotel de Ville, 'one of the beautifullest squares to be found anywhere'. The city's many marvellous fountains were compared with those of Rome and the inns and restaurants were reckoned the equal of any to be found in France. The opera house, built in the early 1700s was one of the finest in Europe. Most of its boxes were heated by individual coal fires and hired by the nobility for the winter season, for the 'conveniency' of their families. The quest for conveniency could go to extraordinary lengths. The Prince de Ligne had a large mirror installed in his box, so placed that he and his party could take dinner in the box and still watch the performance without being seen by the actors or the rest of the audience.

TOURISTS IN THE FRONT LINE

In June 1815 Brussels was a frightened city. Napoleon, defeated and exiled to Elba a year before, was once more the master of Paris. Landing at Fréjus in March, he had marched north to the capital, winning the allegiance of Bourbon generals sent to defeat him, and forcing the Bourbon King, Louis XVIII, to flee into exile. Now, less than one hundred days after his daring return, he was leading a French army against his enemies who had gathered their forces in Belgium. For twelve months Europe had supposed herself freed from his ambitions, and tourist travel had revived. Thousands of English people had crossed the Channel to explore the lands of their former enemy. Many were holidaying in Brussels, among them Fanny Burney, then the wife of the Bourbon courtier Count d'Arblay. Her journal became a vivid record of the days of mounting tension in the Belgian city before Wellington's victory at Waterloo.

She was awakened at five in the morning of Friday 16 June by a bugle call. Running to the window, she saw a platoon of soldiers marching past, then another, and still more. The procession lasted the rest of the morning; Saturday the 17th was a day of confusion and alarm and the dull roar of distant cannon. On Sunday it seemed the artillery was getting nearer; watching from her window, Fanny saw the wounded returning from the battlefield while 'troops of ready-armed and vigorous victims marched past to meet similar destruction'.

Her friends the Boyd family decided to make for Antwerp where they could take a boat for England if Napoleon should actually enter Brussels. Fanny, who was seized with an 'indescribable horror to be so near the field of slaughter', decided to join them. At six o'clock that Sunday morning there was a rapping on her bedroom door. She slipped on a dressing gown, 'always in those times at hand'. From the other side of the door came the agitated voice of Anne Boyd urging her to hurry her packing and to meet them at eight o'clock, ready for the river journey to Antwerp. They set off for the wharf on foot, it being impossible to hire any form of transport whatsoever.

Now and then we heard a growling noise, like distant thunder, but far more dreadful. We were followed by innumerable carriages, and a multitude of persons. Arrived at the wharf, Mr Boyd pointed out to us our barge fully ready for

Sep 10.
1883.

We spent yesterday (Sunday) at Rotterdam. It is a most picturesque place. There are numbers of canals with barges on them and great windmills quite in the town. This morning Father & I started out at about 7. We drew this old house. with great difficulty, for the people crowd round in front just as much as behind you. We next drew a canal, and the Church; while Mother and Willy went to the Zoological Gardens.

A page from Agnes Mary Alexander's watercolour album, 1883

departure; but the crowd so incommoded us that Mr Boyd desired we would enter a large inn, and wait till he could speak with the master, and arrange our luggage and places.

The ladies decided to order breakfast, but before it could be served a troop of soldiers took over the inn. Boyd returned with the news that the French were advancing and every boat on the wharfs had been commandeered by the army. According to the rumours, Brussels was to be evacuated, the campaign being as good as lost. 'The dread reverberation of cannon affrighted us with the probability that we might be personally involved in the carnage; we could only gaze and tremble, listen and shudder.'

So they made their way back to the lodgings in the forlorn hope of finding some form of conveyance to carry them out of the doomed city. 'But every chaise, diligence, cabriolet, calèche, wagon and cart, in short every species of caravan' had been requisitioned for the military. Fanny decided she must take a grip on herself and went up to her room to tidy up her correspondence. Writing at her bureau, she heard a loud 'Hurrah!' in the distance. Her landlord's daughter, a girl of about eighteen, came up to tell the English lady that the battle had in fact been won and Napoleon taken prisoner.

Fanny flew to the window to see 'a noble war-horse in full equipment, a general in the splendid uniform of France, disarmed and, to all appearance, tied to his horse, surrounded, preceded and followed by a crew of roaring wretches, who seemed eager for the moment when they might unhorse, strip, pillage him and divide the spoil'. The triumph in the streets continued, but as she watched from her window during the days that followed, the gentle Englishwoman was more moved by the 'maimed, wounded, bleeding, mutilated, tortured victims that passed by every minute. Many of the Bonapartian prisoners had a mien of ferocious desperation, others, faces of anguish.' To Fanny, and possibly a few other humane spirits, it would have 'demanded an apathy dead to all feeling to see them without commiseration for their sufferings, or admiration for the heroic, however misled enthusiasm' which had brought them to their fate.

The Battle of Waterloo freed Europe from the fear of Napoleon and liberated Brussels from France, but it did not secure her independence. The city was made over to the newly formed kingdom of the Netherlands, becoming joint capital with The Hague. The part played by Britain in the defeat of France was not forgotten by the court however. 'The English are the fashion at court,' wrote a contemporary. 'In all fashionable society English fashions are preferred and the English themselves are heaped with civilities. No wonder they flock to Brussels. Many a one keeps there the company of Kings and Princes, who, at home, would hardly hope to make up a quadrille party in Russell Square or Gower Street.' In the 1830s Belgium at last gained her independence with Brussels as her capital.

OUTSIDE THE CAPITAL

The medieval glories of other Belgian cities, like Brussels and Ghent, were also familiar tourist haunts. For most of the eighteenth century they were subject to the rule of the Habsburg emperors of Austria and in 1780 Ghent was visited by the Emperor Joseph II. Since his was not a formal state visit, he lodged, not in one of the palaces of the town, but at the St Sebastian Inn. Ghent was crowded for the occasion so that one evening, when Joseph and his aide de camp paid a visit to friends staying at another inn, which was on the same side of the square, they made their way under cover of darkness, 'through the little gardens and closes behind the houses along the river, from one house to another'. At last they reached their destination and the landlord ushered the royal visitor into the room, bearing a taper in each hand. From the silence and the candles taken about, the people thought it was the sacrament being administered to some sick person and many knelt in the streets.

Rather less well-known were towns like Namur. The ramparts looked out over flat meadows on the heights above the River Meuse, and the town was surrounded by beautiful walks. The Hotel Harshchamp was one of the finest in Europe but the amenities were unfortunately impaired by the old curfew and warning bell. The bell tower was in the centre of the town and well into the nineteenth century the bell was rung every morning at five o'clock and every evening at nine to signal the opening and closing of the town gate. The bell was cracked and the hotel was uncomfortably near to it. 'To one who has never heard this bell, it is absolutely impossible to convey the slightest idea of the sound.' One was roused at an ungodly hour by this 'claxon of a bell' and had one's evening meal ruined by it.

On his walking tour of the lesser known districts of Belgium in the 1820s the writer Harry Inglis left Namur by the little road that skirted the heights above the valley of the Meuse. Below, there were 'numerous little gardens and many sweet country houses; the full chorus of blackbirds was ascending from the valley below and the meadows wore the aspect of green summer; the thin smoke of the cottages wreathed slowly up into the still air; and the almost cloudless sky canopied all.' One can well believe his claim that there was no more beautiful walk in Europe than this winding river road from Namur to Liège.

Liège itself was an anticlimax – 'the blackest of all the towns that ever consumed coal'. The English traveller compared it unfavourably with

Birmingham and Sheffield, but admired its fine inns, cheap food and good wine, and reckoned that a gentleman of moderate income could live there more comfortably than anywhere else in Europe. Inglis certainly lived well. The *table d'hôte* at the Hotel d'Holand was cheap and good, the company pleasant and the after-dinner music in the Italian taste, rather than the country music favoured at French inns. Inglis was also lucky enough to dine on a number of occasions with the Comte de Rouen and his pretty and affable wife who offered the traveller the hospitality of her box at the opera. It was a pleasant enough way for a gentleman who enjoyed the eccentric English enthusiasm for walking to end his tour of the Low Countries.

A scene from THE FOREIGN TOUR OF MESSRS.
BROWN, JONES AND ROBINSON by Richard Dolye, 1855

PIERRE FILLIOL.

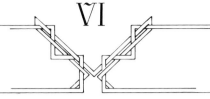

VI

MORE THAN TWO GERMANIES

T he modern tourist who plans to visit Berlin is prepared for various degrees of delay and harassment at the East-West border posts, depending on the political climate. But this is nothing new in German history. As late as 1919, the visitor to Munich, for example, quickly learnt that although it was a member of the greater German empire, ruled from Berlin, Bavaria was also a kingdom with internal self-government. In fact, the proud edifice of Imperial Germany, founded in 1871, was a congeries of more than twenty such lesser kingdoms, grand duchies and principalities of various kinds, whose ruling families were swept away only with the wave of revolutionary movements that flooded the country in the wake of defeat in 1918. During the full flowering of German separatism in

Opposite TOWER OF STRASSBOURG CATHEDRAL John Ruskin
Above   Detail from INTERIOR OF A VILLAGE INN J. P. Horstok

earlier centuries, the country was ruled by as many as three hundred petty courts. This presented the traveller with unexpected delights as well as the inevitable tedium of multitudinous frontiers and customs posts.

'German civility', wrote one of these early travellers, 'extends so far as to introduce a stranger directly into their societies and assemblies.' It was perhaps as well since the inns were atrocious, except for a handful of great hotels in the major cities. Foreigners on the road in the German lands looked, wherever possible, for private accommodation whether in castle or cottage. Touring Bavaria in the 1780s William Beckford, millionaire, writer and eccentric, was charmed with his entertainment by a forester's family. Sitting at the door of his hut in a leafy glade was an old man with long whiskers, 'his white locks tucked under fur cap while two or three beautiful children, with their hair neatly braided, played by him'. Beckford could see the children's mother at the window and, having crossed a stream, he made his way up to the cottage and asked for some refreshment. After a pretty dispute between the children as to who should have the honour of serving the stranger, a little black-eyed girl came shyly over to him with a jug of milk, some bread, and a plate of fresh strawberries.

It was one of those rare idylls which every experienced traveller learns to treasure. Polite society expressed its generosity with more insistence and less elegance. A guide book to Germany, written at about the same time, warned that a stranger was initiated and 'purchased, in a manner of speaking, his freedom by submitting to drink till he has lost the use of his reason. For the Germans think they have never performed their duties of hospitality, until they have over-powered their guests with liquor.' Many inns provided a leather couch at each table for the convenience of those guests too drunk to sit upright, but over-drinking was said to be especially rife in the palaces of ecclesiastical princes where conversational gallantry to the ladies was taboo.

In the time of Shakespeare, when English theatre companies were often to be seen on the roads of Germany, some inns were owned by English landlords and served English beer. A traveller taking a nostalgic pull at his tankard of good ale at a tavern near Oldenburg was highly gratified when a German leant over to compliment the brew which he thought a fine ambassador for England and her virgin queen. Few travellers, though, had a good word for German landlords and their establishments. In place of the bustling and courteous welcome of the English innkeeper, spruce and professional in his long white apron, you were met by 'a huge figure in a great coat, with red worsted cap and a pipe in his mouth, stalking before the door. If he stops, it is to eye you with curiosity and he never bows, or assists you.' The beer, you could be fairly sure, would be muddy and the food atrocious.

In out-of-the-way places it was a wise precaution to show your firearms to the landlord, in casual conversation, before you retired to bed. Sleep must have been difficult. In all but the very best places, both men and women bedded down in a barn along with the staff, the landlord and wife and family, and an assortment of animals. Besides a pair of primed pistols, the wise traveller was also equipped with impregnated leather bed coverings to be laid over the sheets, if any, as a protection against 'the itch venereal, and other diseases'.

There were exceptions. The inns around Leipzig, with its thriving university, were often decent, clean and private; and it was not difficult to find a pretty companion for one's bed. The country girls were glad of the money. Elsewhere, such hotels as the Darmstädter Hof in Karlsruhe, the Hotel Bellevue in Coblenz and the Rheinischen Hof in Mainz, offered superb accommodation for the luxury trade.

Throughout Germany many Englishmen hardly ever saw the inside of any kind of hotel or hostelry. As they were astonished to discover, English travellers were treated as if they were members of the nobility – even at the smallest courts, where distinctions of rank and class were generally an obsession with the natives. Boswell, and he was not alone in this, planned his itinerary so as to stay overnight, whenever possible, in some princely town. It was not difficult – there were so many. This casual hospitality to foreign gentlemen is the more puzzling when in comparison with the rigid hierarchy of class that ruled social contacts between the Germans themselves.

ON THE ROAD

Writing in 1798, the English lady Mariana Starke considered that a visit to Germany was like stepping back a century, 'as the dresses and customs and manners of the people precisely resemble those of our ancestors'. Fifty years later, William Howitt, the English traveller and writer and, incidentally, a pioneer of Australian travel writing, still observed many people in the 'garb of centuries ago'. He was delighted by the gabled and picturesque white buildings, the old squares and markets, and the avenues of limes or dwarf acacias, of the provincial German towns. But such beauties did not compensate, he thought, for the dreadful paving of the streets, of the 'most hobbly and excruciating kind. If an Englishman, accustomed to his well-paved and well-regulated towns, were suddenly set down in a German town at night, he would speedily break his neck or his bones.' Still worse were the 'queer odours' pervading the streets of every town, from the 'peculiar and by no means enviable smell of almost every house, and every hour'.

The roads ranged from the excellent to the unspeakable. Fine metalled highways and posting services linked Frankfurt, Nuremberg and Vienna, and the Alpine passes; the superb Bergstrasse ran from Darmstadt to Heidelberg. Elsewhere the roads were veritable mud tracks. German travel writers warned foreign visitors from bringing their own carriages because of the frequent changes of rut gauge, especially in the north. The ruts on the roads east of Hamburg were wider than those west of the city and if the wheels of one's carriage were not adjustable the vehicle had to leave the road altogether and plough its way through the open fields. Even in the 1840s a traveller might encounter ruts which 'swallowed' the carriage up to the axles and piles of mud which stood, ground up by the action of the wheels, 'like walls'. Many tourists preferred, whenever possible, to travel by water.

Continental river boats interested English visitors. In the 1640s, the diarist John Evelyn boated down the Rhône from Lyons to Avignon, the river being so rapid that the boat merely needed steering. From Geneva one had to buy a boat for the downstream journey and sell it at Lyons, because the current was too strong for the return against the stream. At its best, river travel was speedy and comfortable. In terms of miles per hour it was not dramatically faster than the roads, but the boat traveller could continue his journey in comfort throughout the night. Tom Coryat covered eighty miles in thirty hours on a Rhine river boat; this of course, was on the down-stream journey, boats coming up river needed a team of horses to tow them against the current. For those who could afford it, there was a cabin amidships. However, on difficult stretches all but the most privileged passengers had to take a turn at the oars, a convention observed with some irritation by Fynes Moryson travelling up the Elbe to Hamburg in the 1590s.

Public boats plied regularly on all the major rivers of northern Germany, and on the Danube. From the early 1700s isolated stretches of the German inland waterways were being improved by canal building, but the rivers were not regulated by weirs and locks until the next century. Nor was there a reduction in the numerous tolls levied by the profusion of local authorities. No fewer than thirty-two toll stations had to be passed between Strassburg and the Dutch frontier.

Those who could afford to hire their own river boats could travel in something approaching luxury. In 1748 the Scottish historian and philosopher David Hume made the trip from Regensburg to Vienna down the Danube, in the private party of a wealthy patron. They travelled on a massive log raft, made entirely of fir boards, on which was built a substantial superstructure housing three rooms, one for the gentry, one for their servants, and the third for a kitchen. They ate well during the day and at night lodged in bankside hostelries. When they reached Vienna, the strange craft was dismantled, the wood was sold, and the boatmen made the return journey to Regensburg on foot.

Whatever the mode of travel, political conditions in Germany made movement more difficult than elsewhere in Europe. A visitor to the Frankfurt Book Fair, for example, would find superb accommodation at either the Emperor or the Red House but his troubles had only begun. At least ten currencies were in circulation in the city, even in normal times, among them Reichsthaler, gulden, kreutzers, German gold ducats and Spanish philips. The visitor had to be very astute indeed not to lose a sizable percentage on every transaction he made during his stay. The toll-gates and turnpikes were, of course, a constant drain on the purse, while German transport servants seemed to have had a tariff of additional impositions of their own devising. Charges for horse hire and coach hire were supplemented with *Schmiergeld* for the greasing of the axles; there was *Trinkgeld* for the ostler and a special levy known as *Schwagergeld*, taken by the postilion, whatever all-in charge had been agreed for the journey.

German postilions seem to have enjoyed an even less savoury reputation than their French counterparts. With insufferable impertinence they halted the coach at every wayside tavern for beer, delaying the coach for up to two or three hours while they slaked their thirst. Wordsworth came back to England fuming at the 'heinous' impositions he had endured at their hands in Prussia. He grudged being forced to pay for more horses than he considered necessary; this may, in fact, not have been the fault of the postilions since there were Prussian bye-laws governing the number of horses to be hired for each type of vehicle. The poor state of the roads was the reason given, but each horse was subject to a state tax as well as to the postmaster's hire charge. Under these regulations, even a light carriage taking one passenger and a single trunk had to hire two horses.

A private carriage usually spared one some inconveniences. However, when Boswell trundled into Leipzig on the evening of Saturday 13 October 1764, planning to go on that night to the little town of Gotha, he found that the onward post was already booked. Bribing the postmaster, he hired an extra, but his money failed to ensure prompt changes of horses. At some of the stages he was kept waiting five hours. He resolved never again to take an extra and, being Boswell, contemplated solacing himself with a suitable sexual adventure. 'I strolled about in a village in search of the ugliest woman I could find'; then he restrained himself, reflecting that 'such inclinations are caused by disease'.

NUREMBURG Samuel Prout

BERLIN

Boswell travelled by whatever means that came to hand, and doing so, met people of all kinds, though each with a claim to social distinction, which he meticulously recorded. 'Today I rumbled along in the journalière, a sad machine but cheap, having for company, amongst others, Mademoiselle Dionisius, daughter of the cook of Prince Ferdinand of Prussia.' His accommodation ranged from the magnificent to the unbelievable. At Dessau he was present at a magnificent dinner. 'The whole noblesse of Dessau was assembled. Music played in the next rooms, and by what strange chance I cannot tell, they played among other tunes, the Scottish country dance, "The Campbells is coming, Oho! Oho!" This caused in my mind a most curious mixture of German and Caledonian ideas.'

Even more poignant memories of the home he had left must have come to mind as he contemplated the lodgings offered him at one Hanover inn.

'In the middle of a great German salle, upon straw spread on the floor, was a sheet laid; on one side of me were eight or ten horses, on the other four or five cows. A little way from me sat a cock and many hens; and the cock made my ears ring with his shrill voice, an immense mastiff chained pretty near the head of my bed growled most horribly, and rattled his chain.' The doors to this strange, stable-hostel, were left wide open so that Boswell drowsed off to sleep contemplating the beauties of the evening sky and 'did sleep in this way with much contentment, and much health'.

There were worse shocks in store. In Berlin, he regaled his hosts with Dr Johnson's verses 'On Thames's Banks'. They thought them unpolished. How curious this was, mused Boswell. Here were human beings who did not understand English, and to whom Mr Samuel Johnson did not exist. Despite this unpardonable lapse in their education, his Berlin friends had much to show Boswell.

For a foreign visitor the chief sight of the city was its monarch, the famous Frederick the Great of Prussia. One English knight had already made the trip from London to Potsdam, 'solely to see the king and when he had seen him on the Parade, went quietly home again'. Boswell was not so easy to please; but he was certainly impressed by this king who had 'astonished Europe with his warlike deeds'. When Boswell attended at the palace, Frederick was dressed in a suit of plain blue, with a star and a plain hat with a white feather; he carried a cane. 'The sun shone bright. The king stood before his palace, with an air of iron confidence that could not be opposed. As a loadstone moves needles, a storm blows the lofty oaks, so did Frederick the Great make the Prussian officers submissively bend as he walked majestic in the midst of them.'

Boswell was well pleased with the courtesy and style of the court at

Potsdam. Dr Charles Burney, by contrast, found that it was not reflected in the procedures of the customs officials who watched its frontiers. With some irritation, he found that his 'trunk and writing box were examined as curiously as if I had just arrived at Dover from France'. His bags had been subject to a 'rummage' at the Prussian frontier, and when he reached Berlin he was 'taken in custody by a sentinel' at the town gate. The guard mounted the post wagon in which Burney was travelling and with his musket on his shoulder, and bayonet fixed, led him like a prisoner through the principal streets of the city to the custom house. He was obliged to wait for two hours, shivering in rain-drenched clothes, while everything was searched once again. When that was done he had to complete a questionnaire as to his name, character 'whence, where, when, to whom recommended, business, the length of his intended stay' and other details.

COURT LIFE

Every minor German autocrat throughout the country exercised the same absolute authority within his own frontiers as did the great King of Prussia. For instance, the Prince of Wallerstein ruled a state comprising 320 square miles and 36,000 subjects. The inhabitants of one of his villages greeted him handsomely with a procession of notables, fanfares of trumpets, and a volley of pistol shots. The little pageant delighted a passing tourist – but it infuriated the prince. Why had the bells not been rung? In the Prince's opinion, nothing was to be omitted which might stress, 'through outward signs, the majesty of his lord'. Goethe witnessed a similar village reception for the Duke of Weimar, 'with music, salutes of mortars, rustic arches of honour, garlands, games, dancing and fireworks'. The Duke, apparently, did not mind the silence of the bells.

Delightful as they were, the pageants of the minor courts concealed and distorted overtaxed economies. Stuttgart, with its 250 tailors for its 18,000 inhabitants, was clearly a centre of luxury; but the wealth was generated from rents rather than industry. In the free commercial cities, independent of princely and aristocratic rule, conditions were very different. There, Lady Mary Wortley Montagu observed, was 'an air of commerce and plenty, streets well built and full of people, neatly if plainly dressed; the shops loaded with merchandise, and the commonalty clean and cheerful.' In the minor princely cities, by contrast, she found 'a sort of shabby finery, a number of dirty people of quality, tawdered out; narrow, nasty streets out of repair, wretchedly thin inhabitants, and above half the common sort asking for alms.'

The princely states also suffered from the whims of their rulers; and were dominated by the requirements of the court. The Dukes of Baden-

Würtemberg had a summer capital at Ludwigsburg, one of the many palaces in Europe built to imitate Versailles. Out of the season it was a ghost town, but during the summer months its broad streets and avenues of limes and chestnuts, 'usually so empty, would be thronged with courtiers in brilliant uniform, beside whom the townspeople in their modest civilian clothes formed an inconspicuous minority'. Fêtes were held on the lake, the prettiest girls of the town being enlisted to play the parts of sea nymphs; the market place became a charming toy-town charade of commerce, the stall-holders and their customers all in fancy dress. For the visitor it was delightful, for the citizens, merely a seasonal pantomime.

The summer costume balls given by the Electors of Bavaria were on a still more elaborate scale. Dressed in fanciful versions of the local peasant costumes, the courtiers drove in carnival from the exquisite summer palace of Nymphenburg to the palace of the Residenz in Munich, where they were received by the Elector and Electress, dressed as a village landlord and his wife. The handsome Georgensall was tricked out for the occasion as a rustic inn under the sign of the Bavarian Lion, its elegant furniture cleared to make room for rough wooden painted chairs, and tables laid with earthenware beer mugs and plates. Fortunately the food and drink were of the very best and the dancing which followed was a refined, courtly version of a peasant village green hop. In the 1780s the fashionable world was just discovering what many thought the most abandoned rustic dance to graduate into the polite world. Generations of peasants had whirled away their miseries in the steps of their *Ländler* and *Wälzer*; now the craze was beginning to seize their betters. Visiting Munich towards the end of the century, William Beckford sat entranced at a table in one of the tea rooms of the city 'as old, young, straight, crooked, noble and plebeian, wheeled briskly away in the waltz, round and round in a rapture that would quite astound an English dancer'. It was not long before the waltz craze swept all Europe and crossed the Channel.

The German courts lived in an impressive style; generally well beyond their means. In the Saxon State Calendar for 1733 the list of court officials occupied no fewer than fifty-three pages, and many of the chief officials controlled large households of their own. One of the largest court establishments was the music chapel. It comprised a French choir of twenty, an orchestra of forty-eight players, a separate Polish orchestra (for the Elector of Saxony was also King of Poland) and a ballet company sixty strong. Visitors were duly impressed. Boswell visited Dresden, the Saxon capital, shortly after the war with Prussia. The beautiful city had been heavily damaged by bombardment and, as he strolled the shattered streets, he found his former admiration for King Frederick the Great considerably diminished. The baroque glories of the restored city were destroyed, alas, by Allied bombers in the Second World War.

Travellers were vastly diverted by the sycophancy of Dresden residents to their ruler, and one made notes of the following extract from the city's newspaper for the week ending Saturday 4 February 1795: 'On Tuesday and Friday His Electoral Majesty diverted himself for a few hours with a pheasant shoot in the great park. In the afternoons the Father of the Country, together with his dearest Consort, passed an hour or two in His aquarium.' For Monday 24 May we learn that Prince Anton amused himself by taking a walk. No activity of the royal family, however slight, was too humble for the awed admiration of the subjects.

It was a style which even the smallest courts aimed to emulate. At Kassel sixty people were entertained at the Landgrave's table. This prince lavished a sizable part of his revenues on building and maintaining his Maison des Modeles, 'a singular thing where you have models of all the buildings and gardens of the Prince'. However, some of these princelings were more modest in their expenditure. The streets of the 'pretty town' of Bonn, where Beethoven passed his early years, were 'tolerably well paved in black lava', and the prosperous Prince Bishop of Cologne was content with a palace 'all white without any pretentions'.

German traditions of court pomp and patronage continued into the nineteenth century. In the aftermath of the Napoleonic wars, Bavaria was elevated to the status of a kingdom, and the Electors spent lavishly to maintain their new-found royal dignity. Without King Ludwig of Bavaria, Richard Wagner for example would have been sorely short of funds. The theatre at Bayreuth, which Wagner designed exclusively for the performance of his own operas, was completed in 1872. It has been one of Germany's chief tourist attractions ever since.

The traditions of performance and protocol, piously observed at the annual festival there in the early decades, would not have been out of place at a religious shrine. Stravinsky, when he visited the festival early in the 1900s, was appalled. 'Is not all this brilliant comedy of Bayreuth, with its ridiculous formalities, simply an unconscious aping of a religious rite?' To others, it was all great fun. Gertrude Bell, invited to join the party of the Grand Duke of Hesse when they were shown backstage on their visit to the theatre, found it most entertaining. They were taken into 'every corner, above and below. We descended through trap doors and mounted into Valhalla. We saw all the properties, and all the mechanisms of the Rhine maidens; we explored the dressing rooms, sat in the orchestra and rang the Parsifal bells! We shall feel quite at home when we see it tonight.'

THE GREAT CITIES

The River Rhine has always been one of the scenic glories of Germany and the city of Cologne seemed to many an approaching traveller to be the river's chief jewel. But the once prosperous trading city had lost her trade to Amsterdam during the eighteenth century and, under the reactionary sway of the Prince-Bishops, had steadfastly closed her gates to the Protestant refugees from the Low Countries which had brought vigorous new life to the industries of Prussia.

In the mid-1700s David Hume found the city 'extremely decayed, even falling to ruin; there are marks of past opulence and grandeur, but such present waste and decay as if it had lately escaped a pestilence of famine.' Henry Swinburne, there a few years later, was depressed by the contrast it offered to the pretty town of Bonn. 'There cannot be', he wrote, 'a worse-built, uglier or more dirty city, as black as small coal can make it.' Nor did the cathedral, 'a Gothic structure unfinished' impress him. At that time only the east end was complete. Building did not begin again until the 1820s, after the lapse of close on four centuries.

Coleridge visited Cologne at about that time and was so disgusted by the city, that he celebrated it with a suitable poem:

> In Köln, a town of monks and bones,
> And pavements fang'd with murderous stones
> And rags and hags, and hideous wenches,
> I counted two and seventy stenches,
> All well defined, and several stinks!
> Ye Nymphs that reign o'er sewers and sinks,
> The River Rhine, it is well known,
> But tell me, Nymphs, what power divine
> Shall henceforth wash the River Rhine.

This little squib, so prophetic of the modern concern with matters ecological, was certainly not typical of the reactions of the majority of the poet's contemporaries. They found the Rhine an enchanted river, rolling along, 'mirror smooth, voiceless swift, with trim banks, through the heart of Europe'. From the decks of his river boat the traveller gloried in the sight of ruined castles, well-tended farms and vineyards, a sight 'supremely interesting, instructive and gay'.

Yet perhaps the most renowned of all Germany's river cities was the university town of Heidelberg, on the banks of the Neckar. The students were a tourist attraction in themselves. A sixteenth-century visitor was vastly amused by their slavish scribbling of lecture notes and their habit of rapping on their desks if the professors went too quickly for them. Such earnest attention to the business of learning was not much in evidence during the turbulent years in Europe which followed the French Revolution. Dorothy Wordsworth saw the student population as the 'very spirit of rebellious youth' as they strolled the city streets in their long blond hair and strange clothes; and, like many a visitor, she was intrigued by their passion for the cult of duelling.

The city itself must have seemed an unlikely setting for rebellious youth at the dawn of the nineteenth century. Bayard Taylor was enchanted by the Gothick romanticism of the view as he approached Heidelberg one rosy sunset August evening. Above the river rose the massive bastions, terraces and roofless halls of the famous castle; its arches hung with cascades of ivy. Entering the town, he passed 'peasant girls with baskets on their heads, laden with purple clusters of the Muscatel, and talking to each other gaily over garden walls'. Careless students, pipe in hand, sauntered along the river bank and the sound of guns, firing a salute, crashed from hill to hill, far away into the Odenwald.

The sheer size and diversity of the German-speaking world struck many foreigners. From the great northern entrepôt of Hamburg to the charms of Heidelberg, from the delights of a small princely capital to the grandeur of Berlin or Vienna, the country seemed a world in itself. Prosperous Germans, too, delighted to explore their country and, despite the hardships of travel, were devotees of what we can term internal tourism. From the sixteenth century, the spa towns were among the most popular resorts. They specialized in different treatments. Carlsbad, where the water was rich in chalk, red earth salts, nitre, allum, iron 'and volatile spirits of sulphur', was best for stones. Visiting English found the waters at Wiesbaden comparable to those at Epsom; Baden-Baden, sovereign for a whole range of maladies, was considered especially effective in the treatment of barren women.

Spa society was comparatively democratic, the rich bourgeoisie mixing with members of the nobility in a freedom not permitted in formal society. The main hotel at Baden-Baden had 170 rooms and could cater for 300 people at each meal. In such a crowded public resort, it was virtually impossible to maintain the full social distinction expected at court. To the surprise of some visitors, common bathing for men and women was the norm; gentry took the cure with commoners; and even nuns and monks 'sat altogether in the same water'. Appearances were preserved by a frame of wooden boards that divided the bathers from one another as they passed the time playing cards and knuckle bones on boards floating in front of them.

Of the major German cities, few were as impressive as Leipzig. Its fair,

Castle at St Goarhausen on the Rhine, photographed by
Donald McLeish

held three times yearly, attracted merchants from far and wide. Polish Jews and Russians mingled with Dutchmen and Englishmen, while here and there a Greek was to be seen in his strange garb. But no foreign influence was as marked as that of France. Goethe called Leipzig little Paris. Its prosperity dated back to the Middle Ages, but Leipzig kept up with the times. Unlike many other German towns, it evoked 'no impression of bygone days; its monuments speak of a new and recent epoch'. Its apartment houses 'rose like great castles, or even whole city districts' and the streets were a constant scene of commercial activity and opulent ease.

It overtook its principal rival Frankfurt. Even the Frankfurt Book Fair, which Tom Coryat had found 'a very epitome of all the libraries in Europe', had by Goethe's time lost its pre-eminence to Leipzig. Nevertheless, Frankfurt remained prosperous in a comfortable way. The young Goethe loved his native city. He loved the great bridge over the Main, with the gilded cockerel on its old cross glittering in the sunshine; the old industrial quarters; the arrival of the market boats; the crowds surging round the Church of St Bartholomew. Foreigners were fascinated by the Jewish community in the famous Frankfurt ghetto, and some professed themselves shocked by the insulting treatment Jews often received. But Frankfurters prided themselves on a more generous policy than that of places like Ulm whence the Jews had been expelled. Like Nuremberg, where the foreigner was startled by the croaking of the curfew horn at nightfall and bemused by the ancient medieval town houses, which appeared to the eigtheenth century eye as 'old fashioned and of a grotesque figure', Frankfurt remained a bustling centre although conscious of a more prosperous past.

VIENNA

'Vienna is the best city in Europe to teach the young traveller the manners of the great world.' The elegant society and fashionable riding and fencing schools were admirably supported by large and improving libraries for the education of young gentlemen. The talented and sophisticated Sir Philip Sidney had taken riding lessons from the imperial equerry, John Pietro Pugliano, and in the eighteenth century the city was visited by a stream of British tourists.

Like most foreigners they were not much impressed by the dirty, narrow and dark streets, nor even by the emperor's town palace, 'an old black building, that has neither beauty nor stateliness'. A German gentleman admitted that there were 'more splendid equipages and horses here than in all Paris', but considered there were hardly three squares or palaces in the city which made any 'figure' at all. The only street that was regularly cleaned was the fashionable Prater. For many tourists Vienna's gardens and parks were the most beautiful feature of the city: the Hofgarten, on its island in the Danube, and with its charming shady walks and splendid views across the city; the walks along the majestic Danube, through lofty woods and level fields; and the Prater itself, 'with a long avenue of horsechestnuts, where hinds and stags graze by the river and there is fine scope for riding and driving'.

Here, Prince Galitzin had a pleasure house, or casino, 'a pretty box, in a large grove of old trees, with a little garden', where he entertained privileged visitors at delightful breakfast parties. In the outskirts were the magnificent Belvedere palaces built for Prince Eugen of Savoy, with their immense collection of pictures, their botanical gardens and richly stocked menagerie of strange and exotic animals. They were dwarfed by the Schönbrunn palace, designed for the emperor by the German architect Fischer von Erlach. Many contemporaries thought this unashamed attempt to match the grandiloquence of Versailles somewhat overdone. As to the Gloriette, built in its grounds to celebrate the Austrian victory over Frederick the Great of Prussia at Kolin in 1757, it was a 'long portico-kind of building, as ugly as possible'.

The reputed designer of the Gloriette was Anton Wenzel, Prince of Kaunitz, principal imperial adviser from the 1750s to the 1790s, and rated by some historians as the most astute eighteenth-century statesman. Yet, to a foreigner's eye, he had certain social failings. After a state banquet the prince 'treated the company with the cleaning of his gums, a nauseous operation which lasted a prodigious long time and was accompanied with all manner of noises'. Kaunitz, on the other hand, prided himself as something of a gourmet. He had a special spiral glass for mixing oil and vinegar for salads, which he shook 'with great parade and affectation'. At one memorable dinner, 'the bottle broke in his hands and covered him and the neighbouring ladies and gentlemen with its contents'. The episode no doubt disgusted the guests, but the prince's experimental approach to the pleasures of the table certainly squared with the priorities of the court, where 'carousing and feasting are the chief diversions'.

It was not uncommon for banquets to offer as many as fifty different dishes of meat all served on silver, and followed by an equally lavish battery of desserts, presented in the finest china. A guest at the great aristocratic palaces found a wine list beside his or her plate naming up to eighteen exquisite varieties available from the host's cellars. Champagne was already a famous luxury wine, though it was the opinion of the Prince of Kaunitz that not everybody knew how to treat it. At another dinner which lived long in the memory of those present, a gentleman opened a bottle with a technique of which the prince disapproved. Immediately Kaunitz called for another and, to the great diversion of an English traveller among the guests, proceeded: 'to give the company a lesson in uncorking and frothing the liquor; unluckily he missed the calculation of his parabola and poured the wine into his uplifted sleeve as well as into his waistcoat, etc.'

Humbler tourists missed out on the vaudeville provided by the chief imperial minister up at the palace, but they could dine handsomely at Vienna's public restaurants. While travellers elsewhere in Europe were competing with the hazards of the *table d'hôte*, these establishments were pioneering the *à la carte* menu. For the modest charge of forty-five kreuzers, the diner was offered six courses, for each of which he had an almost embarrassing variety of choice – seven varieties of soup, five of fish, and so on throughout the menu. One fascinated Berliner, haunting the crowded cafés and restaurants and admiring their magnificent mirrors, decorations and paintings, concluded that the Viennese took their food even more seriously than the Bavarians. The novel delicacy of ice cream to be had at stalls in the Kolhmarkt, especially delighted him.

Winter sports were popular, as they were in the Low Countries and northern Germany, and provided Vienna with a new diversion. But the fatigues of a trek into the country to the snow slopes were, in Viennese eyes, a serious drawback. Accordingly, cartloads of snow were brought into town, if by chance the Danube failed to freeze sufficiently hard. When it did freeze over, winter nights in the capital were a sparkling sight. The snow-covered river was dotted with sledges in a riot of fanciful shapes – 'griffins, tygers, swans, scollop shells, etc'. Each cradled a young lady of fashion dressed in velvet lined with rich furs and adorned with laces and jewels. Behind her, feet astride on the sled runners, reins in hand, rode her gallant, controlling the horse with its ribboned and jingling harness. Outriders cantered ahead carrying torches to blaze a way through the fluttering snow flakes. In an age when tourists had little interest in sun-drenched beaches, Vienna on a winter's night was a place of enchantment.

Even the opera was different in Vienna. Lady Mary Wortley Montagu attended a performance at which the stage was built over a large canal. At the beginning of the second act, this stage, 'divided into two parts, discovering the water, on which there immediately came, from different parts, two fleets of little gilded vessels'. The mock naval battle was followed by other sensational moving tableaux, contrived by 'a great variety of machines, and changes of scene, performed with surprising swiftness. The theatre was so large that it was hard to carry the eye to the end of it.' The stage settings and more than one hundred costumes were rumoured to have cost the emperor £30,000; Lady Mary does not even mention the fees of the performers.

By the end of the eighteenth century the Viennese passion for pleasures of all kinds fastened on the new dance, the waltz, to a degree that was to become an obsession over the next fifty years. It spread through Europe at what the staider members of society considered a shocking rate. The Queen of Prussia averted her eyes demurely when it made its début at a Berlin court ball in 1794; the Duke of Devonshire, after watching the couples entwined in each other's arms, vowed he would never marry a girl who waltzed. Yet in the same decade Goethe, the courtier, polymath and poet, found that he had to learn to waltz to be accepted into society in Strasbourg. Twenty years later Joseph Lanner and Johann Strauss launched the dance as a universal craze. Hector Berlioz, in Vienna in the 1830s, was delighted by it all. 'The youth of this city,' he wrote, 'gives rein to its passion for dancing, which has led the Austrians to elevate ballroom dancing to an art.' The composer spent many a night watching the waltzers 'whirling round in great clouds', and in admiring 'the choreographic precision of the quadrilles – two hundred people at a time, drawn up in two long lines'. In the midst of it all stood Strauss, directing his splendid orchestra. When one of his new waltzes made a special hit the dancers stopped to applaud and the ladies threw him their bouquets. In the opinion of Berlioz, it was 'no more than justice; for Strauss is an artist.'

The spa at Bad Leukerbad

VII

THE ALPINE REPUBLIC

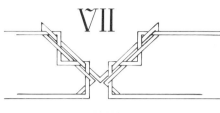

'I am enjoying myself madly. On the Schreckhorn yesterday, at six, we got out into the sunshine on a snow saddle and saw down the other side. I was beginning to think that the Schreckhorn had an absurd reputation, but the hour of *arête* from the saddle to the top made me alter my opinion. It's a capital bit of rock climbing, a razor edge going quite steep down, snow on one side and rock on the other, not quite solid so that you have to take the greatest care, and with a couple of very fine bits of climbing in it.'

This hymn to the joys of mountaineering and the magic of the Alps was written at Grindelwald, on a Sunday morning in the spring of 1901, by that remarkable English traveller Gertrude Bell. At the age of twenty-one

Opposite   Aiguilles du Plan, Blaitiere and Charmoz from Mount Blanc,
photographed by Donald McLeish
Above   Lausanne drawn by Mendelssohn on 7 August 1842

she had been one of the pioneer women graduates at Oxford University. In 1899 she had begun the series of epic journeys in the Middle East which was to culminate in collaboration with T. E. Lawrence in the Arab cause and a major role in the founding of the modern state of Iraq. At the time of this Swiss holiday she was in her early thirties and was making a new reputation as a mountaineer. 'I must tell you,' she wrote home in the following year, 'the guard on the train of the Brunnig line asked me if I were the Miss Bell who climbed the Engelhorn last year. This is fame!' That mention of the railway reveals the change that had come over the world since the founding of the British Alpine Club, nearly half a century earlier.

The first generation of Alpinists had found the snows of Switzerland and the neighbouring Alpine regions an almost unspoiled wilderness. However, others soon followed. In 1871 Leslie Stephen, who had been one of the pioneers, published a book on the Alps which he titled *The Playground of Europe*. In it, he lamented that 'the fortunate generation is passing away, and the charm is perishing. Huge caravanserais replace the old hospitable inn; railways creep to the foot of Monte Rosa and the summit of the Wegern Alp and threaten even the summit of the Jugfrau.' The pastime of the few had opened the way to a new region of mass tourism. Thomas Cook ran his first *voyage accompagné* to Switzerland in the 1860s, barely a decade after the foundation of the British Alpine Club. An official Swiss tourist publication brackets these two events as the foundations on which the country's modern tourist industry is built. By the end of the nineteenth century, an ageing enthusiast for the early days could write: 'Today, the tourist despatches Switzerland as rapidly and thoughtlessly as he does Olympia; and the very name of the Alps, so musical in the ears of those who enjoyed their mysterious charms, suggests little more than the hurry and jostling of the average sight-seeing trip.'

The fashion for Switzerland had its origins in a new attitude towards the beauties of nature which developed during the eighteenth century. Before that time, the wild and remote regions of the Earth were regarded with a fear amounting to awe by most people. To the natural hazards of Alpine travel were added the danger from bandits. Travellers faced the prospect of an Alpine journey with trepidation, and the notion of going out of one's way to enjoy these wild and desolate landscapes was positively eccentric. As the eighteenth century advanced, however, the taste for the wildernesses of Europe developed into something of a cult and formed a strand in the emerging ethos which we know as the Romantic movement. In the 1780s Dr John Moore could write: 'A greater variety of sublime and interesting objects offer themselves to the contemplation of the traveller in Switzerland than can be found in any other part of the globe to the same extent.' Forty years later George Ticknor, the American traveller, had this to say: 'The falls of Niagara may surpass it but I have never seen Niagara, and the Mer de Glace remains solitary in my recollections of the stupendous works and movements of nature.'

Ticknor wrote at the height of the Romantic age, for which 'the stupendous works and movements of nature' were at the heart of the true experience of the natural world. But exploration and scientific curiosity were the impulses that first drove European man up to the mountains. As early as 1741, an English party had made a six-day trip from Geneva to see the glaciers of Chamonix, the mountain village near the point where the borders of France, Italy and Switzerland meet. The expedition was organized by William Windham and Richard Pococke, who is remembered for his travels in the Orient.

Windham and Pococke and six friends were accompanied by five servants and a train of pack horses with their provisions and tents. Perhaps 'expedition' is too strong a word since the party went only as far as the Montanvert Pass, to which a path already existed. Even so, the locals had warned them that the mountains could be dangerous for those unfamiliar with them. In his book *An Account of the Glaciers or Ice Alps in Savoy*, Windham modestly claimed only to have opened the way for others who might have 'curiosity' of the same kind. He recommended any who might follow that way to take a compass, various scientific instruments, and pre-cooked food. Twenty years later the unadventurous tourist did not need to concern himself even with these modest preparations. The 'fashion of climbing mountains and viewing the glaciers' was already catching on to such an extent that the local muleteers were offering day trips to the lower lying Alpine regions.

Mountaineering as an organized sport, like most other organized sports, originated in nineteenth-century Britain. Before that time the idea of climbing mountains for pleasure was virtually unknown. On 26 April 1336 the Italian poet Petrarch climbed Mont Ventoux (6,263 ft) in southern France 'to reach the top and for the glorious view from the summit' as he makes clear in a letter to his father. This is the first recorded ascent of an Alpine peak. The next mountaineering expedition was probably the ascent of Mont Aiguille (6,880 ft). The climb was made by the Seigneur de Beaupré, chamberlain to King Charles VIII of France (d. 1498), on the orders of his master. Having fulfilled his sovereign's command, de Beaupré never climbed another mountain. In the mid-sixteenth century, the Swiss botanist and polymath Konrad von Gessner was climbing a new peak each year – 'at the time when the flowers are at their best' – in search of specimens. Behind this virtuous sense of duty to scholarship lurks, one suspects, the passion of a true mountaineer.

Gessner was unusual in his enjoyment of the mountains, but travel among the Alps was becoming more common. In 1574 Josias Simler of Zurich published a book to help travellers, to detect hidden crevasses, survival techniques that offered the best hope against an avalanche, and on the use of ropes; he even recommended studded shoes and crampons as climbing aids. Over the next two centuries the scientific community became increasingly interested in mountains; as the science of geology emerged into its infancy, practitioners began to see mountains as their research laboratories. Then, in 1760, Horace Bénédict de Saussure made his first visit to Chamonix to begin his study of glaciers – a new age of Alpine travel was about to dawn.

Saussure was enthralled, almost bewitched, by one particular mountain, Mont Blanc. His first thought was to establish a research centre high on its slopes, but the proposal caused horror and disbelief among the local population. They believed that demons and dragons guarded the heights, and nobody was prepared to work for the proposed expedition. But de Saussure could not rid himself of his obsession; at times it seemed to him like a kind of illness. 'I could not even look upon the mountain, which is visible from so many points round about, without being seized with an aching desire.' At length he offered a reward to the first man to reach the summit. The prize was won in August 1786, by a local Chamonix hunter called Jacques Balmat, who made the climb with a young Chamonix doctor, Michel Gabriel Paccard.

At 15,781 ft, Mont Blanc is the highest peak in the Alps; its conquest by two men, with virtually no climbing aids, is one of the great achievements of mountaineering history. The following year de Saussure himself made the climb, with Balmat as guide. He was accompanied by his valet and eighteen porters, carrying scientific equipment and a hamper of wine bottles. The same year Colonel Beaufroy of the Coldstream Guards became the first Englishman to make the climb. 'The fashion of climbing the moutains and viewing the glaciers' was launched; excursions on to the glaciers became more and more common features of tours of Switzerland. The earnest-minded went equipped with botanist's handbook, and with kettle and thermometer for estimating altitude by the temperature of boiling water; the rich engaged an artist for the trip. Wordsworth made a walking holiday in Switzerland during the Cambridge long vacation of 1790. When Europe was opened up by the railways in the next century the middle classes flocked to Switzerland to feel 'the more immediate presence of Him who had reared those tremendous pinnacles'.

In 1863 Miss Jemima Morrell was a member of the party on a dawn trip to the Rigi, to see the mountain panorama at sunrise. It was a motley group.

Some three or four care-for-nobody characters appeared as New Zealand chiefs, wrapped in scarlet blankets. Most of the gentlemen were in buttoned mackintoshes, their neckties of varied qualities and dyes. The peripatetic vendors of carved needle cases, etc., seemed to awake their interest as they offered their itinerating stores. The rising sun on the Rigi, in stately process rises from the dusky mist and with one glance of his ruby eyes suffuses the ashy visages of that snowy congress with the waxen hues of the celestial rose we call 'Maiden's Blush'.

The golden age of Alpine mountaineering is conventionally dated between the mid-1850s and the mid-1860s. The Alpine Club of London was founded in 1857; an Austrian counterpart followed five years later; and the Swiss Alpine Club was set up in 1863. Then, in July 1865, came the conquest of the Matterhorn by the seven-man team led by Edward Whymper, and the accident which turned the jubilant descent of the mountain into tragedy, when four climbers lost their lives. The catastrophe and the subsequent recriminations reverberated around Europe, but the popularity of mountaineering was hardly affected.

The year before the Matterhorn disaster, a fourteen-year-old American boy was brought to Switzerland by his aunt. Marguerite Brevoort, a giant of a woman, was known as that 'great Dutch-American Miss'; her nephew, little William Augustus Brevoort Coolidge, was a frail and sickly child, whose doctor had recommended Alpine air for his health. The pair embarked on a series of energetic Alpine walks, which became increasingly adventurous as the boy gained in strength and vigour. Marguerite was to be the first woman to scale the Matterhorn; William Augustus grew up to be one of the most celebrated of Alpinists. He made six hundred major ascents and was finally elected an honorary member of the Alpine Club of London.

The scientific drive which had inspired the first ascents weakened as the sportsmen took over. But even in the golden age of the sport, a few climbers felt they were first and foremost pioneers exploring unknown territory, and, as such, felt duty bound to record, measure and study. Chief among them were James Forbes, Francis Fox Tuckett and John Tyndal; for all their worthy intentions, they were not immune to the magic of the high places. In his *Hours of Exercise in the Alps* of 1871, Tyndall records one such magic moment on the Weisshorn.

The day was perfect; not a cloud was to be seen; and the gauzy haze of the distant air, though sufficient to soften the outlines and enhance the colouring of the

Mountaineering pioneers in Switzerland in the 1860s

mountains, was far too thin to obscure them. Over the peaks and through the valleys the sunbeams poured unimpeded save by the mountains themselves, which sent their shadows in bars of darkness through the illuminated air. I had never before witnessed a scene which affected me like this one. I opened my notebook to make a few observations but soon relinquished the attempt. There was something incongruous, if not profane, in allowing the scientific faculty to interfere where silent worship seemed the 'reasonable service'.

By the last quarter of the nineteenth century, once historic achievements had become standard climbs. Mont Blanc was scaled by the intermediate class, and even the Matterhorn might be climbed scores of times in a single season. On the nursery slopes, hundreds of tourists disported themselves as 'salon mountaineers'. Crinolined ladies and sportily dressed gentlemen struggled from one accessible rock platform to another with the aid of wooden ladders and burly local guides. Windham and Pococke's trail-blazing adventure to Montanvert had become the highlight of a Cook's tour, tramped in a day's walk by townees, brandishing specially purchased alpenstocks for which they had been grossly overcharged. The valleys around Chamonix reverberated to the roar of the cannon, periodically let off so that the parties might admire the echo. The Alps were no longer the preserve of an adventurous élite; the playground had been opened to the whole of Europe.

CITIES, VILLAGES AND MOUNTAIN PASTURES

Pursuing his sturdy way through the Europe of the 1840s 'with knapsack and staff', Bayard Taylor found the road south from Schaffhausen to Zurich a happy reminder of home. 'The country was so beautiful that we half felt like being in America. The farmhouses were scattered over the country in real American style'. There was an air of peace and prosperity and, above all, a look of freedom. The Swiss exhibited a 'lofty self respect' of which he entirely approved, as he did of the 'noise of employment from mills, furnaces and factories' near Zurich. Such signs of industry were fitting in a republic, and Taylor noted with satisfaction that the 'swift waters of the River Limmat turned many mills'.

From a bridge over the Limmat, Taylor and his friends could look out across the blue lake and down the thronged streets of the city on each side. They strolled along the old battlements of the city, planted with trees and transformed into 'pleasant walks which, being elevated above the city command views of its beautiful environs'. The next morning they went to the Lindenhof, a raised courtyard shaded by immense trees. This was a favourite meeting place for the citizens, the fountains were always surrounded by washerwomen and groups of merry school children could be seen tumbling over the grass. The Americans found the 'social and friendly politeness' of the Zurichers a pleasant change from the indifference of other Europeans. Looking down on the lake they were entranced by the transparent pale green of the water, so clear they could see the white pebbles on the bottom. That evening they left by the eight o'clock steamer, a little boat which 'came like a fiery-eyed monster through the rain and darkness over the water'.

Next day they took a mountain road with glorious views, but lined with beggars 'who dropped on their knees in the rain before us, or placed bars across the way and then took them down again for which they demanded money'. After marvelling at the glories of the pilgrim church at Einsiedeln, they continued along above the shores of Lake Zug, south to the Rossberg. 'The luxuriant fields were spotted with the picturesque chalets and cattle and goats were browsing, their bells tinkling most musically as the little streams fell in foam down the steeps.'

Before the Romantic movement in the arts opened the eyes of the travelling public to the beauties of landscape, Switzerland, with its mountainous roads and thriving towns, had been part of the route to Italy and rarely a destination in its own right. From the mid-sixteenth century, when Zwingli at Zurich, Calvin at Geneva, and other leaders of the Reformation made their headquarters in republican Switzerland, numbers of Protestant visitors were attracted, but they were hardly tourists.

For the eighteenth-century tourist it was the presence of a far from religious celebrity that gave Geneva a special interest. In 1758 Voltaire, the archpriest of sceptical rationalism, bought the nearby estate of Verney. Uninvited, tourists of all kinds flocked to see the house. On one occasion the ageing and tetchy philosopher burst out of the house snarling: 'Well, gentlemen, you now see me. Did you take me for a wild beast or monster that was fit only to be stared at as a show?' Even those with letters of introduction could not be sure of their welcome. Boswell, gratified to be received by two or three footmen, learnt that Voltaire was still abed and was much vexed at the interruption of his rest. Unabashed, the celebrity hunter negotiated a twenty-minute interview, and stayed to dinner, even though the great man returned to his bed. The next day Boswell was granted an invitation as a house guest for one night and a longer conversation. He was, in fact, an occupational hazard for the famous men of his day. Jean-Jacques Rousseau, whose home was near Neufchâtel, was another who found it impossible to avoid receiving him.

The urbane historian Edward Gibbon was a welcome guest at Verney. He received an invitation to a performance of one of Voltaire's plays, in which the author acted one of the parts, and to the dinner and dancing which followed it. The party broke up at four in the morning and their coaches rattled up to Geneva 'just as the town gates were opened'. As a young man, showing dangerous tendencies towards Roman Catholicism, Gibbon had been sent to Lausanne by his father on a kind of Protestant health cure. He enjoyed the town. 'There is scarce an evening without one or two assemblies. There is a sort of Club coffee house where the members are chosen by ballot and the Spring Society of young women, much addicted to English country dances.'

Of the other Swiss towns, Berne appears to have been one of the most attractive. Catherine Romilly found it 'a beautiful city, the streets wide and regularly built, with arches so that you may walk all round the town in bad weather, without being wet; under these arches are the shops; in the middle of the street runs a small stream of water which, with the well-built fountains and cleanliness of the whole, is very agreeable.' The streets were cleaned by gangs of convicts which, to her surprise, included women.

By the time of the Napoleonic wars Switzerland's neutrality was an honoured tradition. However, it did not afford much protection to the English tourists caught in the country in 1803. On the orders of the French controlling power, all those over the age of eighteen were rounded up and interned at Verdun, in France, for the next eleven years. Some did evade capture. The daring young Lord Campbell, for instance, got home safely, disguised as a woman. Dr John Roget, bear leader to two English boys whose age saved them, got his own clearance after an anxious night waking up officials in his native town of Geneva, to assemble the necessary documents proving his Swiss descent.

After the wars more and more foreigners came to Switzerland. Her spas were a special attraction for both clients and spectators. One was intrigued to see 'a lady up to her shoulders in the water taking coffee from off a floating tray'. The bathers sat on a seat running round the inside of the bath below water level, in dark blue or dark red gowns. 'A moustachioed gentleman was cutting leather work on his floating table, whilst one portly, round-shouldered party of about sixty was executing a roving commission across the water to salute some ladies in the opposite corner.'

THE ALPINE PASSES

From Switzerland, the southward journey to Italy lay through one of the four principal passes through the Alps. The route over the Great St Bernard Pass, commonly used in the Middle Ages, declined in popularity. Travellers who had entered Switzerland at Geneva either skirted the northern shores of the lake through Brigue to the Simplon, or headed south through the lands of the Dukes of Savoy to the Mont Cenis. Those coming into Switzerland from the north usually passed through Zurich.

The roads through the passes provided an unforgettable experience. Bayard Taylor described his walk through the St Gotthard with schoolboy enthusiasm. 'The rarefied air we breathed 7,000 feet above the sea, was like exhilarating gas. We felt no fatigue and ran and shouted and threw snowballs in the middle of August.' On his four-day crossing via the Mont Cenis to Turin, a century earlier, Horace Walpole had recoiled from the 'uncouth' rocks and the 'uncomely' inhabitants. Such was the change of attitude to wild scenery, between the Age of Reason and the Age of Romanticism.

Walpole and his party had been obliged to quit their coach at the foot of the pass, so that it could be dismantled and transported by mule train, over the mountains. The passengers went on in carrying chairs, 'swathed in beaver bonnets, beaver gloves, beaver stockings, muffs and bearskins'. Primitive though it was, this mode of travel was diverting enough, and the last leg of the downward journey was an 'agreeable five-hour jaunt'. Twelve men and nine mules were required to carry the passengers, their servants and their baggage. 'The mountaineers ran with us down steeps and frozen precipices, where no man, as we are men now, could possibly walk.'

When Gibbon made the same crossing, he had four porters. One of them was a vigorous fifty-two-year-old who had been working as a mountain porter since the age of eighteen. The team, working in shifts, made the twenty-mile crossing without stopping at all and took the downhill stretch at a run. A humane man, Gibbon 'felt some repugnance at being carried over a fearful mountain by my fellows'; but he did not for one moment think of making the hazardous journey on his own feet.

Gibbon was also of a somewhat timid disposition, but his sense of the 'fearful' in the midst of that wild mountain landscape was very much the standard reaction of the eighteenth-century mind. Even the poet Thomas Gray, whose *Elegy in a Country Churchyard* was one of the works that helped shape the growing Romantic appreciation of nature, considered that the Alps carried 'the permission mountains have of being frightful' rather too far. By contrast, Arthur Young, who made the approach to Lanslebourg down the precipitous slopes by *rammassang*, remained composed to the point of boredom.

As described by Young the *rammassang* actually sounds a very precarious mode of travel. It consisted of a 'machine of four sticks and the weight of two people, passenger and guide, who seated himself in the front and directed the contraption by digging his heels into the snow, was enough to give it motion'. Occasionally, this primitive gravity vehicle veered off the track, and then, for a few seconds, 'the motion was rapid enough to be agreeable'. But for most of the journey, although the gradient was steep, the bends in the winding track slowed them down the trotting pace of 'a good English horse'. From the reports of other travellers, Young had been expecting something altogether more exciting and reckoned that the guides could take a more direct line down the mountain and 'by that means gratify the English with the velocity they admire so much'.

While many Englishmen chose to speed through Switzerland on their way to Italy, it was a popular place of retirement for many others. One tourist to Geneva observed. 'I do not wonder so many English choose it for their residence; the city is very small, neat, prettily built, and extremely populous.' Although a member of the Swiss federation, it was an independent republic and had to look to its defences. The fortifications were rebuilt in the 1730s which gave the place, 'perhaps not of equal extent with Windsor and its two parks', a compact, military air. The citizens appeared happy and confident and maintained an 'exact discipline always as strictly observed as in time of war', which made the city appear a match even for the great powers of Europe.

Gray, who visited Geneva in the autumn of 1739 with his friend Horace Walpole, left the place with happy memories, not least of a trout they shared at a memorable dinner with other guests, and which weighed thirty-seven pounds. Even this monster was not big for the self-esteem of the local fishermen, who claimed that they commonly took trout weighing up to fifty pounds from the waters of the Lake. Certainly, Geneva trout enjoyed a considerable reputation, prize specimen being dressed and dispatched by post chaise to Paris and even as far afield as Madrid. From Geneva, Gray and his companion returned to Lyons to prepare themselves for the arduous journey over the Alps.

They calculated that it would take them two days to reach the foothills of the great range and six more to make the mountain crossing. Winter was already beginning at Lyons and the poet looked forward to the journey with some trepidation. However, they armed themselves as well as possible against the cold, 'with muffs, hoods, and masks of beaver, fur-boots, and bear skins'. It was to prove an eventful crossing.

Much of the journey lay through the mountain valleys, by rivers that forced their way through the mountains with 'a mighty noise, among vast quantities of rocks, that have rolled down from the mountain tops'. The winter was by now so far advanced that the landscape offered few beauties.

On the sixth day of their crossing, the horror and savageness came unpleasantly close. They were now climbing on a narrow track, barely six feet wide, with a great wood of pines on one side, and on the other a vast precipice. Towards mid-day they met 'with an accident odd enough'. Mr Walpole 'had a little fat black spaniel, that he was very fond of, which he sometimes used to set down, and let it run by the chaise side'. Despite the heavy going, the travellers were in good heart as the noon-day sun was, for once, shining brilliantly through the trees which rose sharply up from the road. Then, 'all of a sudden, from the wood-side, out rushed a great wolf, came close to the head of the horses, seized the dog by the throat, and rushed up the hill again with him in his mouth'. The whole episode was over in a matter of seconds and the guides did not have time to level their guns at the marauder before it disappeared in the forest. They were all, naturally, shaken and Walpole was heartbroken at the loss of his pet. But there was little doubt the dog had saved their lives. 'If he had not been there,' wrote Gray to his mother, 'and the creature had thought fit to lay hold on one of the horses; chaise, and we, and all must inevitably have tumbled above fifty fathoms perpendicular down the precipice.'

On the seventh day they came to the foot of the famous Mount Cenis pass. The chaise was dismantled and it, together with the baggage, was transported over the shoulder of the pass by pack mule. The travellers themselves, duly wrapped up in their wardrobe of assorted furs, were 'seated upon a sort of matted chair without legs, carried upon poles in the manner of bier, and so began to ascend by the help of eight men'. It was six miles to the top of the pass and there an immense plain opened out before their astonished eyes. It was covered in deep snow and in the middle was an immensely deep lake 'from whence a river takes its rise, and tumbles over monstrous rocks quite down the other side of the mountain'. The six-mile descent which so diverted Walpole comes vividly alive in Gray's description.

The men perfectly fly down with you, stepping from stone to stone with incredible swiftness in places where none but they could go three paces without falling. The immensity of the precipices, the roaring of the river and torrents that run into it, the huge crags covered with ice and snow, and the clouds below you and about you, are objects it is impossible to conceive without seeing them.

The descent took a mere five hours, and this allowed time for a brief rest at a little village some three-quarters of the way down but still among the clouds. They were in that part of the realm of the King of Sardinia known as Piedmont, today a region of Italy with its capital at Turin. The travellers had time to notice that the language was no longer a variant of French before being plunged on down in headlong journey. The next evening they entered upon 'a fine avenue of nine miles in length, as straight as a line', which led them into Turin, the residence of the King of Sardinia.

VIII

FROM THE ALPS TO THE TIBER

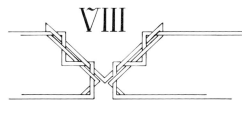

F|or centuries Italy was divided among a number of states, including some of the most prosperous in Europe, based on such historic centres as Venice, Florence and Milan. From the late fifteenth century French and Spanish military interventions reduced their power and prestige and yet they, with many lesser cities such as Parma and Modena, retained traditions of greatness and wealth. Visiting Venice in the later sixteenth century, Montaigne, the French philosopher, noted that the cost of living was as high as in Paris.

No doubt Montaigne's bills were inflated by the Italian convention of plundering all foreigners. As another French visitor observed, 'the common people of Italy look on foreigners as their dupes and frequently

Opposite CANAL SCENE, VENICE J. M. Whistler
Above Orta, Italy, photographed by Donald McLeish

cheat them outrageously, not caring twopence what one says to them.' The tradition endured. An English milord who had the temerity to question his Neapolitan innkeeper in a flagrant case of overcharging, found himself staring down the barrel of a shotgun. Not that other Europeans were the only ones to suffer; the term 'foreigner' was generously interpreted to embrace even Italian travellers whose language or dress betrayed them as citizens of some other region in the peninsula.

A few years after Montaigne pondered disconsolately over his hotel bill, an illuminating little episode was enacted at Indevedro, just below the Simplon pass. It was a crisp, sun-lit winter's day and figures could be seen crossing the river in the valley bottom. A rider clattered along the narrow, unrailed bridge. His horse skittered on the icy planks, lost its footing and plunged into the cold waters. As the rider, a haughty French cavalier, floundered out of his depth, Benvenuto Cellini, Florentine goldsmith and artist, looked back from the safety of the bank with a malicious smile. With uncharacteristic caution, Benvenuto had walked his own horse over, to the Frenchman's jeers. Now, disdainfully, he sent one of his guides to help. But the other guide also demanded payment and, when Benvenuto refused, ran off and came back leading a crowd of people, 'with a great spear in his hand'.

Cellini looked forward to the skirmish. 'I was mounted on my splendid horse, and I lowered my arquebus.' But 'when I had heard the insults die down, I tossed my head and said: 'I'd have done everything needful to prove that I am a man to be reckoned with.'' The little display of machismo was a natural compound of the attitudes of the time, Benvenuto's own fiery temperament, and the hard-edged independence native to a Florentine. He rode off with a swagger, having made his point. The attempt by the locals to extort protection money was not worth a second thought. He was a citizen of Florence, remote and barely known to these rustic mountaineers. As far as they were concerned, he was a foreigner just as surely as the Frenchman.

The behaviour of these frontier villagers was friendly compared with that of the bravos of Venice, 'desperate villains armed with a privy coat of mail and a little sharp dagger called a stilletto'. Between eleven and two in the morning, they lurked in the lightless *calles* and 'if they happen to meet any man that is worth rifling, they will presently stab him, take away all about him that is of any worth, and when they have thoroughly pulled his plumes will throw him into one of the channels'. The stiletto in one form or another was the preferred weapon before the invention of a convenient handgun for thugs all over Italy. The word 'pistol', derived from the adjective pistoian, originally denoted the local stiletto either because daggers were made at Pistoia or because this type was used there so commonly.

Tourists to Italy were not necessarily murdered, but they were certain to be fleeced. 'For the smallest things you are surrounded with men asking for tips: even a man with whom you have made a bargain for a louis will find it very odd if he is not given more when he had carried out the service.' The demand for tips would have been less irksome if the money had ensured decent service and accommodation. It rarely did. 'Give what scope you please to your fancy', wrote one eighteenth-century traveller, 'you will never imagine half the disagreeableness of Italian beds, Italian cooks, Italian postilions and Italian nastiness to an Englishman.'

But whatever the obstacles, every year saw more and more tourists flooding south to explore the beauties of this historic country. Tom Coryat was very nearly seduced from his allegiance to his beloved home town by Mantua 'that sweet paradise' while the dour Scot William Lithgow of Lanark drank happily of Lachryma Christi and 'drew so hard after that same weeping wine, till I found my purse began to weep also'. Everywhere there was novelty. Among the fine things that Coryat saw were those 'which they commonly call in the Italian tongue umbrellas, that is, things that minister shadow unto them for shelter against the scorching heat of the sun'.

A LAND OF MUSIC

Few aspects of life in Italy provided so much delight and surprise to the visitor as the waves of music flooding every town and breaking at every street corner. Even professional musicians, who looked upon Italy as the cradle of their art, were astonished. Dr Burney, who began his Italian tour in Turin found that the entertainment began at his hotel with two girls singing to the accompaniment of two violins, a guitar and a bass. That evening the group took to a stage in the town's main square and sold copies of their ballads. Nearby, on another stage, a man and woman were performing Venetian ballads to a dulcimer. Arriving in Padua, Burney was delighted by a singer and string trio, 'unnoticed here as a small-coalman or oyster woman in England'. Yet they performed so well that 'in any other country of Europe they would have acquired applause'. He soon accepted such entertainment as commonplace and says little more about street musicians. Other travellers fill out the picture. The country people around Naples were 'so jovial and addicted to music, that the very husbandmen almost universally play the guitar, singing and even composing songs to their sweethearts, commonly they go to the field with their fiddles',

Inundated with music in the streets, the Italian got used to ignoring it anywhere. Giving a command performance at the gloomy court of Turin, Signor Pugnani, the greatest virtuoso of his day, 'did not appear to exert himself'. Who can blame him? 'Neither the king nor any one of the numerous royal family, seemed to pay much attention to the music'. One wonders, indeed, how Italian musicians and composers ever won sufficient audience attention to establish their immense reputations. Niccolò Piccini, one of the most famous, unwisely omitted ballet sequences from one of his operas. 'The acts are ... so long', wrote a contemporary, 'that it is wholly impossible to keep up the attention; those who are not talking, or playing cards, usually fall asleep.'

Burney, attending a festival performance in the San Carlo opera house, Naples, in the party of Sir William Hamilton, the British ambassador, was stunned by the grandeur and magnificence of the spectacle. 'The house was doubly illuminated. In front of each box there is a mirror, before which are two large wax tapers; these by reflection being multiplied and added to the lights of the stage and to those within the boxes, make the splendour too much for the aching sight.'

Niccolò Jommelli was the composer. Now respected as a major figure in the history of opera, he was one of the first to 'harness all the musical resources to heighten the dramatic moment'. That night in Naples he need not have bothered. The court was in grand gala, the theatre was immense, and the 'noise of the audience was such that neither voices nor instruments could be heard distinctly'.

In Milan, the theatre which preceded the present Scala was very large and beautiful. Its five hundred boxes were mounted in five tiers, each box holding six people. A broad gallery ran round the house behind each tier, linking the boxes. Across it from each box, was 'a complete room with fireplace in it, and all the conveniences for refreshments and cards'. Serious gamblers who found these private parties too tame generally foregathered in the gallery of the fourth tier where a public faro table was to be found on both sides of the house. The hubbub round the tables was considerable, but the noise in the auditorium was hardly less. People interrupted their conversations only occasionally to listen to an aria. The idea of spending a whole evening in rapt attention to the work of mere musicians would have seemed intolerably quaint: at Naples the king regularly left the theatre in the middle of the second act.

FROM GENOA TO FLORENCE

Many people entered Italy by sea from Marseilles or Nice and, as a result, Genoa was far more commonly found on tourist itineraries than it is today. It was much admired. 'Built in the hollow or bosom of a mountain,' wrote John Evelyn in the seventeenth century, 'it represents the shape of a theatre; the streets and buildings are so ranged one above another, as our seats are in the play-houses; but from their materials, beauty, and structure, never was an artificial scene more beautiful to the eye.' He especially admired the famous Strada Nova, 'built wholly of polished marble, and for the stateliness of the buildings, paving, and evenness of the street, far superior to any in Europe'.

In the next century Thomas Gray was clearly bewitched by the city and on the first day of his visit wrote an effusive letter to an English friend. One feels that, reading it over half way through, he became almost embarrassed by his own enthusiasm. After describing the Annonciata church as 'a most stately structure, the inside wholly marble of various kinds, except where gold and painting take its place', he seems to check himself. 'I should make you sick of marble', he continues, 'if I told you how it was lavished here upon porticoes, the balustrades, and terrases, the lowest of which extends quite to the sea.' The effect was undoubtedly grand, but, within, the buildings were rather less magnificent. The furniture seemed to be as old as the original founder of the family. The famous Palazzo Doria, for example, was full of silver tables embossed with scenes of the great admiral's sea victories; of his reception of the Emperor Charles V; and of his noble refusal of the dogeship. For the rest, Gray saw little more than a tired collection of ancient velvet chairs and 'gothic' tapestry.

But for all this, Genoa dazzled the English poet. He and Walpole arrived there late in the evening of 20 November 1739; early the following morning Gray was out and about. What he saw was 'a vast semi-circular basin, full of fine blue sea, and vessels of all sorts and sizes, some sailing out, some coming in, and others at anchor'. Behind this busy commercial scene rose one of Europe's most beautiful cities. All round the bay could be seen 'palaces and churches peeping over one another's heads, gardens and marble terraces full of orange and cypress trees, fountains and trellis-works covered with vines'. For Gray as for his predecessor John Evelyn, the whole effect was as of a grand theatre.

In the high days of the republic this theatre provided the stage for many magnificent pageants, of which none was more splendid than the Doge's procession. First came the Doge himself, in robes of crimson damask and a cap of the same material, followed by the members of the senate, all in black. The stately cavalcade was accompanied by music of the finest quality and wended its way through the marble streets to the church of Madonna delle Vigne where the image of the Madonna was 'richly dressed out, with a crown of diamonds on her head, another about the child's and a

On the Grand Canal, Venice

constellation of wax lights burning before them'. There the assembly of potentates made their devotions and listened with due solemnity to a sermon.

When Thomas Gray witnessed the procession in 1739, doges had ruled in Genoa for exactly six hundred years. From the tenth century the Ligurian republic, named for the ancient tribe which settled the area, grew to the status of a major maritime power. Together with the men of Pisa, the Genoans drove the Arab invaders from Corsica and Sardinia. As soon as the infidel forces were expelled, the allies naturally became rivals; in the ensuing war Genoa emerged triumphant. Like Venice, the republic made considerable gains from financing and exploiting the Crusades, but in the ensuing wars with Venice she was worsted. Nevertheless, thanks largely to finance provided by the renowned Banco di San Giorgio, Genoa expanded her influence in the hinterland and established commercial colonies from the Crimea to Spain. Her subsequent history was chequered and she came under the domination of Austria until a popular rising in 1746.

Gray, who had expected to spend the winter of 1739–40 in the easy comfort of the south of France, unexpectedly found himself in Italy with Walpole. When the two young men returned to Lyons from a trip to Geneva, they found a letter from Walpole's father, the Prime Minister, desiring that his son would go to Italy. The scheme for wintering in the south of France had to be abandoned but, as Gray reflected, they were to pass the time 'in a much finer country'. Genoa, for all its beauties, was not properly Italy, in the imagination of two young Englishmen on the grand tour. Florence and Rome were, of course, the proper destinations and they made their way there from Genoa, through the papal city of Bologna.

They travelled through Piacenza, 'which made so frippery an appearance, that instead of spending some days there as intended, we only dined'; Parma, where they spent the day visiting the Corregio paintings in the cathedral; Modena, 'an ill-built melancholy place'; and through 'the dominions of his holiness', to Bologna, which had been part of the papal states since the early sixteenth century.

It was a large and populous city, where all the streets had 'porticoes on both sides, such as surround a part of Covent Garden'. The churches, 'mostly old structures of brick', were more remarkable for their paintings than for their architecture, but the numerous palaces were fine enough 'to supply us with somewhat worth seeing from morning till night'. In fact, though he found the country of Lombardy 'one of the most beautiful imaginable', the reader of his letters feels that Genoa was Gray's most remarkable Italian experience, until what was to prove a magical Christmas season in Florence.

Henry Swinburne, at Genoa in the 1770s, described it as the 'city of palaces' and considered the view from the sea to be 'fine beyond description'. Seventy years later Bayard Taylor hastened down to the waterfront as soon as he reached Genoa to observe the famous city in the light of the setting sun. It was 'like some grand painting of a city, rising with its domes and towers, and palaces from the edge of the glorious bay shut in by mountains – the whole scene clad in those deep, delicious, sunny hues which you admire so much in a picture'.

The city of Columbus seemed to him 'deeply tinctured with the magic of history and romance'. The story of the heroic Admiral Andrea Doria, the sixteenth-century father and liberator of his country, fired his imagination. The Doria Palace on the Strada Nova seemed fit to be a monarch's residence. But as Taylor walked the narrow and crooked streets, he was amazed to find many of them 'lined entirely with the splendid dwellings of the Genoese nobility'. These splendours were but faded reminders of past glory. Genoa prospered as a trading and banking centre into the eighteenth century and a French tourist who witnessed the procession of the Doge in the 1730s was duly impressed. Two generations later, however, the venerable republic lost its independence to revolutionary France; in 1814 it was awarded to the King of Sardinia by the congress of Vienna.

In Bayard Taylor's day the glories of the republic were long past, but the ceremonial of the Church brought periodic displays of grandeur to the streets. On the evening of his arrival the city was celebrating a religious *festa*. Banners hung from the windows and floated across the streets. As it was impossible to pass through the dense crowd, the American and his two companions 'slowly moved on with the procession through the city'. Choirboys and nuns preceded the friars in black and white robes carrying the statue of the saint 'with a pyramid of flowers, crosses and blazing wax tapers, while companies of soldiery and monks followed'. Behind them came the band, playing 'solemn airs which alternated with the deep monotonous chanting of the friars. The whole scene, dimly lighted by the wax tapers, produced in me a feeling nearly akin to fear, as if I were witnessing some ghostly, unearthly spectacle.'

From Genoa Taylor embarked for Leghorn, the port of Florence and Pisa. There, through the kind attention of the Saxon Consul, to whom he had some letters, two or three days went by delightfully. There was a large establishment for sea bathers but otherwise the only amusement was the drive along the seashore. The road ended in a large ring 'around which the carriages pass and re-pass, until the sunset has gone out over the sea, when they return to the city as fast as the lean horses can draw them'.

The only other remarkable thing about Leghorn appears to have been the convicts, chained two by two, who swept the streets. They were clothed in coarse, dirty red cloth, with their crime painted on the back – he was dismayed at how many had been convicted for premeditated homicide. After the day's work they were 'dragged away to be incarcerated in damp unwholesome dungeons excavated under the public thoroughfares'.

On the day of his departure, Taylor and his friends had a hurried cup of coffee at the Café Americano, then took the coach for Pisa. At the gates of the town they were 'assailed by the *vetturini*, one of whom hung on us like a leech'. They were only free to walk the town and see the sights after agreeing to engage him for the journey to Florence. The Baptistery, the Campo Santo, the Cathedral and the Leaning Tower together formed a view 'rarely surpassed in Europe for architectural effect'. But the square was melancholy and deserted, with rank grass filling the crevices in the marble pavement. Taylor was surprised by the 'light, airy elegant structure' of the Tower itself, having expected a crumbling black fabric. The Baptistery was not open to the general public, but Taylor's party was lucky enough (or persistent enough) to meet a person with the key. The verger demonstrated the echoes, which ended on 'a dying note as if they were fading away into heaven', so that 'it seemed as if an angel lingered in the temple'.

They spent their first night at the Hotel Lione Bianco, where they met a Dr Boardman, from New York, over dinner at the *table d'hôte*. On his recommendation, they took three large and handsomely furnished rooms in the centre of the city, at the house of a wealthy goldsmith, paying just over five dollars a month; they ate for twenty-five cents a day at the cafés and trattorias. Taylor soon discovered that the Trattoria del Cacciatore was a favourite haunt of the dozen or so American artists in Florence. Congenial company was no doubt welcome. In Pavia they had been 'watched like wild animals' and found the attention 'positively embarrassing'. No doubt the Florentines were equally unapproachable. The famous American art historian Bernard Berenson, trying to argue the Allied case before Italy entered the First World War, was told 'for us Florentines all foreigners are equally hateful'.

This Florentine xenophobia probably had its roots in the underlying contempt for all those members of the human race not born in the city. The original specification of the cathedral called for an edifice 'so magnificent that it shall surpass anything produced in the times of their greatest power by the Greeks and the Romans'. The city whose name is, to northern Europeans, synonymous with the classical Renaissance was as confident in its own superiority to the ancient mentors of European civilization as to its contemporaries. It is to be doubted, therefore, whether the medieval signoria would have appreciated the judgement of a young Irish lady of the 1860s, that the masterpiece of Arnolfo di Cambio and Brunelleschi was like 'an Indian tea chest of inlaid ebony and ivory, on a prodigious scale'.

Modern Florentines might be less concerned. For them Florence is a working city, and its historic past, in the words of the novelist Mary McCarthy, like 'a vast piece of family property whose upkeep is too much for the heirs, who nevertheless find themselves criticized by strangers for letting the old place go to rack and ruin'. After all, the city's wealth was based on commerce and its first great patrons of the arts were businessmen. Even when the Medici family had graduated to the rank of grand dukes they retained memories of their commercial origins. One seventeenth-century visitor, who considered the Pitti Palace the 'most magnificent and regular pile in the world', noted that the duke lived 'after the frugal Italian way, even selling what he can spare of his wines, the wicker bottles dangling even over the chief entrance'.

No doubt there was a certain amount of play acting about this humble, merchant-like posture of the Grand Duke. The wiser members of the Medici family had always pandered to the city's pride in its republican origins. Even old Cosimo who, early in the fifteenth century had established his family's pre-eminence, had steadfastly refused any official title outside the republican repertoire, being happy to be honoured as the city's 'leading citizen' and to pull strings discreetly. By the eighteenth century, when the traditions of the Medici court were established beyond a peradventure, Florence was fully equipped with an aristocracy happy to acknowledge the supremacy of the ruling family. When Horace Walpole visited the city in 1739 the ruling family was away, in Vienna, and 'news was every day of the Great Duchess's delivery; if it be a boy, here will be all sorts of balls, masquerades, operas, and illuminations'; if it was a girl, the city would have to wait until carnival time for such things. Meanwhile, Walpole was received with honour at the Prince of Craon's assembly, the leading potentate in the absence of the Grand Duke, who was 'extremely civil' to the name of Walpole.

He and Thomas Gray were also guests of the Countess Suarez, a favourite of the late Duke, 'and one that gives the first movement to everything gay that is going forward here'. And there was no want of entertainment. The 'famous gallery' alone provided amusement for months and the two companions spent two or three hours every morning there, admiring the 'many hundred antique statues, such as the whole world cannot match, besides the vast collection of paintings, medals and precious stones, such as no other prince was ever master of'. Moreover, the city was so full of palaces and churches that one could hardly place oneself anywhere 'without having some fine one in view, or at least some statue or fountain, magnificently adorned'. And yet, for all this, and despite the fact that Florence had far more palaces than Genoa could boast of, Gray surprised himself with the opinion that Genoa was, in its general appearance, the more beautiful of the two cities.

One of Florence's chief beauties was the prospect it offered to the approaching traveller. Coming there in the summer of 1892, Margaret Fountaine, always on the look-out for a fine, painterly subject, recorded the impact the sight made on her: 'The sky had clouded over rather, but the dark cloud only added to the effect, when I came in sight of the city below, now white and glistening from a chance gleam of sunlight, a marvellous contrast to the dense purple darkness of the mountains beyond.' Gray, visiting the city in winter, had to bring his imagination to bear a little more actively. 'In coming down we could dimly discover Florence, and the beautiful plain about it, through the mists, but enough to convince us, it must be one of the noblest prospects upon the earth in summer.' Before they left, Mr Walpole was received by the great lady of Florence, the Electress Palatine Dowager, sister of the late Grand Duke. She was a stately old lady who never left her palace except to go to church accompanied by guards, her coach drawn by eight horses. She received Walpole with great pomp and ceremony, 'standing under a huge black canopy, and, after a few minutes talking, assured him of her good will, and dismissed him. She never sees anybody but thus in form; and so she passes her life, poor woman!'

We catch another revealing glimpse of the Florentine court a century later in the Taylor's journal. One evening, surveying Florence from his favourite vantage point in the Boboli gardens, he saw the Grand Ducal family preparing for a drive in their carriage. 'One of the little dukes, who seemed a mischievous imp, ran out on a projection of the portico, where considerable persuasion had to be used to induce him to jump into the arms of his royal papa.' The children of the American sculptor Hiram Powers happened to be among the visitors in the gardens and Taylor could not forbear some home-spun philosophy. 'I contrasted involuntarily the destinies of each – one to the enjoyment and proud energy of freedom and one to the confining and vitiating atmosphere of a court.'

It is to be doubted whether the 'little duke' would have accepted the moral. For centuries his family had presided over the prosperous and beautiful world of Florence and, for all its grandiose titles and stuffy protocol, that family still felt itself to be an integral part of the tradition that bewitched the foreign observer. The family collection in the Pitti Palace was, 'thanks to the praiseworthy liberality of the duke', open to the public for six hours every day; their private gardens were regularly opened to visitors. The tourists' Florence was a joint venture by city and rulers.

Carnival was the great time of the year. 'All the morning one makes parties in masque to the shops and coffee houses', wrote Walpole on his visit, 'and all the evenings to operas and balls. Then I have danced. Good gods! How I have danced!' He noted with especial pleasure that the Italians were fond 'to a degree' of English country dances. A generation later, a young lady was delighted to receive invitations to English-style tea parties from her Florentine friends. She was bewitched too by the 'satin softness in the air', even in December, and by the peasant girls in the market place, and was clearly envious of 'their gold and brocaded petticoats, scarlet stockings, real pearl earrings, necklaces of immense size and their braided hair interwoven with coloured cords'.

For the English of the nineteenth century Florence was a place of special enchantment. Florence Nightingale's parents named her after the city, where she was born in 1820; Robert and Elizabeth Barret Browning lived in the Casa Guidi, opposite the Pitti Palace; and Queen Victoria painted watercolours in the hills at Vincigliata. The spell worked upon others. Bayard Taylor was stirred to one of his more purple passages, and provides us with our farewell to the city on the Arno.

Stand with me on the heights of Fiesole, and let us gaze on the grand panorama around which the Apennines stretch with a majestic sweep, wrapping in a robe of purple air, through which shimmer the villas and villages on their sides. Florence lies in front of us, the magnificent cupola of the Duomo crowning its clustered palaces. We see the airy tower of the Palazzo Vecchio and the long front of the Palazzo Pitti, with the dark foliage of the Boboli Gardens behind.

TURIN

One of the classic Italian cities, Turin once provided the first experience of Italian urban architecture for thousands of European tourists. For centuries it was the capital of the dukes of Savoy until, in 1720, the tangled politics of Continental conflict conferred upon them the unexpected title of King of Sardinia.

The majestic buildings and squares that stamp the heart of the city were the result of two chief building periods, from 1666 to about 1685, and again from 1715 to about 1735. The master architect of the first period was Guarino Guarini, whose work includes the Palazzo Carignano and the

Top   ALIGHTING FROM A GONDOLA William Price
Above   FLORENCE - THE PONTE VECCHIO J. F. Lewis

church of San Lorenzo; in the second period Filippo Juvarra designed the great Stupinigi country palace, the Palazzo Madama and the Superga church. Stopping to admire such majestic monuments, many a tourist must have speculated on the source of the funds that paid for their building. The answer, of course, as with all great public works was taxation or extortion. To Edward Gibbon, Turin seemed to be a particularly glaring instance of the oppressions of privilege that held together the European society of his day. 'These palaces', he wrote, 'are cemented with the blood of the people. In a small, poor kingdom like this they must grind the people in order to be equal with other crowned heads. In each gilded ornament I seem to see a village of Savoyards ready to die of hunger, cold and misery.'

To less imaginative visitors the meanness of the royal court was a more serious cause of scandal. Turin seems to have been the one city of aristocratic Europe where introductions were useless. Montesquieu, the French philosopher, noted that a dinner given for a foreigner was a great novelty. While he was there, another French gentleman, the Marquis de Prie, told him that while he had entertained several Piedmontese gentlemen at his own home, 'not one of them offered him so much as a glass of water' while he was visiting in their city. The court was as bad mannered as it was mean. An Englishman who could neither play at the card game faro nor talk Piedmontese had to stand by himself, 'without one of their haughty nobles doing me the honour of speaking to me, whether in Italian or French, the language of polite society everywhere'.

The court at Turin was as punctilious in the mere forms of etiquette as it was lacking in true politeness. The long series of apartments of the various ducal and royal palaces were filled with guards and officers, and a visit to a person of superior rank could not possibly be made without a sword and a formal *chapeau bras*. Above all, the court was dull. The principal amusement seems to have been driving about in a coach in the evening and bowing to the people you met. If the royal family happened to be taking its drive at the same time, 'you had the additional pleasure of stopping to salute them every time they passed'.

The boredom of Turin almost overcame Thomas Gray. He conceded that there was an excellent opera, but it was only in the carnival; there were balls every night, but only in the carnival; there were masquerades too, but only in the carnival. The carnival season lasted from Christmas to Lent, by London standards a miserably short season. Half the remaining part of the year was spent in reminiscing over the last carnival, and the other half looking forward to the next. Having the misfortune to reach the town in mid-November, Gray found the bill of entertainment intolerably slender. The only public diversions for the tourist were an 'execrable' Italian comedy company and a puppet show rejoicing in the title of *A Representation of a Damned Soul*. True, for a member of the élite, there was the occasional invitation to the *conversazione* at the Marquise de Cavaillac's residence, where one could watch the card players. The excitement soon palled. Gray could follow the play at the ombre table, since this three-handed game, played with a pack of forty cards, was popular in fashionable society throughout Europe. However, he was at a loss when he strolled over to the 'Taroc' game. Today almost the exclusive preserve of fortune tellers, the Tarot pack, with its four fourteen-card suits and twenty-two 'triumph' cards, was formerly used in a complicated game which, as he was unable to speak Piedmontese, nobody troubled to explain to the Englishman.

Conscientiously seeing the sights while his more distinguished friend, Walpole, was received at court, poor Gray found little to divert him. 'The palace here in town is the very quintessence of gilding and looking glass; inlaid floors, carved pannels, and painting, wherever they could stick a brush.' The town, it was true, had 'in general a good clean lively appearance', the streets were fine and regular and there many pleasant walks, but the common houses were brick built and disfigured by peeling plaster; windows were of oiled paper which was often in tatters; and everywhere the general impression was of buildings 'apt to tumble down'.

The fortnight he spent in Turin was Gray's first acquaintance with Italy and it was disillusioning. 'I own,' he wrote to his friend Richard West, 'I have not, as yet, anywhere met those grand and simple works of Art, that are to amaze one, and whose sight one is to be the better for: but those of Nature have astonished me beyond expression.' As the tedious days until their departure for Genoa dragged by, he relived in memory some of those astonishing experiences. From Grenoble they had made an excursion to the Grande Chartreuse, the mother house of the Carthusian Order founded by St Bruno in the eleventh century. 'I do not remember to have gone ten paces without an exclamation, that there was no restraining: Not a precipice, not a torrent, not a cliff, but is pregnant with religion and poetry.' It is the creed of true early Romanticism.

The passage of the Alps had reinforced his awe at the marvels of nature, but for all that, his was a rational eighteenth-century mind and he could not view the primitive conditions of life in that harsh terrain with the enthusiasm of our post-anthropological age. The mountains were a little bit too frightful and 'the creatures that inhabit them are, in all respects, below humanity'. He had heard that there was a family of 'these Alpine monsters, that in the middle of winter calmly lay in their stock of provisions and firing, and so are buried in their hut for a month or two under the snow'. Like Livy, whose works provided his vacation reading, he had a horror of these 'unshaven and uncivilized men', preferring the cultivated country of the lowlands.

MILAN

In the eighteenth century it was more common to leave Turin by the southbound road for Genoa, as Gray and Walpole had done. Alternatively, one could follow the Po valley eastwards or head north-east for the great city of Milan. However, the north European tourist with Milan as his destination more generally took a route through the St Gotthard and Splügen passes.

It was along this route that Bayard Taylor left the happy scenes of Switzerland that had so gladdened his republican spirit, and plunged into what he too often found to be the somewhat oppressive atmosphere of Catholic Italy. At first, however, every prospect offered a delightful novelty. The city, the first major Italian centre he had experienced, seemed to resemble a great bazaar as the shops and stores were all open to the street; it was 'odd to see blacksmiths, tailors and shoemakers working unconcernedly in the open air with the crowds continually passing before them'.

In the 1840s music was still part of the Italian street scene as it had been in the days of Dr Charles Burney, though the professionals now included a large contingent of organ grinders. Taylor was delighted by a party of young amateurs in the house opposite his hotel, running through the whole of the opera *La Fille du Regiment*, to a piano accompaniment. 'As I write, they have become somewhat boisterous and appear to be improvising. Occasionally a group of listeners in the street below clap them applause, for as the windows are always open, the whole neighbourhood can enjoy the performance.' He was less enthusiastic about his duty visit to a performance of Rossini's *William Tell* at La Scala. Having but recently come from Switzerland, 'the scene where that glorious historical drama was enacted', he went to see it 'represented in sound'. He found the overture very beautiful but thought the rest of the work unworthy of the reputation of its composer.

Diverted by the music in the streets, Taylor was depressed by the bevies of priests in their cocked hats and black robes, and especially saddened by the sight of a 'bright and beautiful boy of twelve or thirteen years in those gloomy garments'. He reflected that it was 'mournful to see a people oppressed in the name of religion', yet he was overwhelmed by the cathedral which he found 'more interesting than many an entire city'. Solid and vast, the building nevertheless had 'an exquisite and airy look, like some fabric of frostwork which winter traces on the window-panes'. The rest of the city did not detain him long, and 'with the rapidity usual to Americans', he and his companions finished with Milan in a few days.

Genoa, which was to make such an impression on Taylor, was their next destination. After an hour or two's walk in the burning sun, the road they were on petered out at a large stream. There they found a group of workmen building a bridge. The tourists pulled off their boots. Wading through, they 'took a refreshing bath in the clear waters, and walked on through the by-lanes. The sides were lined with luxuriant vines, bending under the ripening vintage. We bought our simple meals at a grocer's, and ate them in the shade of the grape bowers, whose rich clusters added to the repast.' In this way, they 'enjoyed Italy at the expense of a franc a day'.

Before continuing their southward journey, they paused at the little village of Casteggio to look back on the mountain panorama. 'The sky was a heavenly blue without even the shadow of a cloud, and full and fair in the morning sunshine we could see the whole range of the Alps from the lofty peaks which stretch away to Nice and Marseilles to the blue hills of Friuli which sweep down to Venice and the Adriatic.'

Travellers heading eastwards for Venice skirted the foothills of these moutains, and passed through the beautiful cities of Bergamo, Brescia and Verona, past the shores of Lake Garda and through Venetian territory, to the ancient university town of Padua. In bygone centuries it had been as famous for its violent street life as for its learning. Early in the seventeenth century the Scottish traveller Lithgow had commented on the 'narrow passage of the open streets, and of the long galleries and dark ranges of pillars, that go alwhere on every hand of you. The scholars here in the night commit many murders against their private adversaries, and too often execute them upon the stranger and the innocent, and all with gunshot or else stilettoes.' Later in that century, another tourist found the pillars and archways pitted with bullet marks. But in its beauties and dangers, Padua was the gateway to the still more dramatic wonders of Venice.

One could make the last stretch of the journey by the ferry which enjoyed a proverbial reputation. The boat, 'covered with arched hatches', was towed leisurely down the stream, past Dolo and La Mira and Malcontenta, and finally put into the lagoon at Lizza Fusina. As the ferry idled down the river, its passengers 'commonly had pleasant discourse. The proverb saith that the boat shall be drowned when it carries neither monk, nor student, nor courtesan.'

VENICE

Venice, that 'sun-girt city ... Ocean's child', 'that city always putting out to sea', was born from a cluster of island villages in the Dark Ages of Europe. Some time in the late fifth century the scattered fishing communities found themselves flooded by a surge of mainland refugees in flight from the armies of Attila the Hun. The rest of Italy still echoes with memories of ancient Roman greatness: on Lake Garda the poet Catullus had his country retreat; near Mantua Virgil was born; in Padua, the historian Livy. However, during the long *pax romana*, the mud banks and islands at the head of the Adriatic, unsuited for a Roman city, remained a neglected backwater. In the centuries of turmoil and danger that followed the Roman peace, the remote lagoons provided a natural refuge. By the eighth century their sea-going population was already pushing out along the trade routes to the east, preparing the way for a great mercantile empire.

'Last and first the gondola', wrote novelist Mary McCarthy, 'the eternal gondola with its steel prow and witty gondolier.' Shelley called it a funereal bark; Shakespeare regarded it as the very metaphor of the novelties of travel. 'Farewell, Monsieur traveller: look you lisp and wear strange suits ... or I will not think thou hast swam in a gondola.' It is a favourite theme of the painters of Venice, one of the emblems of the Venetian carnival and, with its colourful boatman, the image of holiday romance for generations of Europeans. Sir Henry Wotton, King James I of England's ambassador in Venice, found the gondoliers 'the most vicious and licentious varlets about all the city'. The unwary stranger, unsure of the geography of the floating city and unable to give precise directions as to his destination, could find himself 'carried off where his plumes shall be well pulled before he cometh forth again'. Even today, the wise tourist bargains hard before stepping gingerly aboard, and pays only the agreed fare when he disembarks.

Seventeenth-century Venice had other exotica to offer the tourist. With some we are still familiar, others are long-since forgotten. Landing at the piazza one summer day in 1610, William Lithgow from Lanark 'perceived a great smoke, where was a friar burning quick at St Mark's pillar, for begetting fifteen noble nuns with child, and all within one year; he being also their father confessor'. Jostling eagerly through the throng, Lithgow 'came just to the pillar as the half of his body and right arm fell flatlings in the fire'. The rare treat 'overjoyed' the callous Scot. He missed the equally remarkable, if somewhat less gruesome, delights of the Turkish bath, then unknown in Britain.

The morning after his arrival in Venice, John Evelyn, 'finding myself weary and beaten with my journey, went to one of their bagnios, where you are treated after the Eastern manner'. The treatment consisted of

141

washing with hot and cold water, with oils, and being rubbed with a kind of strigil of seal's skin, which the attendant wore on his hand like a glove. Ruefully, Evelyn records that the bath so opened his pores as to cause him 'one of the greatest colds I ever had in my life'.

The hint of oriental strangeness intrigued the clients of the *bagnio*; a still more exotic atmosphere pervaded the *Ghetto nuevo*. The women there, wrote Tom Coryat, were 'as beautiful as I ever saw; so gorgeous in their apparel, jewels, chains of gold and rings adorned with precious stones, that some of our English countesses do scarce exceed them, having marvellous long trains like princesses that are borne up by waiting women.' Coryat, a contemporary of Shakespeare, was fascinated by the truly alien experience of a Jewish community, the Jews having been banned from England in the thirteenth century. The wave of medieval expulsions which had driven Jews from virtually every country in Europe was completed in 1492 when they were ordered out of Spain. Many of them found refuge in Venice, the cosmopolitan city republic where world-wide commercial interests and business acumen combined in fostering a degree of religious toleration.

From the first, the ghetto was a tourist attraction. The tall buildings were as much a marvel in the early sixteenth century as those of Manhattan were to be in the early twentieth. For fashionable sophisticates, a visit to the ghetto was an opportunity to display their superior wisdom and toleration. In the 1620s the French King's brother, the Duke of Orleans, attended a sermon in the old Spanish synagogue, accompanied by his entourage. The new synagogue, the Tempio Israelitico-Spagnolo, was built in 1655 by Baldassare Longhena, the great architect of baroque Venice. His church of Santa Maria della Salute dominates the entrance to the Grand Canal and his work on the synagogue is a measure of the prosperity of Venetian Jewry of the day.

During the 1650s, while Longhena's beautiful synagogue was still building, Oliver Cromwell re-admitted the Jews to England after a ban of three hundred and fifty years. Shakespeare, by then dead for forty years, had never seen a Jew, just as he had never been to Venice, yet Venice lives on the stage through the eyes of Shylock and Othello. Ever since the first night of *The Merchant of Venice* the world's writers have been building a library of quotations about the city of the lagoons.

John Ruskin devoted a work, *The Stones of Venice*, to the beauties of the place, presided over by the great church of St Mark's, where 'at last, as if in ecstasy, the crests of the arches break into a marbly foam, and toss themselves far into the blue sky in flames, and wreathes of sculptured spray'. Lord Byron, in one stanza, encapsulates the allure of the city in which he swam the Grand Canal and cantered over the Lido:

> I stood in Venice, on the Bridge of Sighs;
> A palace and a prison on each hand;
> I saw from out the wave her structures rise
> As from the stroke of the enchanter's wand:
> A thousand years their cloudy wings expand
> Around me, and a dying Glory smiles
> O'er the far times when many a subject land
> Looked to the winged Lion's marble piles,
> Where Venice sat in state, throned on her hundred isles!

From Giorgione and Titian, to Tintoretto and Veronese, the city's painters have emblazoned the glowing colours of the Venetian imagination on a hundred gallery walls. Canaletto and Guardi, willing employees of the tourists of the past, have left an unequalled record of their native city. The paintings have been called the picture post cards of the grand tour – few tourist resorts can make such a smart boast. But then, by the time of Canaletto, Venice had already been a tourist Mecca for centuries; even the famous carnival had become a calculated tourist attraction. In the late nineteenth century Henry James wrote: 'Venice today is a vast museum. There is nothing left to discover or describe, originality of attitude is utterly impossible.'

We leave the city with a vision of tourism on the truly grand scale, from a world which has faded more completely into history than Venice herself. When Kaiser Wilhelm II of Germany paid a state visit to Italy in his steam yacht the *Hohenzollern*, he demonstrated 'the truly imperial way of arriving'. Among the spectators was Gertrude Bell. Her gondola joined the flotilla of welcome at the entrance to the Grand Canal early in the afternoon. The city dignitaries were 'in gorgeous gondolas hung with streamers and emblems', their gondoliers bedecked in gaudy ceremonial costume. At about three o'clock the *Hohenzollern* steamed in, 'a magnificent great white ship', her decks lined with sailors also in white.

The guns fired, the ships in the harbour saluted and all the people cheered. The imperial yacht anchored nearly opposite the Piazetta and we saw the King and Queen of Italy and a crowd of splendid officers come up in a steam launch all hung with blue. For magnificence there never was anything like a *festa* with the Doge's Palace for a background.

IX

ROME AND
THE SOUTH

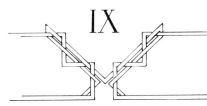

O ne morning, about ten o'clock, we came to a small cluster of houses called La Storta. The driver poured himself a glass of wine and remarked casually, 'Ecco Roma, Signore'; and without turning round indicated with a jerk of his thumb the cross of St Peter's. How can I describe the sudden shock that went through me at the sight of the eternal city, lying afar off in the midst of that vast and desolate plain? At once everything took on an aura of the poetic and the sublime.

Thus Hector Berlioz, the embodiment of the Romantic imagination, caught, as though by chance, his first glimpse of Rome. The city of the emperors, the Eternal City of the Popes, has, for centuries, been the gallery of Europe's cultural memory, more of an idea than a place.

Details from THE OPENING OF THE CARNIVAL David Allen, 1775

'The first entrance to Rome', wrote Gray, 'is prodigiously striking. It is a noble gate, designed by Michelangelo and adorned with statues.' Once inside the gates of the Holy City, Gray was overwhelmed. 'You cannot pass along a street but you have views of some palace, or church, or square, or fountain, the most picturesque and noble one you can imagine.' He was 'struck dumb with wonder' by St Peter's which he visited more than once. He was in Rome at the Easter celebrations and visited the basilica in the evening of Good Friday. 'It was something extremely novel to see that vast church illuminated by thousands of tiny crystal lamps, disposed in the figure of a huge cross at the high altar, and seeming to hang alone in the air. All the light proceded from this, and had the most singular effect imaginable as one entered the great door.'

He counted no fewer than thirty processions of celebrants and worshippers, 'their heads covered with a cowl all over, only two holes to see through left.' Some of the figures were in black, some in red, others in white and still others in parti-coloured robes. As each procession approached the high altar, they were shown 'from a balcony, at a great height', the church's three most precious relics: the spear which had pierced Christ on the cross; St Veronica's handkerchief; and a piece of the True Cross. A fifteenth-century visitor had seen the bodies of St Peter and St Paul, the rope with which Judas had hanged himself, and St Luke's portrait of Christ. The medieval aura of superstition and religious hysteria was still powerful in the eighteenth century. The magical and devout atmosphere of the Easter celebrations was luridly punctuated by 'half a dozen wretched creatures', faces covered but naked to the waist, flagellating themselves with 'scourges full of iron prickles'. Their backs and arms were so raw that at first sight they seemed to be dressed in 'red satin doublet torn, shewing the skin through', were it not for the blood 'plentifully sprinkled about them'.

Outside the sometimes oppressive religiosity of her churches, Rome could offer the lively mind 'some occupation'. The sixteenth-century savant Michel Montaigne, who regarded boredom as the one great enemy, found enough occupation to keep him from tedium: 'visiting the antiquities and the vineyards'; attending sermons and the theological debates that were a regular feature of life in Counter-Reformation Rome; and, occasionally, 'visiting women of the public sort'. But even he had succumbed to the more absurd rituals of the place. Following the suggestion of the French ambassador to the Holy See, Montaigne went to a papal audience and even kissed the papal toe. The ceremony, we are told, involved a kind of zig-zag approach to the pontiff, the visitor going down on each knee alternately. The final stage was to crawl on both knees to the papal slipper itself, where a white chalk cross on the red velvet indicated the exact spot on which to apply the lips. After listening respectfully to a few pontifical platitudes one retired, backwards, as from the presence of royalty.

The distaste felt by the rational Frenchman for his part in this humiliating charade is apparent. He venerated the antique traditions of republican Rome far more highly. He conceived the ambition of obtaining the title of Roman Citizen and set about achieving it with characteristic energy. 'I used all my natural senses to obtain the title, if only for its ancient honour and the religious memory of its authority.' Like most things in Rome at that time, even this pagan honorific was in the gift of the Pope but, in due course, Montaigne received his diploma, dated 'the third day before the Ides of March, 1581'. It was a 'vain title', as he admitted to himself, yet, nevertheless 'I received much pleasure in having obtained it.'

Montaigne, a systematic tourist, had soon dispensed with his French guide in favour of a battery of books and maps, and tramped the ruins daily. A hundred years earlier the Spanish traveller Pero Tafur had been astonished by the desolate aspects of vast tracts of the city: '... there are areas within the walls that are densely wooded and populated with wild beasts. Hares, foxes, wolves, deer and even, so they say, porcupines, breed in the caves.' Conditions were only a little better in Montaigne's day. Over the centuries, the city of the Caesars had been plundered for its stone, left to decay and been rebuilt, piecemeal, a hundred times. Crumbling masonry and the humous of a thousand years of encroaching vegetation had raised the ground level by several feet so that the capitals of lofty colonnades rose only a few feet above street level. As he penetrated the more deserted quarters of the city, Montaigne became convinced, as he told his secretary, that they were walking 'above the roofs of houses still intact'. Yet, for all that, he left Rome reluctantly. It had been 'a pleasant place to live in'.

The Romans would certainly have agreed. As Tafur discovered, few could tell one about the ancient past, 'but they could, without doubt, have informed me fully about the taverns and places of ill fame'. The twenty-three-year-old Cellini found a characteristically novel diversion. A plague was raging at the time and, to raise his spirits, he sought relief in pigeon shooting. He loved to wander among the ancient buildings with his sketch book and, during one of these expeditions, he noted that the ruins sheltered a vast number of pigeons. So, with an assistant to carry the gun, he passed the time, alternately drawing Roman architecture and shooting birds. Of course, being Cellini, he came back 'laden with pigeons, the result of really good marksmanship'. Naturally, his fowling piece 'so bright it shone inside and out like a mirror', was made by himself. Inevitably, he manufactured his own gunpowder, 'discovering the most wonderful secrets that are still unknown to anyone else'.

Despite his brief career as a volunteer officer in the Hampshire Militia, Edward Gibbon did not take his gun with him into the ruins. He found inspiration there, nevertheless, and his trip to Rome must be one of the most momentous in the history of literature. The author of *The Decline and Fall of the Roman Empire* recorded the moment in his *Autobiography*. 'It was at Rome, on the 15th of October, as I sat musing amidst the ruins of the Capitol, while the barefoot friars were singing vespers in the Temple of Jupiter, that the idea of writing the decline and fall of the city first started to my mind.'

A century later, the old city was working its spell on Bayard Taylor, who was thrilled by the prospect of spending New Year in the Eternal City. 'It will', he wrote, 'be something to say in after years that I have seen one year open in *Rome* – that I have walked by the ruins of the Colosseum, and watched the orange groves gleaming with golden fruitage in the Farnese gardens.'

Where the American tourist rhapsodized, that very practical-minded poet John Keats seems to have been as concerned with his victuals as with the glories of architecture and tradition. 'In our first Roman days,' wrote his friend Joseph Severn, 'we got very odd and bad dinners sent in, as the Roman custom is, from a *Trattoria*, or restaurant.' Despite daily complaints to the *padrona*, the 'annoyance' continued unabated. At the beginning of the second week Keats announced that he had 'hit on an expedient' which would ensure good dinners for the remainder of their stay. When the porter, basket in hand, duly arrived and began to set out the meal, Keats stepped forward grinning to his companion and, 'with a "Now, Severn, you shall see it," he opened the window, which was over the front steps, and taking up each dish one after the other he quietly emptied the contents out of the window and returned the plate to the basket – and thus disappeared a fowl, a rice pudding, cauliflower, and a dish of macaroni. He then quietly but very decidedly pointed to the basket for the porter to take away, which he did without demur.' In less than half an hour a first-rate dinner was on the table. They had no further problems, and when the final bill was presented they noticed that the *padrona* had been discreet enough not to charge for the dinners thrown out of the window.

The twenty-three-year-old Keats, already suffering from tuberculosis,

St Giovanni Laterano, Rome, photographed by Donald McLeish

was to die within three years. He had come to Italy for a health cure. Tragically, it was ineffective. But his bright spirit refused to be downcast. A journey to Italy, whatever its purpose, was not to be wasted and he eagerly embraced the opportunity of a visit to Rome.

The lure of Rome was so great that, even during the height of the religious conflicts of the sixteenth century, Protestant Englishmen could not resist it. Henry Wotton, with his 'mighty blue feather in a black hat that he might be taken for no English', was only the most conspicuous of many daring tourists. Half a century later, when the political situation was easier, the celebrations of the Church's great feast days in the papal city were one of the principal tourist sights for an Englishman on the Continent. John Evelyn, there for the Christmas of 1644, wrote: 'I was so desirous of seeing the many extraordinary ceremonies performed then in their churches, as midnight masses and sermons, that I went not to bed and walked from church to church the whole night.'

Evelyn saw baroque Rome at its most dramatic for the coronation procession of Pope Innocent X to the church of St John Lateran. 'The streets this night', he recorded, 'were as light as day, full of bonfires, canon roaring, fountains running wine, all in excess of joy and triumph.' A century later a somewhat disgruntled Horace Walpole noted that he had intended to stay 'for a new popedom, but the old eminences [the cardinals] were cross and obstinate and would not choose one'.

Evelyn took rooms at a Frenchman's house near the Piazza di Spagna. The district was already something of a centre for the foreign community, and when coffee drinking came into fashion English visitors naturally gravitated to the London type of coffee houses there. A serious-minded young man, Evelyn was up early each morning, 'so as to spend no time idly'. He hired a guide or 'sightsman' and set off on a tour of the principal ruins and churches. It is to be hoped that he walked. Fynes Moryson, seeing the sights on mule-back, was jeered at by pilgrims for wishing to ride to heaven while they, poor wretches, had to go on foot without shoes to visit the churches. But Moryson, who was no pilgrim, was indifferent to the jibes. A thoroughly practical tourist, he planned for comfort and speed wherever possible on his travels.

To the supercilious amusement of connoisseurs, the amateur grand tourist allocated no more than six weeks to the city. The young Earl of Carlisle boasted after only a week that he would have finished Rome in three weeks more, by which time he would have seen everything perfectly and the principal things two or three times. By modern standards, he was absurdly conscientious, spending seven or eight hours a day sightseeing. Our culture tours are more along the lines pioneered by another gentleman of the 1760s, who reckoned that the only advantage of sightseeing was the ability to boast of what one had seen. 'Being fully convinced that the business might be dispatched in a short time, he ordered a post-chaise and four horses to be ready early in the morning. 'Driving with all possible expedition, he fairly saw, in two days, all that others beheld during the crawling course of six weeks, even to the most mutilated remnant of a statue.'

Such disrespect for culture was not usual, or at least was not usually exhibited so blatantly. Most English milords of the period, though doubtless just as bored with the sights as the gentleman with the post chaise, cultivated fashionable reputations for taste by purchasing everything they could lay their hands on. The Italians said: 'If the Colosseum were portable, the English would carry it away.' As it was, they returned home with wagon-loads of antiques and wagon-loads more of fakes and so earned themselves 'the glorious title of Golden Asses all over Italy'. Maybe the jibe was born as much from envy of the foreigners' immense wealth as from contempt for their indiscriminating purchases. Certainly, enough genuine stuff was brought home in those wagons to make the country houses of England still the world's greatest treasury of Italian art outside Italy. Perhaps it was the thought that there would be nothing to buy at the Villa Borghese that determined Lord Baltimore's approach to the place. Engaging the services of the distinguished German scholar Johann Wincklemann, he went through the collection in the record time of ten minutes. His guide reflected that the young man had 'wearied of everything' in spite of, or perhaps because of, his income of £30,000 a year as proprietor of Maryland in America.

The judgement was not entirely fair. Lord Baltimore had eight ladies in his entourage and when asked, in Vienna, to identify the one who was his wife, replied that he was an Englishman and did not discuss his private affairs with foreigners. Baltimore and his harem were a peripatetic marvel for the towns he passed through, every bit as fascinating to them as any of the sights they might have to offer could be to him.

Another visitor to the Borghese considered it to be 'a vast collection of pictures, but not a good room in it'. Perhaps he would have liked the place better had he been invited to the entertainments mounted there in the 1770s, when the prince 'gave music and refreshments with many sorts of diversions such as tilting at the ring, and grand balls in the evening'. Those not privileged to attend such private parties had to content themselves with the parade of high society on the Corso. There the Maltese ambassador, making use of his privilege, drove in splendour down the centre of the street. There too, members of the nobility could be seen proceeding to the costume balls, dressed like Turks, in exotic garbs of blue and white. After supper, one could make one's way to the masquerades in the Teatro Alberti, which began at midnight. Beautifully presented, they could, nevertheless, be rather dull on occasion. A somewhat sombre allegory in the repertoire for February 1779 concerned itself with Britain's rebellious American colonies. They were represented by thirteen men and women 'meant for Quakers, dressed in round pink hats, encircled with ribbons, the men wearing long beards. There was no fun, no noise, no gaiety, no humorous characters.'

The last decades of eighteenth-century Rome were presided over by Pope Pius VI. His tall, majestic figure was occasionally to be seen striding through the Piazza di Spagna. Rumour said that he was immensely rich. The Romans long remembered him for his ill-fated attempt to drain the Pontine Marshes; the art lover can revere his memory as the inspiration of the inauguration of the Vatican Museum, begun during the reign of his predecessor Clement XIV. The museum soon attracted streams of visitors, though some were critical of the display of the exhibits and of 'the false lights they are all of them placed in'. An imaginative group of Russians decided to examine the statues by torchlight and were delighted to discover 'what a different effect they have, and how much better the expression and merits are understood by these means'.

The aura of tradition, splendour and authority that surrounded the papal court, gripped the imagination of all sophisticated visitors, whether Catholic or Protestant. In 1639, as a young man, John Milton passed a memorable evening in the Casa Barberini. The reigning Pope, Urban VIII, was a member of the Barberini family, and his nephew, a cardinal, was the patron of Milton's friend in Rome. Years later, the poet was to serve in the bleak government of Oliver Cromwell, but on this evening he listened 'with rapt soul sitting in his eyes' to an opera. A woman soprano, Leonara Baroni, took the leading role, and the sets were designed by the renowned sculptor and artist Bernini.

The actions of the popes absorbed Romans as they do today; foreigners were equally intrigued. Innocent X delighted everybody when he instituted the custom of flooding the Piazza Navonna during the dusty days of August. He acted at the request of his sister-in-law, Olympia Maidalchina, whose residence overlooked the piazza and who wished to refresh the air for the guests at her receptions. The livelier members of Roman Society and visiting noblemen enjoyed great 'sport, driving their coaches about it all night'. The gossips had still greater sport debating the influence that Donna Olympia seemed to exert over his Holiness in more weighty matters, which 'gave rise to gross scandal'.

Scandal or no, it was the sumptuous ritual of the Catholic Church in its capital city that was the great draw. In the words of a modern writer, the Good Friday services in the Sistine Chapel and the Easter Day Service at St Peter's became 'an almost obligatory fixture in the tourist itinerary'. The great moment in the Sistine chapel's order of service was the singing of the Miserere by Gregorio Allegri. Ever since the composer's death in 1652, the full details of this music and its performance were the jealously guarded secrets of the papal choir. Then, in Holy Week 1770, so tradition has it, the secret of the music was stolen. Among the foreign visitors crowding the congregation was the fourteen-year-old Wolfgang Amadeus Mozart. After the service he hurried back with his father to their lodgings and there copied down, it is said, the entire work, including its final nine-part chorus, from memory.

If this legendary escapade actually took place as described, the papal court seems to have been unaware of it at the time. Two months later, Clement XIV received the boy genius in audience and made him a *cavaliere* of the Order of the Golden Spur. Mozart himself had nothing to say of his act of piracy in his letters home, though they were full of the wonders of the city. Writing to his sister on 25 April he told her that 'we have been to the Campidoglio and have seen several fine things. If I were to write down all I have seen, this small sheet would not suffice.' More exciting was the game of *boccia* which he promised to teach her when he got home. Three days later he was setting his mother's mind at rest as to his safety. 'I have not yet seen any scorpions or spiders nor do people talk or hear anything about them'.

His departure to Naples was delayed because the roads were infested with highwaymen, and several people had been killed, some by them and others by the troops who cleared the road. In Naples young 'Wolfgango in Germania, Amadeo Mozart in Italia' as he signed himself, met all the important people. Besides the composer Niccolò Jomelli, he was also introduced to Marchese Tanucci, the principal minister, and the English ambassador William (afterwards Sir William) Hamilton and his first wife, Catherine. The lady had a great reputation as a musician, and yet, Leopold Mozart recorded, she trembled to play before his renowned son.

NAPLES

'From the reports of divers experienced and curious persons,' wrote John Evelyn in the seventeenth century, 'I had been assured that there was little more to be seen in the rest of the civil world, after France, Flanders and the Low Countries, and Italy north of Naples, but plain prodigious barbarism.' It was the conventional view. Later, the principal towns of

THE COLOSSEUM William Pars

Germany were admitted to the itinerary of the 'civil world', and with the discovery of the ancient Roman cities of Herculaneum and Pompeii in the mid-eighteenth century, it extended its curious gaze a little southward of Naples. Beyond that, however, only the most investigative traveller ventured into the barbarous south. Edward Lear was to find northern ignorance and contempt fully reciprocated. In southern Calabria he heard the position and attributes of England described by a village wiseacre. 'The English had no fruit of any sort, and all our bread came from Egypt and India. As for our race, with a broad contempt for minute distinctions, he said that we were all "a sort of Frenchmen".'

But Naples herself, the metropolis of southern Italy, bewitched all her visitors, 'What traveller has looked unmoved on its splendour? Midday, and the wide blue stillness of the sleeping sea, the swish of its quiet swell making long slow folds in the silky water.' The romantic soul of Hector Berlioz naturally went out to the place. Even Lord Macaulay, the great historian, fell under its spell. For him it overflowed with life and was the only place in Italy to have 'the same sort of vitality which you will find in all the great English ports and cities'. To another traveller it was, 'the pleasantest place in all Europe. The neighbouring country abounds with corn, wine and oil which are excellent. Its wines, above all the Lachryma Christi, are the best in Italy.' Goethe became positively sentimental: 'Naples is a paradise; in it everyone lives in a sort of intoxicated forgetfulness. I too. Yesterday I said to myself: 'Either you have always been mad, or you are mad now!''

With a population of 300,000 people, Naples was the third largest city in eighteenth-century Europe, and the largest in Italy. Her name, literally 'Neapolis', betrays her origins as an ancient Greek colony. In the fourth century BC she was absorbed into the Roman state, but the conquerors fell under the spell of the queenly city, enthroned upon her blue Mediterranean bay. The poet Virgil was just one of the many successful Romans who ended their days there.

Late in the thirteenth century the Pope conferred southern Italy as a kingdom upon the French Prince, Charles of Anjou, with Naples as his capital. Early in the 1500s it fell, with Sicily, under Spanish rule and two centuries of imperial exploitation ensued. After a brief interlude as a province of Austria, the joint kingdom regained a measure of independence under the Spanish Bourbon Prince Charles. Under his government, from 1734 to 1759, a generation of modest prosperity was enjoyed and this was apparent to travellers as they journeyed south from Rome.

Once the frontier with the papal states was crossed, the countryside changed dramatically.

The face of things begins to change from wide uncultivated plains to olive groves and well-tilled fields of corn, intermixed with ranks of elms, every one of which has its vine twining about it, and hanging in festoons between the rows from one tree to another. The great old fig-trees, the oranges in full bloom, and myrtles in every hedge, make one of the delightfullest scenes you can conceive.

Under Charles, the city itself was a thriving metropolis. 'The streets are one continued market, and thronged with populace so much that a coach can hardly pass.' In those days, Neapolitans were more industrious than the average Italian; they worked late into the evening and then strolled the streets or the seaside, many with lute or guitar in hand.

The golden years did not last long. Under Charles's son, Ferdinand, and his Queen, the Austrian-born Marie Caroline, sister of Marie Antoinette, reaction set in again. For thirty years they presided over a court that upheld the privileges of the nobility, oppressed the mass of their subjects, and diverted Europe with its buffooneries and amorous intrigue.

There was something in the air of Naples. That adventurous Victorian young lady, Margaret Fountaine, accepted an invitation 'to go out together' from a young Scotsman she met on her first day there, without hesitation. He was a good enough sort of fellow but, almost at once, 'his attentions were entirely supplanted by those of an Italian, Signor Scafidi, also staying at the Pension'. The shy Scot left the following day and only then did Margaret realize the deep impression she had made on him. Rather pensively her diary records that, instead of attempting to 'further win the esteem of this good man' she had listened to the empty compliments of a 'worthless buffoon'. For all that, the buffoon nearly won a kiss from her and the flirtation was clearly relished by both parties. 'Quite earnestly and in a manner which amused', Scafidi confided that he would like to be a pin-seller and in a half-whisper added 'If you would buy the pins' – Neapolitan pin-sellers were paid in kisses by their female customers. But Signor Scafidi was cheated of his reward by the arrival of Margaret's friends who, 'finding the turn things had taken', never rested till they had got the Italian out of the house.

By the 1890s, it seems clear, one's Italian fellow travellers could be something of a hazard. Three centuries before there were very real dangers on the road. Fynes Moryson joined a party which had hired sixty musketeers. On the way they passed the quartered bodies of numerous thieves. Italian banditti were moderately indifferent to the barbarous penalities of the law – what worried them was the competition from the Turkish and Barbary corsairs who infested the coastal waters, marauded deep inland and layed waste villages, destroying their churches, and taking their young men for slaves and their virgins for concubines.

A century later the danger had abated, and many travellers took passage on the *feluccas* that sailed the coastal waters. The *felucca* was an open boat with a stern awning to protect passengers; it was rowed by upward of a dozen oarsmen, assisted by a lateen-rigged sail. The larger boats could take a post chaise on board, amidships. By this time, too, the roads were generally safe, and some *vetturini* offered a fortnight round trip from Rome for fifteen crowns. The price did not cover accommodation, but did include all ferry charges, two meals a day while on the road, and excursions from Naples to Vesuvius and to Pozzuoli, with its Roman amphitheatre, and the nearby springs of Solfatara. Allowing for these trips and the journey time from Rome, the tourist could count on four full days in Naples. Few did not regret the briefness of their stay.

'See Naples and die' went the saying, yet the enthusiasm of some earlier travellers may seem a little overstrained. Evelyn found the streets well paved and the drains sweet and clean; another visitor spoke of its pure air, 'serene and healthful'. These are not the aspects of Naples that first appeal today, and even then they may have required the nose of faith. In the 1770s a pernickety Englishman observed with distaste that 'the porticoes and colonnades seemed made for people to relieve themselves whenever they felt the urge'. People of quality did not hesitate to order a halt when they felt the call of nature, descending from their carriage to make use of some convenient courtyard or house porch, landings and staircases were casually fouled in the same way. Not that Neapolitans were unique in this: caught short on the great staircases at Versailles, courtiers did not discommode themselves by looking for a closet. It comes as a surprise to learn that Ferdinand of Naples was thought ill-mannered for breaking wind in public.

Whatever the occasional stenches, all visitors were swept up in the vitality and vigour of the city's life. For Stendhal, the Strada Toledo was 'the most populous and gayest street in the world'. Like many other streets in the capital it was paved with lava blocks from the slopes of Vesuvius, but the traffic here was so heavy that it had to be repaved every five to seven years. No doubt the high level of maintenance was partly due to the fact that this was part of the town most frequented by the court. In February 1776 it was the scene of a great court pageant.

The street was lined with a double row of guards behind ropes, yet the procession of coaches could force its way through the crush of footmen only with difficulty. The windows, hung with tapestry and silk hangings, were crowded with spectators. After dark the pageant made its way back down the route, brilliantly illuminated by torches and flambeaux with 'a pretty brisk firework on the front of each car'. The hunters, horsemen and hounds who had taken part in the day's hunting brought up the rear. After all this there was a ball, followed by an excellent hot supper of pies, hams, wines and fruit. It was served in a somewhat novel manner, 'each person eating off his knees, in the best manner he could'.

State functions did not always take place smoothly. On one occasion Queen Marie Caroline ended a ball and furiously ordered the guests to leave, in a fit of jealousy at the flirtation of the court favourite, the Duchess of Lucciana. The Queen was also bitterly jealous of the dancer Rossi, another beauty admired by the King. Gossip said that the jealousy was political, not sexual; that the Queen hounded her rivals so as to maintain her prestige and her influence over the King. She herself was notorious throughout Europe for her own affaires.

The setting for these court routs was the royal palace of Caserta. Building had begun on his father's instructions, when Ferdinand was just a year old, in 1752. The architect, Luigi Vanvitelli, was commissioned to design an edifice that would rival Versailles and the Escorial. His building is a vast open rectangle with wings connecting the centres of all four sides to a large central octagon. The palace has 1,200 rooms and is set in an immense formal park. Although never completely finished, work on the building taxed the already impoverished kingdom to the limit.

Privileged visitors did not worry about such things. They were too engrossed in the grand functions and the intrigue of the court. When the extensive works on the water gardens were complete, Ferdinand arranged a great hunt. At the signal of a gun fired by the King himself, the water was released. As it soared down the cascades, beaters in the high ground let off pistols and firecrackers to drive the game towards the foaming waterfalls, where the royal party picked off the animals at their leisure.

The candle-lit drawing rooms were the settings for more piquant dramas. The Queen, determined to break the influence of Spain, worked for an English alliance; Britain's ambassador Sir William Hamilton, and his second wife, Emma, were honoured friends. Emma Hamilton, whose brilliant position, fame and beauty had much influence. When, during the Napoleonic Wars, the British Fleet under Horatio Nelson put into Naples, court society there became the setting for one of the most famous romances in history, between the hero and Lady Hamilton. The intrigues of the Queen's clique, both amorous and political kept the court in a perennial fever of speculation and scandal and the Nelson touch spread its notoriety all over the continent.

Other English residents at Naples, besides the Hamiltons, included the forceful Lady Orford, estranged wife of Lord Orford. She was an ardent whist player, and her companion, Mrs Sperme, lived in terror of the card table. One dreadful evening she was dealt all thirteen trumps. The game, which was played on a January evening in 1777, must be unique in the history of card games, since the odds against Mrs Sperme's hand are many million to one. The poor lady, unaware of her statistical fame, was rightly terrified of the jealous anger of her mistress.

Outside the privileged walls of the palace, Naples teemed with life. Down at the waterfront *lazzaroni* were to be seen 'walking and sporting on the shore perfectly naked, without the least ceremony'. In the streets, soldiers, priests, barrow boys and the inevitable street musicians jostled with the city's ten thousand prostitutes plying for trade, and 'little brown children jumping about stark naked'. They were joined for a few days, in the summer of 1776, by the Prince of San Lorenzo who paraded stark naked in the Strada Toledo, before being taken in charge.

Tourists who explored as far south as Apulia were equally bemused by the *tarantella* 'a low dance consisting of turns on the heel, much footing and snapping of the fingers'. The legend that the dance is the cure for the spider's bite still persists, yet two centuries ago, the Italian physician Dr Cirillo was convinced that 'not only the cure but the malady itself was a fraud, and that the dance was an imposition practised by the people of Apulia to gain money'.

The villages in the environs of Naples could not offer such exotic diversions, but they appeared friendly and hospitable to travellers lucky enough to have friends at the royal court. Throughout Europe the aristocracy expected, as of right, to be entertained by the villagers when a day in the country took their fancy. One foreigner, invited to join such an expedition from Naples, recorded that they dined at a cottage where they had 'grapes curiously dried with pineapple kernels in each and some good buffalo cheese, called Caccio de Cavallo and excellent wine, which is bought by merchants and carried out to sea for a few months, and then sold in Naples as French wine'.

During the eighteenth century the kingdom of Naples became renowned for the most remarkable tourist attractions in the history of modern travel. In 1709 an accidental find in the countryside at the foot of Vesuvius, on the Bay of Naples led to excavations that laid bare over the years the remains of the ancient Roman city of Herculaneum, buried by the eruption of the volcano in AD 79. The result was a sight which could not be parallelled 'in all the known world, a Roman city entire of that age, and that has not been corrupted with modern repairs'. 'Have you ever heard of subterranean town? A whole Roman town, with all its edifices, remaining under the ground.' When systematic excavations revealed another such city at the site of Pompeii, the chorus of admiration swelled further. For Hector Berlioz 'those bones of the ruined town had a melancholy fascination'.

Berlioz was still more deeply stirred by the awful prospect of the volcano itself. In the seventeenth century, John Evelyn, as befitted a future member of the Royal Society of London, spent several hours clambering around the crater in search of geological specimens. Berlioz, the Romantic, was not concerned with such scientific curiosity. On a midnight excursion to the crater he luxuriated 'in a vague thrill of fear at the rumble of its subterranean thunders, the roar forced up from its vitals' and visualized 'the explosion hurling heavenwards like flaming blasphemies great lumps of molten rock which, falling, roll down till they form a huge fiery necklace round the throat of the volcano'.

A tourist in the 1770s marvelled at the sight of the volcano's slopes covered by snow after one of its periodic minor eruptions. Taking a coach into the vineyards to the spot where the lava had stopped some days before, he found that it had just blocked up the road, overturned a cottage, and buried an entire vineyard. It was still burning hot to the touch, and night flames flickered over the uneven and broken surface. 'During the daylight there is only a trembling vapour which indicates the heat under it.'

Drawing by D. T. Gevers van Endegeest (1793–1877) of himself and his Sicilian guide on a grand tour of Sicily in 1825

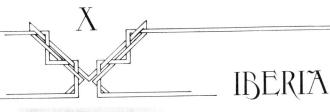

X

IBERIA

'S pain', said Voltaire, 'is a country of which we know no more than of the most savage parts of Africa, and it is not worth the trouble of being known. If a man would travel there, he must carry his bed.'

Compared with the army that tramped southwards over Europe to Italy, comparatively few travellers investigated Spain. The reports brought back by the adventurous few differed considerably. George Keith, Earl Marischal of Scotland, who lived in Spain during the middle decades of the eighteenth century, spoke eloquently in the country's praises when he met Boswell. Keith talked of the beautiful country, the charming climate, the excellent people who were never known to betray their trust – but he had nothing to say about the rigours of travel in the country, of the slow and

Opposite   The Alhambra, Granada J. F. Lewis
Above   Sketch of a Spanish Woman J. F. Lewis

dull muleteers of Madrid, of the woefully bad roads, or the 'wretched hovels called inns'.

ON THE ROAD

In one critical respect Voltaire was right – many an early traveller would have confirmed that it was wise to carry a bed roll in Spain. 'As we carry beds and provisions with us,' wrote one eighteenth-century Englishman to his family at home, 'we have been able to put up with the inns. Without these precautions one would often run the risk of lying down upon the floor, supperless.' Even those who were fortunate enough to be offered a decent bed were disconcerted by the Spanish hotelier's convention of sleeping four guests to a room. Sir Arthur de Capell, an English diplomat, found himself drawing lots with the other gentlemen passengers to determine who should share the ladies' room; the ladies took it all quite good humouredly; Sir Arthur was mildly titillated by the proceedings. His fellow countryman Francis Willoughby, able to afford only low-class lodgings found that virtually every inn outside Catalonia employed 'whores who dress the meat and do all the business, with great impudence, lewdness, and immodest behaviour and practice'. It is not clear whether they outraged his moral sensibilities or not since he reports that 'they are to be hired at a very cheap rate'.

Henry Swinburne could supplement the rigours of Spanish inns with the hospitality of the communities of British settlers, which were particularly common in the coastal towns, and who loaded him with 'civilities, wine and provisions', but in May 1818 the wealthy young American George Ticknor was totally nonplussed by 'a country such as this, where all comfortable and decent means of travelling fail'. It took him thirteen days to reach Madrid from Barcelona, the roads being so bad that, even travelling from four in the morning to seven at night, their coach never made more than twenty-three miles a day. After leaving Barcelona he never stayed at any inn where the lower story was not a stable and on two occasions he was served his supper along with the mules. He only slept in a bed twice. After Madrid, he preferred to ride post-horse and the improvement was considerable, at least as to the speed of his journey. One September morning he left La Carolina at four o'clock and was in Cordoba, a distance of sixty-three miles, by eleven. In the later nineteenth century, travel in Spain began to improve somewhat and, for those who did it in style, could be positively comfortable. Miss Betham-Edwards, a fine example of young Victorian womanhood, operated on the principle that 'luggage and good clothes ensure you good places, general civility, and infinity of minor comforts'. Luggage, she and her companion had in plenty. They travelled in a first-class compartment, which they did not have entirely to themselves, and piled 'an infinite variety of packages' under the seats, on the seats and in the racks above the seats. In addition to the standard requirements, such as medicine chest, provisions and sketching equipment, their supplies included: a folding india-rubber bath, opera glasses, an air cushion and a teapot. In wry self mockery, the young lady admitted that in no country but 'patient' Spain would two young women have been allowed to fill the compartment as they did.

Whatever the hardships of the road, the courtesy of the Spaniards delighted and impressed many travellers. On his journey to Madrid, Ticknor had travelled with the new director of the Madrid Academy of Arts and two army officers, whose 'genuine courtesy and hearty dignified kindness' made it the gayest journey of his life. But then, as he observed, life in Spain in time of peace, was at an altogether friendlier and more civilized pace than elsewhere. 'When you have crossed the Pyrenees you have gone back a couple of centuries in your chronology, and find the people still in that kind of poetical existence which we have not only long since lost, but which we have long since ceased to credit on the reports of our ancestors.'

BARCELONA TO MADRID

The palaces of the kings and viceroys of the once powerful medieval kingdom of Aragon held little interest for the nineteenth-century visitor to Barcelona. For him, the city was a staging post on the road south to Valencia and Andalucia, or eastwards to Madrid. However, in the 1780s, Henry Swinburne made the then unusual journey to the nearby monastery of Montserrat, and its famous Black Madonna. He found the monastery 'one of the greatest curiosities of the world. Its pyramidal rocks, the hermitages dispersed among its precipices, more like the nests of eagles than the dwellings of men, and the situation of the convent in a cleft of the mountain, are most singular and romantic.'

A vast pilgrim hostel now stands there, but the aura of the place was still powerful when the present writer stayed there in 1958. In the cleft of that immense rock rises an ice-cold spring of water. Like other visitors we filled a bottle to drink during the sultry night. Later, the water bottle full and tightly stoppered on the night table between the narrow beds, we were joking irreverently about the mysterious little Madonna, when a crack like a pistol shot rang out. To slake our parched throats, we nervously lifted the bottle. The bottom, as though sliced off by a jeweller's gem cutter, remained on the table and the water gushed to the floor. Schoolboy science explained the effect. The icy water expanding in the warm room had cracked the glass. For a medieval pilgrim it would have been a sure sign of the Madonna's wrath. Even we wondered why the effect should have coincided with a particularly outrageous blasphemy. Our cynical ribaldries faltered, and soon the only sound in the cell-like room was the soughing of the wind in the trees which climbed the precipitous mountain-side behind our window.

Such superstitious worries did not disturb George Ticknor as he trundled between the dreadful hostelries on the road to Madrid, whiling away the time with readings from *Don Quixote* for his Spanish companions. Once in the capital, he lodged with a family recommended by the American minister and was a regular guest of the diplomatic corps.

A German traveller had found a dearth of amusements in Madrid which were 'therefore supplied by devotion, and its sister passion, love'. Christian Augustus Fischer found that after dark 'third-class courtesans threw their arms round men's necks and covered their mouths with kisses, asking "Do you want to see my little bed?"' Swinburne preferred hunting with the court, though that could be a hazardous entertainment. 'King Charles III has already shot several persons in his shooting parties from his badness of sight, which does not diminish his passion for the amusement.' In Ticknor's time the Bourbon royal house was represented by Ferdinand VII, 'a vulgar blackguard'; the capital was far from handsome; and the new buildings going up in the Retiro and elsewhere were 'worse than all that has been done before'.

The chief glory of the place was the Prado promenade, ornamented with three fine fountains and eight rows of trees and statues, with marble seats between them. At five in the afternoon the double walks and carriage-ways were watered to lay the dust. Just before sundown the carriages began to appear and, for about half an hour, made a splendid procession.

On your left hand are two rows of carriages, forming a complete line, slowly moving up and down each side while King Ferdinand and the Infantas dash up and down in the middle with all the privileges of royalty and compel everybody to take off his hat as he passes, and everybody in a carriage to stop and stand up.

Ticknor spent some of his happiest hours in the theatres of Madrid. When the play was over, it was customary to end the evening with a dancing display. 'The stage was converted into a magnificent apartment and a dancer and his partner come forth from opposite sides, each in graceful Andalucian costume, which seems invented for dancing, and dart towards each other as if they had been seeking each other.' As Ticknor returned to the city after an evening's walk he encountered half a dozen groups of the 'lower class' of people dancing to their pipes and castanets.

In Spain dance was almost a part of the landscape. A flamenco display in a wooded glade in Granada quite captured the heart of Miss Betham-Edwards.

Your pulses are quickened to gipsy pitch, you are ready to make love and war. We were a company of ladies and gentlemen whose utmost vagabondage had not exceeded boiling a picnic kettle in Epsom Forest and we felt thankful to Senor Antonio for having given us so full an experience of wild life in the space of a few minutes.

Before he left Madrid, George Ticknor made a five-day excursion by post-horse to the Escorial palace. After thirty miles of dreary, barren waste he came to the forests of the royal domains and saw the 'domes and towers of the convent springing up on the dark, barren sides of the mountain'. Later, he visited Segovia and marvelled at the Roman aqueduct there, 'which still serves the purpose for which it was built'. The general commandant of the military school showed him round the Alcazar fortress and, after a hard gallop over the mountains, he was back in Madrid the following afternoon at four o'clock. Being a wealthy young gentleman, Ticknor believed in doing things in style and at ten o'clock that evening he attended the ball at the town palace of Prince Scilla where he danced until midnight.

Senoritas and Bull Fights

Naturally the young American attended a bull fight. As the day of the 'bull feast' approached, country carts loaded with chains and spears began rumbling into town. Foreigners were astonished that even society ladies adopted famous matadors and picadors, presenting them with jewelled costumes and fine horses. The French Marquis de Custine quite revised his admiration for the beautiful ladies of Spain as he watched their lovely faces contort with excitement in the *plaza de toros*.

At the turn of the nineteenth century bull fighting from horseback, practised to this day in Portugal, was still to be seen in Spanish bull rings. None of the horses had any kind of protection. The picador's function, then as now, was to weaken the bull's neck muscles with a heavy lance while the torero, though he might begin the encounter on horseback, generally dismounted for the final stages. Mariano Ceballos, a renowned Argentinian nicknamed 'the Indian', caused something of a sensation by making the kill from the saddle.

There was much more variety than in the modern bull fight, much more barbarity, and much more danger. A Basque torero received the charging bull while seated on a chair; or leapt upon it from a table with his ankles

The Alcazar, Segovia David Roberts

CASTELLO DE LA KALAORRA, CORDOVA David Roberts

manacled together. La Pajualera of Zaragossa, was fêted for her skill on horseback, as well as for the fact that she was a woman. Juanito Apinani would pole vault over the animal, just before it seemed about to charge him down. Banderilleros entertained the crowd by tying fire-crackers to their darts before planting them in the tormented beast. 'The Indian' actually fought one bull from the back of another. This almost unbelievable exploit, depicted in an engraving by Goya, is confirmed in the letters of a contemporary English tourist: 'At a bull feast in Madrid I saw an Indian from Buenos Ayres who hampered and fastened a bull with a rope to a post; then got on him, cut the rope, and killed another bull.'

Such hazardous circus acts delighted a public eager for bloody violence; women were among the most eager spectators. The fire and passion of Spanish women astonished many foreign visitors. 'Their constitutions may be said to be made up of the most combustible ingredients and prone to love in a degree that natives of the more northern latitudes can have no idea of.' Even the embrace of greeting, then more customary throughout Europe than it is today, 'set Spaniards on fire', if exchanged between members of the opposite sex. The German traveller Augustus Fischer found that the Spanish women had 'character of energy and sublimity that would carry you away in spite of your better judgement and all your philosophy. Slender in form, majestic in bearing, sonorous of voice and with a black brilliant eye.' In these circumstances it is hardly surprising that, during his travels in Spain, Casanova discovered scope for 'a great deal of libertinage in the capital', despite a 'luxury of precaution' which he supposed was maintained on the orders of the Inquisition. 'If you dine alone in a Madrid tavern,' he wrote in his memoirs, 'the waiter will remain constantly on guard to be sure that you do nothing else but eat and drink.'

MADRID TO GRANADA

South from the capital, lay the magical little city of Toledo. The house of El Greco was not the place of pilgrimage that it is today, and the cathedral appealed little to eighteenth-century taste. 'There is more gilding in the church here than in all the palaces of France put together', observed one visitor in disgust. Ticknor seems to have bypassed the place on his journey to the south. At La Carolina he noted a change in climate 'to be expected from passing a considerable chain of mountains. The balmy mildness of the evening air; the reappearance of large groves of olives, so meagre in Castile; are the infallible signs.' He rode on till he came to the banks of the Guadalquivir, which he kept in view until the turrets and domes of Cordova appeared on the horizon.

The beauties of the landscape were no more remarkable than the change in the people. 'Where the Castilians are gay in their private circles, the Andalucians are gay always and everywhere with open-heartedness towards strangers.' Fischer attributed the characteristics of the people to the burning climate. Everything, he thought, was 'immoderate without restraint and above all in what regards the sexes'. Impulses and passions were at their most unruly when the *solano* wind blew. 'Then the very air they breath is on fire and all the senses are involuntarily inebriated. If anything could moderate this ferment of the blood it would be sea-bathing, of which both sexes make frequent use.' Women bathed from a separate part of the beach, under a cavalry guard, which seems to have been pretty easily outwitted by determined lovers. The German even claimed to have seen mixed nude bathing when the tide was well out at low water.

But such titillations were only of passing interest to the real travellers who explored Europe in the grand days of tourism. Even today, few visitors to the Andalusian city of Cordova fail to be overwhelmed by its great mosque; though few will have had the magical experience of Henry Swinburne, who saw it illuminated by candlelight. It had, of course, long been converted to use as a Christian temple, but for George Ticknor it was the lingering aura of Arabian mystery that provided the magic of the place.

You enter by the court and portico where the Faithful once put off their shoes, the very fountains still flow there which flowed for their ablutions and the orange trees and cypresses still form a refreshing shade. Within, one is entranced by the beauty of its marbles and the minute delicacy of its ornaments, combined with the grand effect produced by the whole imposing mass of the edifice, whose thousand columns make you feel as if you were in the labyrinths of a forest.

At Granada, Ticknor, in characteristic style, lodged as a guest of the Archbishop in his palace. Once again the luxurious style of the 'Arabian' architecture, 'the immense halls of the moorish palaces, the light and gay toilet-rooms of their queens', exercised its spell. He wandered for hours in the Alhambra, resting under the shade of a palm tree and luxuriating in the refreshing coolness of the 'minute fountains the Arabs invented only to temper the heat' or enjoying the magnificent view from the Generalife. As the sun set, the twilight began to fade on the plain below, 'traversed by its four streams and bounded by mountains'. Over an evening glass of wine with the Archbishop, he enthusiastically described his day of sightseeing; he found a keen listener for 'in his veneration for this wonderful ruin the old gentleman was little better than a Mohametan'. Ticknor tells us that he went to bed that night and dreamt of the Alhambra.

The next morning he was off again, before dawn, to the enchanted hill-top palace. 'The mountains passed from grey to purple, from purple to gold as I gazed upon them. The birds where everywhere rejoicing at the return of day, in the groves and gardens of the Alhambra, and the convents of the city were just ringing their matins.' He would have been there the next morning too, but the company of merchants he was travelling with to Malaga, were to leave at five and the roads were so infested with robbers that it was not safe to travel alone. The caravan set out thirty strong with one hundred mules in the train and six other travellers, like the American, taking advantage of the protection. Passing a plantation of sugar cane, which proved to Ticknor that he was now in a tropical climate, they entered the busy little town of Malaga at nine that morning.

FROM GIBRALTAR THROUGH SOUTHERN SPAIN TO LISBON
From Malaga he went on to the British garrison colony of Gibraltar, which had been tenaciously held, despite French and Spanish sieges, for a century and more. The tourist who approached the Rock down the coast of Valencia was likely to be somewhat startled by the sight of slaves working in the dry dock at Cartagena. This was kept clear of water by a massive pump manned by a force of 1,400 men working twelve-hour shifts. It was, as Henry Swinburne observed, 'an unpleasant sight for a man of the least humanity. The labour was so severe, the place so unwholesome, that they frequently dropped down dead at the pump.'

For Swinburne, Gibraltar had proved a welcome reminder of home. The life of the garrison was the focus of society. The British and Hanoverian soldiery, who looked like giants, were part of the scene which gave an English visitor

no small satisfaction to be once more on British ground, to hear one's own language spoken and to see so many jolly roast beef faces, after having so long been used to swarthy, peaked countenances and small limbed people. The Hanoverians are quick, good-natured people, keeping much together and being disliked by none of the wine houses.

The hurry and pomp of military music and the parades, and the good manners and hospitality of the officers helped the arrival to pass the week or so pleasantly enough. But once one had 'heard all the marches and all the signals, had dined round and seen everything to be seen', life on the Rock soon palled. In the second week of their stay, Swinburne and his friends were impatiently waiting for a passage to Morocco. Three times they were ready to embark, but were forced to abandon the plan by consistently contrary winds. Perhaps it was just as well. The Spanish fleet was preparing for an attack on Algiers at the time, but rumour said that Gibraltar was its true objective. Swinburne was soon heading north towards Cadiz.

There he was feasted and made much of by the English community. As it rained solidly for more than a month, he spent much of his time at the theatre. The French theatre surpassed anything the Englishman had seen outside Paris; the Spanish playhouse was merely adequate; the dancers at the Italian opera, infamous. However, attending the theatre was not merely a matter of seeing the show; fortunately, the companies staggered their performances so that it was possible for any 'bon ton person to make his appearance at the three houses in the course of the evening'.

Otherwise, apart from gambling, the Cadiz night scene offered only a few private dances and conversation evenings. Even the Mardi Gras carnival proved a damp squib, as the 'old fool of a governor' had put a ban on all public assemblies; the swarms of footpads roaming the city kept all but the most adventurous off the streets after nightfall. The foreign community was catered for by hotels under English, Irish and French managements – mostly with women proprietors. Foreigners who stayed at Spanish hotels, however, could find life exciting.

In the 1730s the French priest Father Labat, himself not averse to a little adventure, was accosted in the street one evening by a lady whom he suspected was in fact his landlady. The ladies of southern Spain, even those of high rank, were known to divert themselves of a summer night, parading the streets in the anonymous guise of tapadas. Heavily veiled in a hood that left only one eye uncovered, they accosted likely looking passers-by in the hope of starting an intrigue. Keen to confirm his suspicions, Father Labat tried to follow the lady, but soon lost her among a crowd of other 'animals of the species' in the dimly-lit interior of a nearby church. The next day, the wily priest made a secret mark on his landlady's mantilla and when, later that afternoon, she once again boldly addressed him in her disguise of a street walker, he threw her into a considerable 'tizz' by identifying her.

From Cadiz, Swinburne went on to Seville where the gardens of the Alcazar were like 'a fairy land with galleries, water-works, myrtle and yellow jasmine hedges, and orange groves'. He wandered down to the tench-filled pond where a Spanish king had once fished by torchlight, and rode through the groves of orange trees outside the city. These picturesque scenes appealed to him far more than the cathedral, 'not so light and airy' as York Minster. But the great church stirred the imagination of George Ticknor, as 'altogether one of the most pure, solemn and imposing specimens of the genuine, uncorrupted Gothic style'. Even so, one feels that Ticknor was more moved by the 'decayed glories', as he termed them, of the city. At Roman Italica, on the outskirts, he found the amphitheatre a crumbling ruin with its mosaics part of a sheepfold and reflected, romantically, that at the time of its glory the place had been the birth-place of the Emperor Trajan. He says nothing of the tobacco factory where, forty years before, Swinburne had seen five hundred people in one room, making cigars. But then the factory of Seville had not yet been made famous by Bizet's *Carmen*. Towards the end of the nineteenth century, after the opera had brought it a certain notoriety, a French visitor described it as a horrible place and the faces of the women workers 'pale, drawn, and poisoned by vitiated air, while beside many of the tables, swaddled infants lay sleeping in their cots'.

Leaving Seville, Ticknor continued his European tour on the road to Lisbon. On 23 October 1818 he saw the 'splendid bosom of the Tagus' stretching along the horizon. The city and its suburbs lay along the bank for a distance of some eight miles; the long line of buildings was 'broken by hills that finally tower above the river and are covered with gardens vineyards, and orange groves'. The multitude of ships crowding the river heightened the drama of the view, but the city itself was a sad anticlimax, 'Besides the extreme filthiness of the streets, there is little curious, interesting or beautiful in the buildings or architecture.' The most remarkable structure was the aqueduct, completed by King John V in

Engraving of a matador pole vaulting a charging bull by Goya

1732. It carried the city's principal water supply through a covered channel supported on thirty-five enormous arches, so well designed and constructed that they had survived the tremendous earthquake of 1755 unscathed.

Above all, the American traveller remembered Lisbon for the happy days he passed with the family of Baron Castel Branco at his villa in Cintra. During the day Ticknor roamed among the opulent country houses, 'scattered on the declivity and in the dells of a precipitous mountain, whose sides are covered about two-thirds of the way to the summit with beautiful and various woods and broken by innumerable little cascades that come rushing down over its rocks'. Every morning he joined the family at the Villa Branco for breakfast and sometimes stayed with them until midnight, when he would return to his own lodgings to dream of the beauty and happy conversation of the day.

A scene from THE FOREIGN TOUR OF MESSRS. BROWN, JONES AND ROBINSON by Richard Dolye, 1855

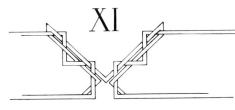

XI

HELLAS UNDER THE CRESCENT

T he first guide book we know of is the *Itinerary of Greece*, written by Pausanias about the year AD 170. Probably a native of one of the Greek cities of Asia Minor (modern Turkey), Pausanias travelled the ancient Greek world at a time when the glorious achievements of its architects and sculptors were still largely intact. Politically, the city states which made up the Greek world had lost their independence and been absorbed into the Roman Empire; but the centuries of barbarian invasion and destruction that ruined the monuments of classical Greece lay in the future. For us, therefore, Pausanias's descriptions are an invaluable record of a departed glory.

The Emperor, Marcus Aurelius, was a devotee of all things Greek, and

Opposite   Evzone Grec Eugene Delacroix
Above   Nineteenth-century photograph of a Greek musician at
Phaestos, Crete

the prosperous citizens of his empire, while they regarded the political weakness of the Greeks with patronizing tolerance, generally acknowledged their cultural superiority and eagerly visited the sights of the country. Pausanias provided these Roman tourists with a complete guide to the topography, descriptions of the monuments and explanations of the principal myths and legends of the towns or temples on the itinerary. Greece was to the Romans what Italy became to later generations of European travellers: the cradle of their culture. By the 1600s, when the culture safari soon to be known as the grand tour was beginning to gather momentum, the literature of ancient Greece was held in high veneration, but the country itself rarely featured on the itinerary of the gentlemen travellers. Greece was not merely remote, it was also, by this time, a province of the Moslem Turkish Empire. Those few adventurers who did make the arduous journey to this distant land found the hazards of travel over the appalling mountain roads compounded by the need to observe the strange conventions of an alien culture and religion.

When Sir George Wheler visited Athens in 1676, he found the temples on the Acropolis being used as Turkish garrison buildings and the Erechtheum reserved as the house of an officer's family. Wheler is one of the very few Englishmen to have seen the temple of the Parthenon in its undamaged glory. For two thousand years this exquisite building stood almost unchanged, as it had been left by the architects of Periclean Athens, although during the Middle Ages it had been reconsecrated as a church of the Blessed Virgin Mary. The Turks had commandeered it as part of a military base, but still the majestic structure survived. Then, in 1689, during one of the recurrent wars between the republic of Venice and the Turkish sultans, a gunner in the Venetian army of Francesco Morosini skilfully lobbed a mortar bomb into the ancient sanctuary, which the Turks were then using as a powder magazine.

It was during the next hundred years that the antiquities of Greece, particularly the shattered temple on the Acropolis, began to win a growing reputation among the cognoscenti in Europe. In 1776 another Englishman, Robert Chandler, was commissioned by the London Society of Dilettanti to make a tour of the monuments of Greece. His report, accompanied by the drawings of the expedition's artist Mr Pars, not only gives a comprehensive account of the classical buildings but also describes life in Turkish Greece at the time.

To his great delight, Chandler was greeted at Piraeus by a dignitary bearing the proud and ancient classical title of 'archon'. In ancient Athens the three archons had been the principal officers of state. Two thousand years later the name was merely a quaint survival. Apart from their title, the archons were distinguished from 'the inferior classes' merely by a tall fur cap and somewhat better clothes. In the 1770s ordinary Athenians wore a red skull cap, a jacket and sash, baggy trousers tied with a large knot; a long cloak lined with wool or fur was worn during cold weather. Chandler, who had travelled elsewhere in the Turkish Empire, found the Turks living in Athens 'more polite, social and affable than is common in that stately race'. Yet walking or riding in the street, the Turkish gentleman displayed the badge of his race: the pipe, carried by an attendant. It was an elaborate piece of equipment: the long flexible tube of the hookah was often embellished with a small silver pendant crescent and the tobacco was kept in a silken embroidered bag, tucked into the gentleman's sash.

The Turks lived on more or less equal terms with the subject people and seemed to be acquiring some aspects of the Greek character. There were, in fact, only some three thousand Turkish families in and about Athens, but, in Chandler's opinion, there were enough to maintain the Sultan's authority: 'because the Turks possess from their childhood an habitual superiority, and can awe with a look the loftiest vassal.'

Athens was an impressive town. The houses were mean and straggled along irregular, narrow streets. Christian churches and convents mingled with mosques and Turkish bath houses. Classical paganism, Islam and Christianity jostled one another in a townscape unique in the experience of the north European traveller. The ruined Parthenon now housed a small mosque, built within its shattered columns after the 1689 disaster. The Greek inhabitants loved to reminisce over the glories of the eastern Roman Empire, ruled for a thousand years from Constantinople before its conquest by the Turks in the mid-fifteenth century. They called themselves and their language Roman, reserving the term Hellenic for classical Greek; yet they celebrated saints' days with dances, which, according to tradition, went back to Theseus, the legendary king of pagan Athens. Turks mingled with the Christian idlers watching these celebrations, just as the Greeks enjoyed watching the celebrations attending the circumcision of sons of wealthy Turkish families.

'The principal Turks on horses richly caparisoned, attended the boys, who were neatly dressed, their white turbans glittering with tinsel ornaments, to a place without the city, where carpets were spread for them on the ground, in the shade.' There were foot races which were followed by Turkish wrestling at a spot near the temple of Olympian Zeus. These wrestlers were naked except for tight-fitting shorts and their bodies were oiled.

A foreigner was a rare sight in eighteenth-century Athens, yet Chandler's party found themselves readily accepted into both Greek and

Turkish society. During the month of Ramadan they entertained their Turkish friends after dusk with 'sweet meats, pipes, coffee and sherbert much to their satisfaction, though they were distressed by our chairs. Some tried to collect their legs under them on the seats, and some squatted down by the sides.'

At the return party given for Chandler by his Turkish friends the Englishman found himself in an exotic, fairy-tale world. Sweet gums were scattered on glowing coals held in little braziers set before the sofas on which the guests were seated, to perfume their moustaches and clothes. After a rich supper of numerous dishes they took their leave with due etiquette; as they were ushered out into the warm night servants at the door sprinkled them with rosewater from specially designed silver shakers. They were received with equal cordiality by leading Greek families and, to their surprise, found many similarities between the household arrangements of the Christians and Moslems. The hospitality did not stop short at the doors of their hosts' homes. Each day, they found presents of freshly picked flowers, pomegranates, oranges and lemons and baskets of pastries delivered to their lodgings.

Nothing intrigued Chandler more than the position of women in Athens. He found that 'the liberty of the fair sex, was almost equally abridged by Turks and Greeks'. Strangers were, of course, forbidden entry to the harem, but it was also unwise for the passer-by to look at the building itself with too much curiosity. If you encountered a woman in the street, it was the custom to turn your face to the wall and stay in that position until she had passed. Not that such encounters were likely. The Turkish women were allowed to walk in the streets only on one day a week and were 'enwrapped and beclothed in such a manner it is impossible to discern whether they are young or old, handsome or ugly.'

Greek ladies were similarly swathed from prying eyes when they left the house, but a Greek husband did sometimes admit a privileged friend to his wife's *gynecaeum* or 'women's quarters'. Chandler, allowed such a privilege by one of his Greek friends, was enraptured.

Her white and delicate feet were naked; the nailes tinged with red. Her trowsers, of thin gauze, hung losely about her limbs; the lower portion embroidered with flowers and appearing beneath the shift which had the sleeves wide and open, and the seams and edges curiously adorned with needlework. Her vest was of silk, exactly fitted to the form of the bosom which it covers rather than conceals. A rich zone [girdle] encompassed her waist and was fastened before by clasps of gold set with precious stones. She had bracelets of gold on her wrists and like Aurora the goddess of Dawn was rosy fingered, the tips being stained. At her cheeks there was a lock of hair made to curl toward the face and down her back falls a profusion of tresses. She was painted blue round the eyes and the insides of the sockets, with the edges of the lashes, were tinged with black.

Neither Turk nor Greek could hope for such a vision of his wife before marriage. Indeed, he was not permitted even to speak to her, but had to rely on descriptions from his female relations who might see the bride-to-be in visits to her home or in the public baths. Throughout the Turkish Empire, the women's bathhouse was an important institution in the larger towns. Lady Mary Wortley Montagu, who visited the one in Sofia in 1717, described it as the women's coffee house. It was the place to exchange gossip and news and, for the older women, to vet the girls proposed as marriage candidates for the menfolk of their families.

A Greek marriage was a beautiful ritual. As the priest read the service, bride and groom stood side by side each holding a lighted taper. The sealing of the union was symbolized by a ring and a gilded wreath or crown, and, at the end of the ceremony, a little boy or girl was led to the bride to kiss her hand. The bride was then enthroned on a chair, the husband standing at a respectful distance with his hands crossed. In due course she was escorted away by the women and the men adjourned to another apartment to carouse. The bride's hands were daubed with paint and, if her family was wealthy, might have her forehead and cheeks decorated with gold leaf.

From his account, Chandler seems to have gone everywhere and seen everything there was to see in Athens. The city fascinated him and almost everything he saw delighted him. However, when he comes to describe the food one detects a certain note of disillusion. It was good enough and certainly cheap but, apart from a few delicacies like the little sychophas bird 'eaten roasted entire wrapped in a vine leaf', not outstanding. Snails and octopus were frequently served, but he found octopus, beaten to make it tender and then boiled, rather flavourless. As to the wine, while it was wholesome, it had a taste 'to which strangers are not immediately reconciled' thanks to the infusion of pine-pitch to preserve it.

When he turned from the enjoyments of modern Athenian life to the study of the ancient monuments that were the object of his journey, his journal becomes a lament. The dilapidated structure of the Parthenon was a tragedy in stone and he surmised with heavy heart that 'so much admirable sculpture as is still extant about this fabric should be all likely to perish from ignorant contempt and brutal violence'. Many carvings had simply disappeared and those that remained suffered almost daily 'barbarism in defacing of them'. During his walks about the city he observed two fine fragments of the Parthenon frieze which had been mounted over the lintels of private houses and bought them forthwith; a few days later, when his interest in the old statues was known, he was presented with a beautiful torso 'which had fallen from the metopes and lay neglected in the garden of a Turk'. About twenty years later another Briton took steps to preserve the statuary. While he was serving as ambassador to Turkey from 1799 to 1802, the Scot, Lord Elgin, resolved to save what he could of the marble sculptures of the Parthenon. As we know from Chandler's journal, they had been decaying for generations from neglect and the thoughtless plunder of the local population. Soon after, Captain Abercrombie Trant deplored the 'mania of destruction which actuates all those who visit Athens, among them, be it said, untutored British sailors. A stone is seized and applied as a hammer to one of the finest bas-reliefs; off flies a fragment, if the head or leg of a statue, so much the better,' Elgin did a deal with the Turkish authorities, permitting him to remove many of the carvings from the temple. The majestic sculptures that now rest in the British Museum as the 'Elgin Marbles' vindicate his decision, being better preserved than the carvings still left on the site.

But Chandler was in Athens to record rather than collect. Back in the 1670s the French ambassador to Turkey had employed a painter to record the great frieze round the top of the temple, but since he had worked from ground level, the results were far from satisfactory. Chandler's artist, Mr Pars, made his drawings from a precarious vantage point on the architrave of the colonnade. He did a professional and thorough job, but not without angry complaints from the officers living in the garrison houses on the Acropolis. There were even threats against the expedition because the artist was often in a position to overlook the private quarters, and the householders had to move their women 'to prevent their being seen from this exalted station'.

His work at Athens complete, Chandler toured other sites in Greece, with Pausanias's *Itinerary* as his principal guide. At Marathon, field of the famous Greek victory over the Persians, Chandler turned to the description by the ancient writer. 'The funeral barrow of the Athenians is in the plain and on it are the pillars containing the names of the dead, under those of the tribes to which they belonged. At night are to be heard the neighing of horses and the clash of arms.' Chandler says nothing about hearing these ghostly sounds of ancient battle; perhaps his was a more prosaic mind. At the Bay of Salamis, scene of the great Athenian naval victory over Persia, the antiquarian dilettante 'supped on turkey which our men roasted on the shore', and then lay among the rocks waiting for the moon to set. On previous nights, looking out over the gulf from his apartment, he had been delighted by dancing fires that flickered along the waters almost till sunrise. They were, he had discovered, the local fishing fleet at work. Now he was preparing to go out with the fisherman. When, at last, the moon had sunk from the sky, the boats put out to sea. In the lead were the net boats, two by two, a net stretched between each pair. Once these were in position the others drove the shoals of fish towards them by waving lighted torches over the water. It was the kind of experience a tourist never forgets, and yet the view of the flickering fires from the shore seems to have impressed Chandler still more.

Another day, looking out from his window over Salamis Bay he saw a water spout run its course.

The weather had changed from settled and pleasant and clouds now resided on the mountains, black and awful. About seven in the morning a cloud tapering to a point descended into the gulf between the islands of Aegina and Salamis. Round it at the bottom was a shining mist. After a minute or more it began gradually to contract itself, and retired very leisurely up into the sky.

The Greco-Turkish world Chandler described died in the Greek struggle for independence of the 1820s. To the English, the war is forever associated with the name of Byron, who died of fever at the siege of Missolonghi, on the Gulf of Corinth, in 1824. The Greeks honoured his memory with almost as much veneration as they did that of the Greek hero Botzari. Byron's birthday was on 22 January and in that fateful year he was thirty-seven. That morning:

Lord Byron came from his apartment where Colonel Stanhope and some friends were assembled and said with a smile: 'You were complaining the other day that I never write poetry now. This is my birthday, and I have just finished something which I think is better than what I usually write'. He then read to us the poem which ended with the prophetic verses:

> If thou regrett'st thy youth, why live?
> The land of honourable death
> Is here: – up to the field, and give
> Away they breath.

> Seek out – less often sought than found
> A soldier's grave, for thee the best;
> Then look around and chose thy ground,
> And take thy rest.

The romantic version of the Greek liberation war, which gained currency in England, and the noble story of Byron's death made Greece a more popular tourist destination than its classical past had ever done. Even so, it remained a destination for the hardy and the adventurous

EAST FRONT OF THE PARTHENON William Pars

throughout the nineteenth century. In 1830, when the struggle against the Turks was in its last stages, Captain Trant observed: 'Travelling in Greece is conducted in so different a manner from that of any other country, that a person who does not make up his mind to experience every kind of hardship and annoyance will be much disappointed.' The horses were poor, the roads non-existent, inns unheard of, and food meagre and scarce. Moreover, the traveller ran the risk of being fired at, or robbed, by marauding soldiers.

Twenty-five years later conditions were not noticeably better. Murray's handbook commented, optimistically, that 'no small portion of the pleasures of travel in Greece arise from sheer hardship which increases so much of our real enjoyments by endowing us with a frame of mind and of body at once to enjoy and endure'. A few wealthy men were beginning to explore the Greek islands from their personal yachts or hired boats, but, apart from this privileged class, few visited Greece for a holiday. Foreigners, in general, came to the country on business, as an educational experience or, in the case of the English, to visit the Byronic shrines.

Missolonghi was not merely a place of pilgrimage, it was also conveniently near to the route inland from the Gulf of Corinth to Delphi, site of the ancient oracle. In 1876 Mr Young, an Oxford academic, made the trip by mule.

We began to ascend the rising ground which forms the roots, so to speak, of Parnassus, behind us was the beautiful view of the Bay of Krissa. We continued the ascent, the path becoming, if possible rougher, and the stones thicker, till at last we rounded a curve and Delphi, in the shade of its two beetling crags, lay in a hollow below us.

He found the place one of intense gloominess and depression, but was pleasantly surprised by the beautiful peasant girls at the Castalian spring. His lodging was a straggling broken down barn and he slept, as usual, on the floor.

Young gave as his sole excuse for publishing his 'trifling book of travel', the fact that it was about a country of which many parts were not on the regularly beaten track of tourists. He felt that the beautiful scenery of the interior of Greece, and the friendly hospitality of most of its inhabitants, deserved greater credit. He acknowledged that the fear of brigands was still general among his fellow countrymen. In 1854 Murray was encouraging his readers with the thought that 'there are now few instances of travellers being attacked when travelling with one of the regular Athenian couriers and nowadays, in the Levant, a Frank runs very little risk from open violence'. Assurances like these rang hollow when news broke of the ambush of Lord and Lady Muncaster and their party, travelling with military escort to Marathon in 1870. An immense ransom of £32,000 was demanded and Muncaster, sent back to Athens to raise it as best he could, was also instructed to negotiate with the government for free pardons for the bandits and the release of some of their gaoled friends. But the Greek government mounted an expedition against the brigands and four of the hostages were murdered in the ensuing battle.

The wary reader of Mr Young's book would not have been unduly astonished by the Muncaster tragedy. The author described a very instructive little play which he saw in Athens, dealing with brigand life. 'One of the scenes represented an "at home" of villains; and, if one might judge from the clapping and cheering which ensued, it would seem as if the sympathies of the audience were not altogether with the Government against brigandage.' No doubt, as he commented in his preface, the British consul had declared the whole of the Peloponnese to be perfectly safe, but many readers must have had their doubts.

Not that it was difficult to reach the country. By the middle of the nineteenth century one could make the journey with reasonable speed and comfort. The chief routes were by P & O steamer to Malta, or overland across France to Marseilles and thence to Malta. From there one had the choice of the British Royal Mail packet to Corfu and neighbouring islands, on the 12th and 31st of every month, or French government steamers direct to Athens three times a month. Later there was the still more pleasant route by rail to Trieste from Ostend, and then by Austrian Lloyd steamer, via the Adriatic, to the Gulf of Corinth. The trip took only ten days, and the all-in first-class single fare was ten pounds.

The problems of internal Greek travel of course remained. The private yacht contingent were advised to take some 'tokens of remembrance' for local officials – a few pairs of English pistols, Sheffield steel knives, pocket telescopes, and even 'prints of the Queen and her chief ministers', were reckoned to be ideal for the purpose. Less prosperous travellers were urged to consider the merits of Mr Levinge's bell-tent-cum-sleeping bag apparatus of calico and muslin as a protection against vermin – no amount of pistols or photographs would secure decent hotel accommodation outside Athens.

In the 1840s the indefatigable topographical painter Edward Lear disembarked at Salonika to begin a painting tour of Greece. He was stunned by his reception. Crowds of black-turbanned porters tore him from the boat, 'with the most unsatisfactory zeal', and then threw themselves on his luggage: 'each portion was claimed by ten or twelve frenzied agitators, who pulled this way and that until I stood apart, resigned to whatever might happen.' It was only with the aid of 'a half score of police' that the porters were finally driven off. It had been an unnerving experience for the timid painter.

Travellers in Greece needed a hardy spirit and the intrepid butterfly hunter Margaret Fountaine showed herself equal to even the most intimidating hazards. In 1902 she was trudging the tracks of Crete, with her Greek guide Roussos, in quest of the rare, tiny brown butterfly *Lycaena pslylorita*. They found their quarry at last on the approach to the Plain of Ida and that afternoon cast about for a place to camp for the night. An apparently comfortable cave had to be abandoned when Roussos discovered that it was dripping with water and crowded with pigeons. Further searching led them to a shepherd's hut, built of large stones in the shape of a beehive and with an entrance little more than four feet high. In the heat of the afternoon the hovel was pleasantly cool, but as night drew on the interior became distinctly chilly.

As the two travellers huddled round their little camp fire they were joined by a group of rough-looking shepherds. Next a couple of Cretan soldiers turned up, proclaiming their intention to help the 'foreign lady'. 'It was', wrote Miss Fountaine in her diary, 'a delicate little attention which rather pleased me.' Eventually the soldiers strode off into the night and were followed shortly after by the shepherds. So far as one can tell the middle-class English gentlewoman was hardly aware of the horrid possibilities of this evening encounter with a bunch of virile foreign peasants. But then, she had already more than a decade of travel through Europe and Syria behind her and had become the secret mistress of one of her Arab guides. Even so, her courage was to fail momentarily during the long night ahead.

Roussos made up her bed of dry brush-wood and rugs and she was much too tired to worry about the rough accommodation. More disturbing was the thought that the shepherds to whom the hut belonged might return while she was asleep. Apart from a few flimsy wax tapers that soon burnt out, she was without light, 'and then the darkness was intense'. There was no lock on the hut's makeshift door; she therefore secured it as well as she could with a boulder and so 'obstructed the one outlet to this gruesome abode; I began to feel rather as though I were spending the night in a tomb'. But it had been a very hard day climbing the mountain tracks and she soon fell into an exhausted sleep. At about two in the morning she was awoken by the sound of sheep bells and the cries of shepherds. Miss Fountaine looked to her defences and found them slight in the extreme. She decided that if the shepherds should manage to break into the hut, she would rise up from her bed, 'a tall, white figure in the gloom, and pretend to be a ghost'. No doubt the superstitious peasants would scatter in sheer horror at the sight and never dare enter the hut again. Yet there was, of course, the possibility that one of the hardier peasants would take a potshot at the ghost, 'and that might have been a trifle awkward'.

All turned out well. The sound of rough voices and tinkling bells died away and the would-be ghost in the beehive hut concluded that the flocks were merely changing pasture during the night. She recovered her courage as best she could in the shivering dark and, 'as the grey dawn began creeping through the chinks of the doorway', she was finally roused by a loud banging on the door. Roussos, who had spent the night crouched over the fire, could stand the cold no longer and the two thankfully prepared for an early start.

After a night like that, even the accommodation provided by the monasteries, where they often slept, appeared in a kindlier light. Miss Fountaine was impressed by the kindness and generous hospitality of the monks and the welcome they gave to strangers but, she observed, it was 'much to be deplored that they are not a little more inclined to bear in mind that "cleanliness is next to godliness"'. Every time she prepared for bed in the guest quarters of some friendly but remote monastery, she had cause to regret that she was not 'literally a bug hunter'; and every time she rode out into the fresh morning air 'vainly hoping for better luck next time'.

Margaret Fountaine, whose travels took her to India, South Africa and South America, as well as the Middle East, was a woman with a mission. Even in Crete, the mythical home of the Minotaur and the heroic exploits of Theseus, it was a little brown butterfly rather than the legends of ancient Greece that held her imagination. The Victorian writer Alexander Kinglake had more conventional sensibilities. Visiting Cyprus, he recalled its legendary associations with the cult of Aphrodite. He noted 'the bewitching power attributed at this day to the women of Cyprus' and found in it a 'curious connection with the worship of the sweet goddess who called their island her own'. Kinglake concurred with the general Greek opinion that

in face the women of Cyprus are less beautiful than their majestic sisters of Smyrna ... yet there is a high-souled meaning and expression, a seeming consciousness of gentle empire, that speaks in the wavy lines of the shoulder, and winds itself around the slender waist; then the richly-abounding hair (not enviously gathered together under the head-dress) descends the neck, and passes the waist in sumptuous braids.

The mysterious beauties of Cyprus were, apparently, renowned throughout the Greek world, even though the girls of Smyrna were rated higher on the aesthetic scale. The Greek seaman of Kinglake's day reckoned that he could 'trust himself to one and all of the bright cities of the Agean, and may still weigh anchor with heart entire, but that so surely as he ventures upon the enchanted isle of Cyprus, so surely will he know the rapture or the bitterness of love'. The Greeks attributed this to the Cypriots' 'politike', that is 'their tact and bewitching ways'. Kinglake, we know, preferred to see in it the lingering power of pagan Aphrodite, goddess of Love.

He had no interest in ruins as such, though he did make one pilgrimage to a temple site in the hope that he could fulfil his 'pagan soul's desire to speak out my resolves to the listening Jove, and hear him answer with approving thunder'. Far more fascinating for him, was to hear the great names of the classical past, spoken in the dialect of the people. A luncheon in Limasol was especially memorable. The children of the family 'all had immortal names – names, too, which they owed to tradition, and certainly not to any classical enthusiasm'. As the meal progressed the mother, to Kinglake's delight, maintained discipline with cries of 'Themistocles, my love, don't fight' and 'Socrates, do put down that cup'.

The family in question was that of a Greek who had 'hoisted his flag' as the English vice-consul at Limasol. His little house had nothing else to distinguish it from the others in the street and one senses that it was as much self-importance as hospitality that prompted him to invite the English gentleman to a formal lunch. Kinglake, no doubt embarrassed as well as amused by the pretentiousness of the proposal 'induced him to allow my dining with his family, instead of banqueting all alone with the representative of my sovereign in consular state and dignity'. The lady of the house was very shy about sitting down at table with a strange man, as might be expected from a woman used to the conventions of the gynecaeum, but finally submitted to her husband's request. 'He reminded her, I fancy, that she was theoretically an Englishwoman, by virtue of the flag that waved over her roof, and that she was bound to show her nationality by sitting at meat with me.' It required yet more persuasion to get her to agree to the children joining the adults but finally she did so and the family party went off very well. When it was over the vice-consul and his guest retired to the roof, 'for that is the lounging place in Eastern climes', to discuss, at the vice-consul's request, the British Constitution.

Two days later, at the village of Baffa, Kinglake was again entertained by a 'representative of his sovereign'. This time it was 'a Greek husbandman who, for the sake of the dignity and protection it afforded, had got leave from the man at Limasol to hoist his flag as a sort of deputy-provisionarysubvice-pro-acting-consul'. Having first changed his Greek headgear 'for the cap of consular dignity', he, too, insisted on entertaining the Englishman to lunch. He seized a club and 'with the quietly determined air of a brave man resolved to do some deed of note', went into the poultry yard behind his cottage, 'stood for a moment quite calm – collecting his strength; and then suddenly rushed into the midst and began to deal death and destruction on all sides'. The dead and dying were carried off and, in less than hour, were brought to table 'deeply buried in mounds of snowy rice'.

Embarrassed by the lavish entertainment he had received but equally embarrassed to offer money, Kinglake made a present, instead, of 'a rather handsome clasp-dagger' he had bought in Vienna. The Greek, 'in all respects a fine generous fellow', overwhelmed his guest with thanks and, a few minutes later, came 'bounding and shouting' down the road with a large goat's milk cheese in his hand. As he rode on his way, the English traveller remembered, with pleasure, that two thousand and more years earlier Theocritus had written of a shepherd rewarded for his songs with just such a cheese.

At the time of Kinglake's visit Cyprus was still under the dominion of the Ottoman Empire yet, as the names they gave their children suggest, the island's Greek population retained a proud sense of their descent from a remote but illustrious past. On the Greek mainland this strong national pride was reinforced by memories of the recent heroes in the war of liberation against the Turks which established, with the aid of the great powers, an independent kingdom of the Hellenes in 1832. In the closing years of the struggle the country was in a sorry state. Waiting for his horses, to carry him from Cape Katacolo in the western Peloponnese to Pyrgos, Captain Trant, wrote that he

tried to look with admiration on the classic ground around me: I called to mind that I was treading on the land which had produced those great and virtuous men whose exploits and glorious deeds had been the theme of my early lessons, and that within a few miles of me was the celebrated Olympia, where in former days, the fiery youths were seen eagerly contending for the prize. But instead of viewing any of the fancied forms of ancient heroes, I perceived a tattered, dirty-looking wretch driving before him three miserable little horses.

It was an accurate summary of the sad state to which Greece had sunk. In the 1870s Princess Victoria of Prussia made a highly interesting proposal so that 'poor little Greece would become rich at once'. Daughter of Queen Victoria of England, and mother-in-law of King Constantine of Greece, she suggested that Mr Thomas Cook should be invited to Athens, so that he might examine the possibilities of extending the tourist trade to Greece. Mr Cook's commercial instincts satisfied him that the time was not ripe for such a venture and the scheme came to nothing.

Cook's opinion contrasts oddly with the picture of Greece drawn for us by a foreign resident there in the 1890s. It was, he recalled, 'an astonishing little kingdom, the like of which, outside pure fiction, will never again exist in Europe'. The reign of its first king, a Bavarian Prince crowned as Otto I in 1832, had done little for the country. His authoritarian régime was overthrown in 1862 and a Danish Prince adopted as King George I. The Greek royals were connected with those of England, Russia and Germany and this family of 'eminent personages with the best will in the world set themselves to be truly royal and thoroughly democratic'. The effect was intriguing.

King George lived in a monstrous white palace overlooking the square; a bugler was stationed by the front door in the long portico of Doric columns who blew soul-stirring blasts in a great hurry whenever a royal personage emerged ... Sometimes the royal personage was only a royal baby in its perambulator, and the slightly self-conscious nursery-maid hastened to convey her charge into the garden away from these trumpetings.

King George clearly recognized the importance of protocol in royal affairs, but foreigners found him remarkably approachable, nevertheless. One had only to be cleared by one's legation in Athens to obtain a quarter of an hour's audience: Queen Olga was equally gracious. Indeed, 'American ladies flocked to Athens because (as one of them stated with the most engaging frankness) "The royal family of Greece is the easiest royal family to become acquainted with."' Tourists enjoyed a special dispensation for these encounters with royalty. King George generally expected to receive visitors dressed in top hats and frock coats but, 'since few travellers carried such articles in their luggage, they were permitted to wear dress-clothes and white ties'. The results could be delightful. 'About eleven o'clock on a broiling morning I observed the pleasant spectacle of an obese pilgrim emerging from the Grand Hotel in a dress suit (slightly green in the strong sunlight), pumps and a straw hat, and making his way across the stony desert in front of the palace for his chat.'

At this time Athens's most distinguished visitor was the Dowager Empress of Germany, mother of the Greek Queen, who moved to the Greek capital to await the birth of her grandchild. She passed her days sketching at the Acropolis surrounded by a group of idlers and tourists who all 'stood around her spitting and smoking' until a gentleman-in-waiting approached, bare-headed, to inform Her Majesty that her carriage was waiting to carry her back to the palace. The Empress Frederick, daughter of Queen Victoria, was by no means the only royal tourist to visit Athens in these halcyon days. The Princess of Wales came to see her sister and the Czarevitch came to visit his uncle, the King, and his cousins, 'and all the Greeks thought they had come to render homage to the land of Hellenic culture'.

In the mid-1890s the proposal to revive the Olympic Games and to hold them at Athens was eagerly taken up by the Greek government. A foreign visitor has recorded for us the mood in the Greek capital.

The youth of Athens instantly went crazy over athleticism. Strings of young men in shorts trotted about the streets of Athens all day, occasionally bursting into sprints ... the extremely bumpy roads to Phalerum and Kephissia were thick with flashing bicycles, and one day I saw two stout and elderly gentlemen solemnly wrestling together, by the columns of the temple of Zeus.

The ancient stadium was renovated with finance provided by a patriotic millionaire and everything was ready for spring 1896. A number of foreign athletes turned up, and the opening ceremony, performed by King George, was cheered by a crowd who looked forward to the coming games as a contest between Greece and the rest of the world. Unfortunately, most of the events went to other nations, but the Marathon, regarded as the Blue Riband, was triumphantly and conclusively won by a young Greek called Loues. So large was his margin of victory that some of his rivals hinted that he had 'possibly been assisted by occasionally placing his hand on the stirrup of the Greek cavalry officer who rode beside him with words of encouragement'. Such slanders were ignored in the wave of national rejoicing at the victory. He received the olive crown of victory at the hands of the King; the Athens-Corinth railway awarded him an unlimited free pass; and the municipality of Athens voted him a free dinner every day for the rest of his life.

Later that year war broke out between Greece and Turkey, sparked by Turkish atrocities in Crete. In 1897 the Turks successfully invaded Thessaly from the north, and the tourists in Athens watched from their hotel windows as streams of penniless refugees poured into the city. The Turkish victory worried the great powers of Europe; the Turks were ordered out of Thessaly, and Crete was handed over to Greece. One more district of the historic domain of the ancient Hellenic lands had been liberated from the oppression of the Crescent, but it was hardly a glorious victory and the golden years of the reign of King George were past forever.

XII

NEW DEPARTURES

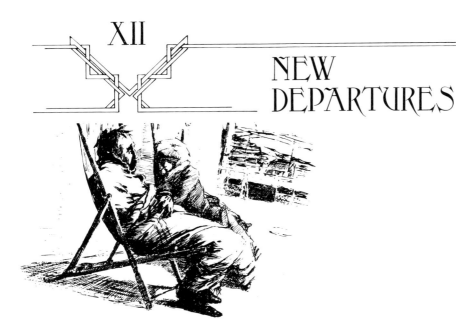

E|arly one spring morning in the year 1803 a remarkable contraption clattered up the Tottenham Court Road in London. It looked like a carriage, but there was no horse. The wheels were eight feet high, a flicker of fiery coals could be seen in the darkness, and a belching plume of smoke and steam waved behind. Leaning from her window, fuddled with sleep, a dazed London housewife whimpered defiance at the Devil and his coachman. 'Tally Ho! For Cornwall', floated up in broad west-country accents through the greying light. In fact Captain Trevithick and his friend Vivian ended their little jaunt in disaster a few miles further on, and coached back home in the normal way.

The portable high-pressure-steam engine pioneered by Richard

Opposite   OFF TO SEA FOR EASTER, a late nineteenth-century photograph
taken at Waterloo station, London
Above   MAL-DE-MER Arthur Briscoe

Trevithick around 1800 was the pivotal invention upon which the nineteenth-century revolution in transport turned. A year after his London venture, to settle a bet, Trevithick demonstrated its traction power on a colliery tramway in south Wales, becoming the first man to run a steam locomotive on a railroad. In 1808 he was again in London, this time as impressario of a sideshow near Euston. For a shilling a ride, the passer-by could trundle round a circular track in a carriage dragged by a little steam horse called 'Catch Me Who Can'. Regency London disdained such provincial novelties, and the fertile genius of Trevithick had no time to waste on exploiting just one invention. It was left to the dour George Stephenson to put the world's first regular railways on the map of England – coals from Stockton to Darlington in 1825, and a regular passenger service from Liverpool to Manchester in 1830.

Little steam packet boats were already plying profitably round the coasts of Britain. William Symington of Glasgow patented a steam boat as early as 1789, and his prototype, the *Charlotte Dundas*, towed a seventy-ton line of barges some twenty miles along the Forth and Clyde Canal in 1802. Between 1812 and 1820, his fellow citizen Henry Bell was operating the steamboat *Comet* on a ferry service between Glasgow, Oban and Fort William; the first cross-Channel steam passenger service (Brighton to Le Havre) sailed in 1816; in 1820 the *Rob Roy* began working out of Dover, and when, two years later, the new French ambassador, the Vicomte de Chateaubriand, used the service, steam travel at sea had become so well accepted that the crossing receives merely a passing reference in his journal. A ship could easily accommodate the clumsy steam engines that had been in use for a hundred years to pump water from mine shafts, but it was a challenge to adapt them to land transport. Trevithick showed the way; Stephenson demonstrated its profitablity. It is largely thanks to them that modern travellers sometimes like to think of the often vexatious adventures of the grand tour as a golden age of leisure and aristocratic elegance.

THE SHIPS

Bayard Taylor's Atlantic crossing on the sailing ship *Oxford* took twenty-six days, four days longer than scheduled because they were becalmed for three days off Newfoundland. In May 1861 Charles Francis Adams, the Federal American minister to Britain, made the voyage in the steamship *Niagara* in thirteen days, which he found a convenient time to read Macaulay's *History of England* in preparation for his ambassadorial duties. The cut in travel time was much appreciated by Mr George Ticknor, who was delighted with the progress in sea travel since his first journey at the age of twenty-seven, in 1818.

The sense of progress is epitomized for us by Hector Berlioz in the journal of his Austrian tour of 1845. Having missed the steamer at Regensburg, he 'had the mortification, instead of steaming down the Danube, of being laboriously conveyed along its banks, reflecting on the centuries of progress which separate the two modes of travel'. At Linz he left the Middle Ages and 'stepped aboard a handsome, swift-looking steamer and was back in 1845'.

The first trans-Atlantic crossing by steam had been made in eighteen days by the *Sirius* in March-April 1838. It was a brief triumph. The *Sirius*, sailing out of Cork in Ireland, docked in New York harbour only hours before the *Great Western*, designed by Isambard Kingdom Brunel, which had left Bristol three days behind *Sirius* and completed the longer crossing in just fifteen days. Then, in 1840, a merchant from Nova Scotia won a contract with the Royal Mail to run a regular steam service between Liverpool and Boston, via Halifax. The Royal Mail contract was the foundation of the line's prosperity and, in the early days, the standards of passenger comfort left something to be desired. When Dickens sailed in the *Britannia* in 1842, he found the saloon, 'a long narrow compartment, not unlike a gigantic hearse with windows in the side'. During the night the boat shipped a heavy sea which 'crashed down through the skylights and flooded down into the ladies' cabin'.

By the time Ambassador Adams sailed to take up his London posting, the steamship companies were already providing considerable luxury for their clients on the premier services, though conditions on the smaller boats remained variable, Robert Louis Stevenson, bound for the Continent, boarded his ocean steamer at Greenock. 'There she lay in mid-river, a street of white deckhouses, an aspiring forest of spars, larger than a church and soon to be as populous as any incorporated town.' But even this proud vessel did little for her tourist passengers.

At breakfast we had a choice between tea and coffee for beverage; I found that I could sleep after the coffee and lay awake after the tea, which is proof conclusive of some chemical disparity; and even by the palate I could distinguish a smack of snuff in the former from the flavour of boiling dishcloths in the second.

Not that the shipping companies could be blamed for the most usual complaint of sea travellers. Effie Ruskin, crossing by steamer from Folkestone to Calais in 1848 found that, although it was a lovely day, the ladies' cabin was already full, so she stretched herself out in the general cabin, with 'a gentleman ditto at each end and so on all round with one or two on the floor'. The ship was barely under way before all the ladies were ill; soon, 'the whole assembly rose *en masse* from their reclining positions,

197

dreadfully sick'. Fortunately, the stewards were 'very attentive and brought me some nice eau de cologne which revived me a little'. Such palliatives, however, were of no avail for a German, or Frenchman whose moustache, imperial and beard nearly covered his face. A very large man, he was in a dreadful state and 'moaned and roared terribly'.

During the 1820s and early 1830s, when steamboat services were well established but the railway network of northern France was still being developed, many travellers continued their journey from Le Havre by the steamboat *Navrais* down the Seine to Rouen. It was a pleasant jaunt. 'The river winds at the foot of the gentle hills along the Seine with small villages and pretty churches concealed in the thick foliage of the trees along the bank'. Passengers could dine on deck and so catch their first sight of Rouen, magnificently dominated by its cathedral, the trees of the city's boulevards mingling with masts of the shipping at the quays.

Europe's most popular river journey, then as now, was down the Rhine. The Coblenz steamers were so full of English travellers that the idea of being in a foreign land required some imagination. 'English faces met the eye on every side and our native language proceeded from the mouths of all.' Maintaining their reputation for extravagance, the English preferred to travel in the 'pavilion', a well-appointed apartment in the stern 'reserved for those who prefer a high price to a low price and will on no account travel without a partition between themselves and their inferiors in wealth'. Sometimes, the passengers stayed overnight at riverside inns; when the steamer had sleeping berths, the finest were the select few which gave on to the pavilion. The larger steamers could also carry the horses and carriages of the wealthier passengers.

THE RAILWAYS

Europe's rail networks grew at varying rates, and horse and coach long remained the only way to explore the country outside the principal centres. John Murray's *Handbook of Travel Talk* of 1847 gives a whole section to the all-important business of horse trading. A decent horse might cost as much as eighty guineas, but one could be hired for three guineas a week with an additional guinea charged if the horse was to be used to hunt. If one intended to hire a coach, it was vital to come to terms over the return of the vehicle; some hirers paid for this, others had arrangements with coaching inns along the route.

Murray's book gave a number of searching questions for the traveller to use in such situations, but there were also more detailed matters of importance for the convenience of the Victorian traveller. Phrases in French, German and Italian, enabled one to demand, for example, more leather straps on the roof to secure sticks, umbrellas, parasols and the like; venetian blinds at the windows of the coach; a leather dickey mounted at the back for servants; or 'an elegant, new-fashioned carriage suitable for driving about town'.

As we saw in chapter one, really dedicated travellers like the Ruskin family commissioned the coach at home to their own detailed specifications. For John Ruskin this remained the ideal way to see the world. 'Going by railroad,' he commented once, 'I do not consider travelling at all; it is merely being "sent" to a place, and very little different from becoming a parcel'. Nevertheless, as soon as railways became available he made use of them. When he and Effie crossed to France in 1848, it was not with their usual cumbersome coach. The Boulogne-Abbeville railway was opened that year and so the link from the coast to Paris was complete. With ten trains a day from London to Folkestone, and a steamer with every tide, London to Paris became a miraculously rapid and convenient journey. One could cover the one hundred and seventy miles from Boulogne in barely nine hours, where the fastest diligence had taken more than fifteen. The French carriages were as large as those on Brunel's broad gauge Great Western line and even better padded. If railways revolutionized the life of the traveller, they also transformed the towns and countryside they passed through. In July 1848 a line was opened from Dieppe to Rouen; it had been built by British navvies, financed by French and English capital. The Rouen council recognized the importance of the occasion with a grand ceremonial opening. Cannons thundered from the old castle and the church bells pealed out all day. That night, balls and dances were held throughout the town and as dawn broke the choral society of Rouen gave a concert of *aubades* composed for the occasion, under the windows of the company directors. The navvies' banquet, later in the day, was a roistering, boisterous affair.

The 1840s and 1850s witnessed a veritable railway mania with new lines being opened all over Britain and Europe. In the next generation luxury was added to speed. In America the pioneer was Pullman. In Europe the first sleeping car was introduced by the Cie International des Wagons Lits, formed by the Belgian Georges Nagelmackers. A decade later he introduced his first restaurant car. In England both sleepers and dining cars were owned by the railway companies but in Europe Nagelmackers found it hard to get his rolling stock accepted by the companies.

Wherever they were introduced, the new facilities transformed the conditions of travel. The standard of food provided by the contractors who won catering concessions on the stations was atrocious; the cuisine on the early dining cars approached the finest standards of the best hotels and

Midland Railway Sleeping Car *c.* 1905

restaurants. It was matched by the opulence of the decor. Small chandeliers, hanging from elegant, stuccoed ceilings, cast their glow on gleaming white napiery and richly upholstered chairs. The wine list rivalled the very best, without regard to the damage done to a fine wine by hours of shaking in the rocking motion of the train. Handsomely wined and dined, the customers returned to their compartments where attendants had transformed the seats into comfortable single beds.

In the nineteenth century travel entered a new time dimension. When he began his European journeys, George Ticknor had travelled in the height of luxury, enjoying the hospitality of the best houses. But, until the coming of the railways, little could be done about the sluggish progress on the road from one splendid household to another. On his trip of 1856, he could write: 'We did not reach Southampton till the five o'clock train had been gone ten minutes. So we made ourselves comfortable, with a mutton chop and a cup of tea at an excellent inn, and at fifteen minutes past seven took the next train, reaching London at ten and Rutland Gate at half past ten.'

The new pattern of travel can be seen in the record of the Roget family's journey from their London home to the Continent in 1844. 'On the morning of 26 July, boxes and bags were seen descending the staircase and forming a pile in the entrance hall. At nine, a hackney coach, followed by a cab, drove up to the door.' They drove to Fenchurch Street railway station and took the train to Blackwall. Arriving at the quay three-quarters of an hour before the boat was due to sail, they secured their berth aboard the steamship *Soho* by placing their overnight bags 'upon certain shelves with bed-clothes upon them in a kind of dark cupboard'. With the pile of luggage on the deck at 'its maximum height' a few late arrivals hurried aboard, the gangway was removed and 'an impatient splashing was heard underneath'. With the paddle wheel churning steadily, they glided majestically down the Thames.

Dusk fell as they steamed out across the North Sea. The calmness of the sea and the brightness of the moon 'produced a visible change'. Ladies who had been keeping themselves quiet below stairs and amusing themselves with a few volumes of Blackwood's magazine, appeared on deck. A young gentleman in a shooting jacket 'immediately ordered some fowls and ale which he was presently seen devouring with great avidity in the dining room'. When the Roget family retired to bed, they found some difficulty in getting to sleep, 'because of the draught from the aperture which served as a window, the noise of the engine in the next compartment, and the cramped position which limited the size of the berths'. They approached the Belgian coast the next morning in a sickly dawn light, instead of the bright sun which had been shining over the Thames, and a depressing drizzle.

Although the early steam ships did not move significantly faster than a square-rigger with a good wind and quarters on board could be pretty uncomfortable, it was the fact that man had at last made himself independent of the wind that made the little cross-Channel steam packets seem so revolutionary. Regular and reliable schedules were now possible and actual travel times were slashed. The very dimensions of the globe seemed to have been reduced and if the Atlantic had not, quite yet, become the 'herring pond' it had become a negotiable obstacle to many more thousands of travellers than had dared consider the trip to Europe before.

A SHRUNKEN WORLD

The opening of the Paris-Rouen and Paris-Orleans railways in 1843 prompted the poet Heinrich Heine to troubled reflections on the import of the railway age. The revolution in travel would, he believed, work as profound a change in human awareness as had the invention of gunpowder and the invention of printing. Perhaps the effect would be more profound since 'even the elementary concepts of time and space have begun to vacillate'. He went on: 'Space is killed by the railways, and we are left with time alone.' Thanks to the railway, the travel time between the capital and the two great provincial centres had been reduced to four and a half hours. 'Just imagine what will happen when the lines to Belgium and Germany are completed ... I feel as if the mountains and forests of all countries were advancing on Paris. Even now, I can smell the German linden trees; the North Sea's breakers are rolling against my door.'

A few years before, the British *Quarterly Review* had pointed to the impact of steam power on the dimensions of the globe itself:

We have seen the power of steam suddenly dry up the great Atlantic ocean to less than half its breadth ... The Mediterranean, which is now only a week from us, has before our eyes shrunk into a lake; our British and Irish channels are scarcely broader than the old Firth of Forth; the Rhine, the Danube, the Thames and the Ganges have contracted their streams ... and the great lakes of the world are rapidly drying into ponds.

Travellers and travel agents noted more practical results. Murray's handbook for France of 1848 noted that 'the high road to Paris is nearly deserted now that the railway from Boulogne is open to Paris'. The same guidebook had a whole page reset in order to take in a footnote describing the relaxation in the French passport regulations, following the introduction of railroads. Murray discovered that the upsurge in travel brought about by the railroads created a new phenomenon, which threatened the reputation of his company. A 'Caution to Innkeepers and Others', reveals that travellers were quick to realize how the sudden increase in their numbers, made possible by the railway, transformed their importance in the economic calculations of hoteliers.

The Editor of the hand-books [wrote Murray] has learned that persons have of late been extorting money from innkeepers on the Continent, under pretext of procuring recommendations and favourable notices of them and their establishments in the Hand-books for Travellers. Recommendations in the Hand-books are not to be obtained by purchase and the persons alluded to are totally unknown to us. Notices to this effect have been inserted by the Editor in the principal English and foreign newspapers.

The tourist industry and the average tourist responded enthusiastically to the transformation brought to the travel scene by the new technology. The philosphically minded addressed themselves to its supposedly deep impact on the human psyche. Thomas De Quincey wrote:

Seated in the old mail-coach we needed no evidence out of ourselves to indicate the velocity. The vital experience of the glad animal sensibilities made doubts impossible on the question of our speed; we heard our speed, we saw it, we felt it as thrilling; and this speed was not the product of blind insensate agencies, but was incarnated in the fiery eyeballs of the noblest among brutes, in his dilated nostril, spasmodic muscles, and thunder-beating hoofs.

De Quincey's thrilling evocation of the coach horse might have surprised the average traveller of the pre-railway age, all-too familiar with the broken-down hacks that so often haled him laboriously across the potholed routes of the Continent. But many a traveller noted the alien nature of mechanized travel. 'The flowers by the side of the road are no longer flowers but flecks; there are no longer any points, everything becomes a streak; from time to time, a shadow, a shape, a spectre appears and disappears with lightning speed behind the window: it's a railway guard.'

It was the astonishing speed of the railway that made the deepest impression on the average traveller. Even in the first generation of the steam age people observed the parallel between the railway train and a projectile. 'The train shoots right through the landscape like a bullet.' The American writer D. Lardner quantified the comparison. He calculated that a train moving at seventy-five miles an hour 'would have a velocity only four times less than a cannon ball'. Mistakenly, but not unreasonably, medical opinion debated the possibility of physiological damage resulting from such un-human velocity.

The rapidity and variety of the impressions necessarily fatigue both the eye and the brain. The constantly varying distance at which the objects are placed involves an incessant shifting of the adaptive apparatus by which they are focussed upon the retina; ... scarcely less productive of cerebral wear because it is unconscious.

For the railway companies themselves, the speed of their locomotives produced a severe problem of the most practical nature. In the days when even a fast coach took the best part of a day to cover the distance between London and Reading the four minutes difference in time between the two cities was of no consequence. But the railway, in the words of Heine, had 'killed space and left us with time alone'. The companies had to standardize the times over their routes. The novelty of the idea is revealed by the cumbersome daily procedure employed. Each morning an Admiralty official carried a watch bearing the correct time to the guard on the down Irish Mail of the Grand Junction Railway leaving Euston for Holyhead. 'On arrival at Holyhead the time was passed to officials on the Kingston boat who carried it over to Dublin. On the return mail to Euston the watch was carried back to the Admiralty messenger at Euston once more.'

This railway time governed the schedules on the routes and for years each company had its own schedule time. Eventually the companies agreed to co-operate in a uniform national railway time for the national rail network. Greenwich time was adopted as valid for all lines, but it still applied only to the schedules of the companies. By 1880 the railways had unified the country to such an extent that it was seen to be unreasonable to retain local times for any purpose. Thus the transport revolution had effected a truly fundamental change in human awareness. Greenwich time became standard across Britain, even though sunrise there was almost half an hour ahead of the most westerly part of the country, and before the end of the century the entire globe was divided into artificial 'time zones' by international conference.

THE PRIVATE JOURNEY

Where some lamented the loss of landscape in the speed of railway travel, the American Matthew Ward, touring England in the 1850s, saw things in a different light:

The beauties of England being those of a dream, should be as fleeting ... They never appear so charming as when dashing on after a locomotive at forty miles an hour. Nothing by the way requires study, or demands meditation, and though objects immediately at hand seem tearing wildly by, yet the distant fields and scattered trees, ... dwell long enough in the eye to leave their undying impression

... I love to dream through these placid beauties whilst sailing in the air, quick, as if astride a tornado.

The general concensus among travellers, on the other hand, seems to have been that dreaming, not to say sleeping, was about all rail travel was fit for. John Ruskin opined that 'travelling becomes dull in exact proportion to its rapidity', while Gustave Flaubert confessed: 'I get so bored on the train that I am about to howl with tedium after five minutes of it.' The novelist's complaint is a little ironical since in the same decade a French conference heard that 'practically everybody passes the time reading while travelling on the train. This is so common that one rarely sees members of a certain social class embark on a journey without first purchasing the means whereby they can enjoy the pastime.' A few years earlier, a German writer, anticipating modern railway publicity, observed that rail travel was so smooth that one could not only read but even write during the journey, so that professional men 'need no longer rest or interrupt their regular routine while travelling, but can pursue it while sitting in the steam-car'.

As befitted the home of the railway, it was in England that booksellers saw the potential of the new market. By 1850 W. H. Smith had won the franchise for the entire London and North-western Railway network, while at Paddington, the headquarters of the Great Western, there was even a railway lending library. Publishers quickly followed the trend. Routledge began a series called the *Railway Library*, while the house of Murray, involved for fifty years in the business of publishing travel books, launched *Literature for the Rail*. Soon after this the French firm of Hachette, with all the pride of an original discovery, announced their intention to establish a 'railway library'. The traveller, they observed, was condemned to idleness as soon as he entered the carriage and the monotony of the trip soon took effect, what was worse: 'impatience engulfs the unfortunate traveller, pulled along by the machine like a piece of baggage.'

The members of that 'certain social class' who could remember the old days commented on the way the isolation of the railway carriage, the speed and hence brevity of the journey and the numerous changes of personel in the compartment at the various stations along the line had killed one of the great pleasures of travel – conversation. 'In the coach,' wrote a Frenchman, 'conversation got off to an easy start after a few moments of preliminary study of one's companions; at the moment of parting, one often regretted the end of the journey, having almost made friends.' How different things were on the train. We remember how Dr Burney's fellow travellers in the diligence burst out in spontaneous applause when a pretty girl at last joined the company; such a demonstration would have been impossible in a railway compartment of the next century.

By the end of the century the new travel mode had established its conventions. In England, at least, there were very few people of the upper classes who would expect, or desire, to engage in conversation with strangers on a train. There were times, however when even British reticence broke down. Shortly after the publication of his *Book of Nonsense*, Edward Lear was on a journey, sharing the compartment with two other gentlemen. The two friends were discussing the immense success of the new book by a hitherto unknown author. One of them, claiming inside knowledge of the 'facts', loftily assured his dubious companion that he knew for certain that the name was in fact a pseudonym adopted by Edward, Earl of Derby, clinching his argument with the observation that 'Lear' was an anagram of 'Earl'. Astounded, the usually timid author took up his hat and, displaying the name tape on the inside band, conclusively squashed his 'would-be extinguisher'.

The speed and privacy of rail travel was eagerly exploited by those with the money to pay. When her doctor ordered Rachel Fountaine to the south of France as a cure for pleurisy, the family dug into its considerable resources to ensure the smoothest possible journey from the fogs and grey skies of Bath to the warmth and sunshine of Mentone. Her sister, Margaret, was dispatched to Cook's London head office to arrange the bookings from Dover to the south of France while the doctor, Mr Bannatyne, arranged transport from the family's home town to Dover.

On the day of departure, Rachel was escorted to Bath station where a private coach was waiting in a siding. It was fitted out luxuriously. 'A lavatory communicated with two separate compartments on either side. In one was slung a large basket bed and there Rachel lay through the long hours of this tedious journey.' Margaret, who had returned so as to accompany her sister on the whole journey, sat with Dr Bannatyne in the other compartment while the nurse watched over the invalid. The luggage of the three travellers was accommodated in a private van coupled to the coach, and the two vehicles were duly detached, shunted and recoupled when the time came to change trains at Reading.

They reached Dover late in the afternoon to find that the bath-chair they had ordered was already waiting on the platform to convey Rachel to the Lord Warden hotel. The next morning she was wheeled out along the pier to the steam packet. The Channel crossing was uneventful and, although Margaret and Dr Bannatyne were agreed that 'of all the dismal, dreary places we had ever seen, Calais took the cake', Rachel was shown to a splendid room in the Hotel Terminus. It was 'full of red winter sunlight' and there was, 'of course, a blazing fire roaring in the grate'.

Despite a suite in the wagon lit to Mentone, the twenty-three hour journey was depressing. But when they eventually arrived, and Rachel had been safely ensconced in the Hotel d'Orient, Margaret and Dr Bannatyne went on to Monte Carlo, where they had a successful little flutter at the tables. The next day Bannatyne returned home.

The journey of the two Miss Fountaines and their medical escort would have been unusual, but hardly remarkable by the standards of their day. They came from a prosperous middle-class family of no special distinction. For herself, Margaret preferred a bicycling holiday or adventurous rough travel in the remoter parts of the world. She would never have contemplated joining one of the package tours which, already by the 1890s, were a commonplace of the travel scene. She was, it is to be feared, something of an élitist. 'It is curious', she had recorded in her diary, 'how once a place becomes frequented by foreign tourists the manners of its inhabitants deteriorate.' Thanks largely to the efforts of Mr Cook who had so discreetly arranged her sister's journey to the sun, Europe was yearly frequented by thousands of foreign tourists.

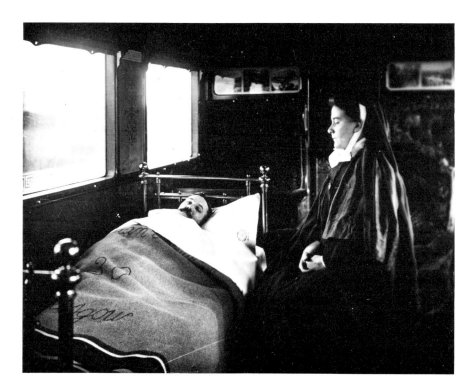

Invalid Saloon on the Caledonian Railway

XIII

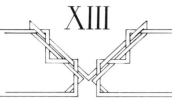

THE GREAT STEAM PACKAGE

B|y the 1820s British travellers were flooding into Europe at the rate of 150,000 a year; the numbers increased dramatically once the possibilities of cheap rail travel began to open up. It was not only the British who availed themselves of the growing rail network with its opportunities for cheaper travel. As the nineteenth century progressed, tourists became increasingly familiar throughout the Continent, and even the once select spa towns were crowded. At Marienbad, Mark Twain found that the crowds along the promenade 'speak a lot of languages that you have not encountered before'. The curative springs had been known for centuries, but 'there was never a boom here until a quarter of a century ago.'

Opposite   Promenaders on the Casino Terrace, Monte Carlo,
photographed by Donald McLeish
Above   Swiss steam engine

The railways were not solely responsible for the revolution in travel. The boom in trade experienced by places like Marienbad derived in large measure from the simplification of travel introduced by the tourist agents. To increase their own profitability the agents rationalized the whole business and their work benefited the whole travelling public.

When Mark Twain toured Switzerland in the late 1890s, he bought his tickets 'of Thomas Cook & Sons, of course – nowadays shortened to "Cook's", to save time and words'. By no means the only tourist agent in the field, Cook's, thanks largely to the energy and acumen of the founder's son, had established its reputation as a household name. In the early days, as Twain recalled, 'to be a "Cook's tourist" was a thing to be ashamed of, and everybody felt privileged to make fun of Cook's "personally conducted" gangs of economical provincials'. Things had certainly changed by 1897. People of all sorts and conditions made their bookings through the company, if only because it was all so much simpler.

In the early days of the railway, travel in Europe had been made 'hateful and humiliating by the wanton difficulties, hindrances and vexations, put upon it by stupid and disobliging transportation officials,' and the sensible traveller who could afford it hired a personal courier rather than 'risk going mad'. One could not buy a rail ticket in advance of the day of the intended journey and, even then, had to wait until fifteen minutes before departure time. There was a weight limit on trunks and cases, all of which had to be weighed – and excess baggage paid for – in that same fifteen minutes. If there was not enough time one simply had to abandon 'such trunks as failed to pass the scales', for if you missed the train you could not travel on the next one on the same ticket. A long journey, involving changes of train could be a hazardous undertaking as even booking clerks were appallingly vague on the details. It was not unusual for a long-distance traveller to find himself with a ticket which suddenly became invalid along the way because it had not been correctly drawn at the departure point.

Cook [wrote Mark Twain] has remedied all these things and made travel simple, easy, and a pleasure. He will sell you a ticket to any place on the globe ... good for all trains of its class, and its baggage is weighable at all hours. It provides hotels for you everywhere, if you so desire; and you cannot be overcharged, for the coupons show just how much you must pay.

The company's agents and couriers met the trains at all the principal rail stations on the continent to deal with clients' problems. They would 'get you a cab, tell you how much to pay cabmen and porters, procure guides for you, or horses, donkeys, camels, bicycles, or anything else you want'. If you decided to break the journey the company was prepared to refund the unused portion of the ticket at a mere ten per cent discount. By the time that Mark Twain came to write this glowing encomium, Cook's had been in business some four decades. The beginnings had been humble.

THE START OF MASS TOURISM

In August 1838, less than ten years after the opening of the world's first passenger railway between Manchester and Liverpool, the Whitby-Pickering railway in the county of Yorkshire offered a special group booking for an excursion to a church bazaar. That year, too, a special train form Wadebridge in Cornwall to the neighbouring town of Bodmin, was chartered by a large part of the town's population to attend the public hanging of a notorious Wadebridge murderer at the Bodmin assizes. They got a fine view, even without leaving the train, as the gallows had been erected in Bodmin station yard. From the beginning, bargain travel offered a wide range of possibilities.

The exploitation of cheap group travel was opened up still further by the northern working men's associations. In June 1840 the Leeds Mechanics' Institute organized an excursion to York, inclusive of high tea, for half the normal rail fare. In July the Leicester and Nottingham institutes ran exchange excursions at concessionary rail fares. The newspaper report of the excursions, which had been run on the Midland Railway's Derby-Rugby line, was read by a Mr Thomas Cook, a baptist temperance worker, and planted an idea that was to germinate over the next few weeks. Then, one day, travelling on the same line, at a point 'about midway between Market Harborough and Leicester', a thought flashed through his brain: 'what a glorious thing it would be if the newly developed powers of railways and locomotion could be made subservient to the promotion of temperance!'

Thomas Cook planned his grand scheme thoroughly and, on Monday 5 July 1841, 570 people, travelling in open, seatless, third-class carriages, arrived in Loughborough for a grand temperance gala and a tea of ham and loaves in the park of a Mr Paget. The return journey, of eleven miles, cost one shilling. For many years, the basis of Cook's expanding travel business was his continuing devotion to the temperance cause.

Cook is justly remembered as the founding father of mass tourism, but he quickly found others developing the same field with equal success. In 1844 Joseph Crisp of Liverpool contracted with the Grand Junction and the London and Birmingham Railways for a five per cent commission on all business he introduced to their services. He was so successful that they were soon regretting their casual agreement to his terms. The same year, another English entrepreneur had introduced the idea of the package tour to the Continent. Henry Gaze ran a tour to Paris, taking his clients by steamship down the Thames to Boulogne and then on to Paris by diligence. Soon he was offering package tours to the battlefields of Waterloo and the city of Brussels and, later, tours to the Oberammagau Passion Play. The history of this highly successful business, which appeared in 1881, uses the term 'tourist agent' for the first time in print.

Thomas Cook, whose company was to prove the most successful of these first tourist agents, was less adventurous than his early rivals. His first tour outside England went no further afield than Scotland, but it showed he had an eye for the main attractions. The advertisement for this 1846 tour featured a special stop in Gretna Green, 'should any demand be made by the ladies and gentlemen for the special services of Mr Linton and Mr Murray, the famous blacksmiths'. The tour was a success, but Cook continued to operate only within the United Kingdom, though his excursions became increasingly ambitious. They entered a new dimension, when, in 1851, the tenth anniversary of his historic Loughborough excursion, Cook laid on a grand series of excursions to the Great Exhibition in London. No fewer than 165,000 clients took advantage of the cheap rates he offered and the success of packaging touring was clear. In fact, the Cook tours of Scotland proved so successful that the Scottish railway companies decided to dispense with this enterprising middleman and run excursions to their own profit. At last, Cook turned his attention to the possibilities of Continental travel.

The Paris Exhibition of 1855 provided the natural opportunity for Cook's new departure. But he planned something more ambitious for cut-rate travel to the French capital and back. According to one client 'Mr Cook mapped out a most delightful route' to Paris, by way of Antwerp, Brussels, Cologne, Mainz, Mannheim, Heidelburg, Strassburg and, finally, Paris. One of the most comprehensive foreign tours yet offered to a discerning public, the itinerary was successfully marketed the following year. The outcome was another holiday for the expanding brochure of Cook's organization. One group of travellers on the 1856 tour decided to leave the main party for a private sortie into Switzerland. Cook followed the reports of their venture with close interest and was to record that the difficulties they encountered 'started in my mind an idea of Swiss tours'.

He was not the first to see the possibilities. In 1858 Henry Gaze published his *Switzerland and How to See it For Ten Pounds*. But when Cook did run his first tour in 1864, five hundred people applied for bookings. When the younger Thomas Cook entered his father's business, the firm expanded still further. Far-sighted and able, young Cook began negotiations with the German Rhenish Railway Company for concessionary fares for his tours on their network. At first the company refused, on the ground that the arrangement would erode their profits. Finally, expecting to put a stop to his badgering, they agreed in principle, on condition that he pledged himself to sell the seemingly impossible figure of at least five hundred first-class fare equivalents in the first year. To their dismay, within a month of signing the contract, young Cook reported back that the year's bookings were sold out. Mass tourism was established beyond question.

THE TOURIST MENACE

'The bar of England is scattered over the face of the earth', wrote Charles Dickens in the early 1850s, 'in Switzerland, at a French watering place, on the canals of Venice, at the second cataract of the Nile, in the baths of Germany.' A staff writer on the magazine *All the Year Round*, which the great novelist ran during the 1860s, heartily approved the development. 'Now surely, this is a good kind of thing, that a hardworking man can, in his fortnight's holiday, betake himself to some place as far away from his ordinary abode as lies within the reach of his purse.' He concluded that it had all been made possible 'by the aid of such providers as the excursion agent'.

It was true. Thanks to the new excursions of agents, thousands of moderately well-to-do artisans and professional people, who were an essential class in the prosperity of mid-Victorian England, found new and liberating horizons opening before them. But the chorus of complaint from those priding themselves as 'the better sort of people' was already beginning to swell. 'A contemptuous old lady', encountered by a journalist in the Scottish Highlands, 'thought that places of rare interest should be excluded from the gaze of common people and be kept only for the interest of the "select" society.' *Punch*, which had jeered at Gaze's book on its first appearance, delighted to publish cartoons of encounters with Cook's tourists in foreign hotels. 'Elderly gentleman politely to middle-aged Spinster, evidently one of Cook's tourists: "And where, may I ask, are you going next?" Spinster: "Oh! Let me see – I'm going to Geneva." E. G.: "Going to Geneva. Why, you *are* in Geneva."'

Charles James Lever, the British consul in Trieste, declaimed against Continental excursionists. 'The cities of Italy are deluged with droves of these creatures, you see them forty in number pouring along a street with their director circling them like a sheepdog.' He reckoned that if the flood of 'unlettered' British excursionists was allowed to go on, 'nothing short of another war, and another Wellington, will ever place us where we once were in the opinion of Europe.' (In our own day such carpings are still a favourite theme of the self-estimated sophisticates of the media. The classic target of the modern 'liberal' concensus is the fish-and-chip shop on the Costa Brava catering for the contemporary British excursionist. For reasons understood only by the commentators, the British penchant for familiar food is risible in a way that the Italian, Greek and Chinese passion for establishing their own particular cuisines in foreign climes is not.)

As for the Iron Duke, he instantly identified the railway as a dangerously democratic invention, opening travel to all and sundry. The complaint was even then as old-fashioned as it was reactionary. A Mr Cresset, writing in 1662, had deplored the increase in stage coaches which annihilated the distance between Brighton and London by travelling it in three days under summer conditions. This sort of thing would, he argued, encourage the country gentry to come up to London 'merely to have their hair cut, or such like frivolity', and give their wives a 'habit of idleness and love of pleasure'. William Wilberforce, recommended a health cure in the Lake District by his doctor in the 1790s, had found Lake Windermere 'as populous as Piccadilly'. A few years before, Edward Gibbon had lamented the summer infestation of Lausanne with English: 'I am told that upwards of forty thousand English masters and servants are absent on the continent; and I am sure that Lausanne has its full proportion.'

To this way of thinking, the railway made things infinitely worse. But the bastions of élitism were quickly conquered by the seductions of convenience. In the winter of 1870–71, Archbishop Tait of Canterbury commissioned the firm of Cook to organize his journey to a rest cure on the French Riviera. The route through Paris was closed because of the Franco-German war and so Cook's sent the party via Ostende, Germany and Austria. The archiepiscopal family and household were delighted. One of the ladies in the party wrote:

From the start we always found most comfortable saloon carriages ready for us and the landlord of each night's hotel met us at the station in advance; beautifully appointed carriages were in readiness to convey our party to the hotel, where we found the name of each member of the party over the doors of the rooms they were to occupy, including the names of the ladies' maids.

No eighteenth-century gentleman could have made a more stately progress on the grand tour than this one, arranged by the father of popular mass travel.

Archbishop Tait and his entourage were only the latest in a long line of English people to take refuge from their dank native climate on the sunny

214

shores of the French Riviera. The English had begun exploring the southern coast of France as far back as the 1770s in their quest of sunshine. The sea view, though not in those days the sea bathing, was an additional pleasure. At Antibes the view was particularly fine, as Arthur Young noted in the 1780s.

For enjoying it in greater perfection, the inhabitants have an admirable contrivance. A long row of houses a quarter of a mile long, has flat roofs which are covered with a stucco floor, forming a noble terrace and this is raised above the dirt and annoyance of the street, and equally free from the sand and shingle of the beach.

Before the railway age, transport was something of a problem. Unable to hire carriage, horse or mule, Young had been obliged to walk from Cannes; but Antibes was undoubtedly flourishing, 'owing very much to the resort of foreigners, principally the English, who pass the winter here'. The previous winter there had been fifty-seven English visitors to only nine French, and when Young visited the town in 1789 he found its inhabitants worried by the news of the revolution which, they foresaw, would ruin their prosperous little tourist trade.

There is surely some irony in the fact that the revolution in transport which killed the grand tour as an institution of privilege, at the same time provided the privileged classes with a standard of luxury superior to anything that could have been imagined by even the wealthiest traveller a century earlier. However, privilege could prove its own enemy. In 1873 Baron Alphonse de Rothschilde had an engagement to dine in Brussels with Leopold, King of the Belgians. Just before the Belgian frontier the train in which he was travelling incognito was shunted on to a loop line. A 'special', commissioned apparently by some other plutocrat, thundered past and the Paris-Brussels express arrived so late that the baron missed his royal dinner. When he at last reached his hotel, it was to find his evening wear already unpacked, neatly laid out, and waiting. His valet in Paris had forgotten it and, to make good his oversight, had cleverly ordered the offending 'special'. Only the absurdly rich, the baron may have reflected, can be side-tracked by their own dinner jacket.

The tour organizers and the railway companies seemed to conspire to help the less privileged. Thomas Cook, opening up the American market in the 1870s, made a virtue of the fact that his transatlantic customers entered Britain at Liverpool and not in the capital. 'Our tickets from Liverpool', ran a notice in his firm's *Excursionist and Tourist Advertiser* for April 1874, 'provide for the journey by the Midland Railway, because we believe it to be the best route either for the direct traveller or the tourist with time to linger.' The reason: the line passed through the Derbyshire Peak District with stations where one could alight for Chatsworth House, the residence of the Duke of Devonshire, already in the stately home business.

By this time, Cook's Continental operation had extended into Italy. The railway was the basis of these tours, but the journey over the Alps was still by diligence over the Mont Cenis pass. From Susa, one had a special train to Turin and then the night train to Florence. The organizer had problems, even when the transport ran smoothly. 'Young and active gentlemen' were liable to dash off from the station to the hotel, to grab the best rooms. Cook devised a two-pronged strategy to deal with the menace. Hoteliers were asked, as a matter of policy, to send the first comers, 'as the most vigorous', to the highest rooms; secondly, and more effectively, the company sent its own couriers on ahead to the hotels with specified reservation lists.

At this time, Cook was organizing tours for select parties from the middle-class. However, John Frame, like Cook a temperance enthusiast, ran a tour aimed at lower paid clerks and skilled artisans in 1881, and Henry Lunn ran an Easter tour to Rome in 1893, for only twenty guineas. He expected fifty or sixty clients, but in fact got a response of four hundred and fifty. Cook's representative had warned him that his company had never been able to make even a twenty-five guinea tour pay, but this, observed Lunn, was 'simply because they aimed at small parties'. Lunn was subsequently to take parties of Eton and Harrow shoolboys to the Bernese Oberland (resulting in the formation of the Public Schools Alpine Sports Club), and win a knighthood for his enterprise. Then, in 1900, Dean and Dawson organized a company outing to Paris for fifteen hundred employees of Lever Brothers. The steam revolution was reducing foreign travel from a major expedition to a spontaneous jaunt. But from the Orient came occasional reminders of how to travel in style. An Indian prince, touring Europe a few years before the Lever Brothers company spree was accompanied by select members of his household establishment – two hundred servants, fifty family attendants, twenty chefs, ten elephants and thirty-three tame tigers, not to mention a small howitzer for the occasional royal salute.

By comparison, the wealthiest Europeans had to be content with the status symbols of opulence. 'How you travel is who you are', opined Lucius Beebe, America's arbiter of fashion and the high life. In 1920 the Ladies' Page of the *Illustrated London News* advised: 'By their luggage you shall know whether they be well-born folk or not.' The writer recommended a set of luggage from Waring and Gillow, 'of the finest cowhide, finished in a nut-brown colour and fitted with the best nickel-plated locks'.

The cataclysm of the Great 1914–18 War proved merely a hiatus in the expanding story of European holiday travel. The great glamour trains, like the Golden Arrow, the Engadine Express and the Blue Train from London (Victoria) to the south of France, which let you 'sleep your way from the city's fog to the Riviera sunshine', sped once again across the Continent. Their luxury sleeping cars and dining cars revived for the new generation of moneyed classes and war-profiteers the splendours of pre-war Wagons Lits and Pullman travel. Naturally, the fashionable German resorts of the Edwardian age, Bad Homburg, Marienbad and the rest were not in vogue. Instead, the seekers after winter sun headed in swelling numbers to the French Riviera from Monte Carlo to Cannes. The cultured, or those who wished to seem so, still took their Baedeker guides to the great Italian cities.

In 1923 more than half a million tourists entered Italy by rail, twenty-eight per cent of them travelling first class. Six years later the percentage of first-class bookings had dropped to fifteen, but the total of rail passengers had risen sharply to 976,800. Apparently, the decline in first class percentages reflected not so much a decline in prosperity as a large increase in less well-to-do travellers. And there was something else of significance about the Italian tourist statistics for 1929. More than 120,000 visitors arrived by car; the following year, Swiss border records showed that 163,000 motorists had crossed their frontiers.

After 1919, in Europe as in America, the motor car, once the plaything of privilege, became available on the mass market. The painted motor chariots of the rich – the Rolls Royces, the Hispano-Suizas, the Daimlers and Bugattis – found themselves increasingly jostled on the highway by charabancs, adventurous motor-cyclists and distressingly numerous plebeian saloons of low horse-power. Unsatisfactory as all this no doubt was for the right ordering of society, it meant money to many a European exchequer.

In his book, *England's Treasure by Forraign Trade*, published in 1664, Thomas Mun had some prescient remarks on the idea of the balance of trade. 'There are', he wrote, 'some other petty things which seem to have reference to this ballance, of which the officers of his majesties customs can take no notice, to bring them into accompt; as namely, the expences of travellers.' Two and a half centuries later, governments were finding ways of taking such expenditures into account and discovering that they were by no means petty. Today, there is hardly a government in the world for which the 'expences of travellers' is not considered an important source of revenue.

In the Middle Ages, towns and churches fortunate enough to be custodians of some sacred relic made the fleecing of pilgrims a systematic and lucrative business. The English milords on the grand tour were seen as lambs for the slaughter by innkeepers, postilions and curio dealers throughout Europe. Less grandiose, and perhaps more canny, than their predecessors, today's tourists are eagerly courted for their custom by historic cities, sun-drenched seaside towns, and vacation parks of every kind.

Few now venture abroad as a religious penance, and even the notion of travel as an education to broaden the mind is a trifle outmoded. Few would say with smug James Boswell: 'Before I left, I was idle and dissipated. Now I am very different and have a character which I am proud of.' For real travellers, there is an itch to see beyond the horizon, an excitement about the very idea of abroad. For them, the true patron is not the comforting figure of St Christopher but, rather, bustling Tom Coryat of Somerset, who died on his travels in India in 1623. 'I do confess', wrote this irrepressible adventurer, 'that the mere superscription of a letter from oversea doth set me up like a top.'

France, October 1909: on the left a 1909 Daimler and on the right a 1908 Rolls-Royce 'Silver Rogue'

BIBLIOGRAPHY

Archenholtz, J. W. von, A Picture of England (1791)

Baldick, Robert, translator, The Memoirs of Chateaubriand (1961)

Bell, Gertrude, The Letters of Gertrude Bell (1953) ed. Lady Richmond

Benson, E. F., As We Were: A Victorian Peepshow (1930)

Bird, Anthony, Roads and Vehicles (1969)

Blom, Eric, editor, and Emily Anderson, translator, Mozart's Letters (1956)

Boswell, James, An Account of Corsica, Germany and Switzerland (1953 edition)

Brownwell, William C., French Traits (1893)

Bruford, W. H., Germany in the Eighteenth Century (1953)

Bull, George, translator, The Autobiography of Benvenuto Cellini (1956)

Cairns, David, translator, The Memoirs of Hector Berlioz (1970)

Cobbett, William, Rural Rides (1830)

Edwards, Mathilda Betham-, Through Spain to the Sahara (1868)

Epton, Nina, Love and the Spanish (1954)

Evelyn, John, The Diary of John Evelyn, ed. E. S. de Beer

Fountaine, Margaret, Love Among the Butterflies, edited from the Journals of Margaret Fountaine
    by W. F. Cater (1980)

George, Daniel, A Book of Anecdotes (1958)

Glover, Cedric Howard, Dr Charles Burney's Continental Travels (1927)

Gray, Thomas, The Letters of Thomas Gray (1925), ed. John Beresford

Hindley, Geoffrey, A History of Roads (1971)
    England in the Age of Caxton (1978), Saladin: A Biography (1976)

Hitti, Philip K., An Arab Syrian Gentleman of the Crusades (1929)

Hull, Raymona E., Nathaniel Hawthorne: The English Experience, 1853–64 (1981)

Kendall, Alan, Medieval Pilgrims (1970)

Kinglake, Alexander William, Eothen (1844)

Hibbert, Christopher, The Grand Tour (1969)

Lear, Edward, Journal of a Landscape Painter in Southern Calabria, ed. H. van Thal (1952)

Links, J. G., The Ruskins in Normandy (1968), Travellers in Europe (1980)

Lloyd, Christopher, editor, The Diary of Fanny Burney (1948)

McCarthy, Mary, Florence and Venice (1972 edition)

Mitchell, R. J., The Spring Voyage (1965)

Moritz, Karl Philip, Journeys of a German in England (1782)

Murray, John, Handbook for Travellers in Holland, Belgium and North Germany (1836)

Ogilvie, F., The Tourist Movement: an Economic Study (1933)

Pudney, The Thomas Cook Story (1953)

Roget, S. R., Travel in the Last Two Centuries of Three Generations (1921)

Schivelbusch, Wolfgang, The Railway Journey (1979)

Searight, Sarah, The British in the Middle East (1969)

Seymour, M. C., Mandeville's Travels (1968)

Stevenson, Robert Louis, Essays of Travel (1905)

Swinburne, Henry, The Courts of Europe at the End of the Last Century (1895)

Swinglehurst, The Romantic Journey (1974)

Taylor, Bayard, Views Afoot; or Europe Seen With Knapsack and Staff (1856)

Trant, Captain Abercrombie, Narrative of a Journey Through Greece (1830)

Trease, Geoffrey, The Grand Tour (1967)

Twain, Mark, Europe and Elsewhere (1923)

Tyndall, John, Hours of Exercise in the Alps (1871)

Wenderborn, F. A., A View of England Towards the Close of the Eighteenth Century (1791)

Young, Arthur, Travels in France (1890 edition)

INDEX

ACKNOWLEDGEMENTS

The author and publishers wish to thank the following for permission to reproduce photographs:

Art Institute of Chicago, page 58; BBC Hulton Picture Library, pages 19, 59 and 194; Birmingham Reference Library, pages 67, 75 and 128/129; Bodleian Library, Oxford, page 18; City of Birmingham Museums and Art Gallery, pages 34 and 169; Christie Manson & Woods, page 40 *above*; Courtauld Institute of Art, pages 122, 154/155, 162 and 184/185; Fine Art Society Ltd, page 176; Fisher & Son, *Syria, The Holy Land and Asia Minor* illustrated by W. H. Bartlett, W. Purser etc. with descriptions by J. Carne, 1836–38, page 33; Robert Harding Picture Library, page 109; Historisch Museum Rotterdam, Atlas van Stolk Collection, pages 76, 91 and 161; National Maritime Museum, page 40 *below*; National Motor Museum, page 218; National Railway Museum, York, pages 200 and 207; Popperfoto, pages 77, 82/83, 103, 108, 123, 149 and 208; Royal Borough of Kensington and Chelsea Libraries and Arts Service, page 86; Rodney Searight, page 27; Stanhope Shelton, page 3; Sotheby Parke Bernet & Co, pages 16, 35, 96, 136 *above*, 136 *below*, 163 and 168; Swiss National Tourist Office, pages 114/115 and 209; Teredo Books Ltd, *Arthur Briscoe-Marine Artist* by Alex A. Hurst, 1974, page 195; University of Texas at Austin, Humanities Research Centre, pages 50/51; Whitworth Art Gallery, University of Manchester, page 90; R. Williams, page 177.

The illustration on page 174 is from the author's collection.

The illustrations on pages 6, 7, 12/13, 144 and 145 are reproduced by Gracious Permission of Her Majesty The Queen.